Depression-Free for Life

BOOKS BY GABRIEL COUSENS, M.D.

Conscious Eating, new revised edition
Spiritual Nutrition and the Rainbow Diet
Sevenfold Peace
Tachyon Energy: A New Paradigm in Holistic Healing

BOOKS BY MARK MAYELL

Natural Energy
Off-the-Shelf Natural Health
52 Simple Steps to Natural Health
The Natural Health First-Aid Guide

Depression-Free for Life

....

A Physician's All-Natural,
5-Step Plan

....

Gabriel Cousens, M.D.
with Mark Mayell

HARPER

NEW YORK • LONDON • TORONTO • SYDNEY

A hardcover edition of this book was published in 2000 by William Morrow, an imprint of HarperCollins Publishers.

HarperCollins books may be purchased for educational, business, or sales promotional use. For information please write: Special Markets Department, HarperCollins Publishers Inc., 10 East 53rd Street, New York, NY 10022.

First Quill edition published 2001.

Designed by Susan Hood

The Library of Congress has catalogued the hardcover edition as follows:

Cousens, Gabriel.
   Depression-free for life : an all-natural, 5-step plan to reclaim your zest for
   living / by Gabriel Cousens with Mark Mayell.
      p.   cm.
   Includes bibliographical references and index.
   ISBN 0-688-16500-1
   1. Depression, Mental—Popular works. 2. Depression, Mental—Alternative
   treatment. I. Mayell, Mark. II. Title.

   RC537.C747 2000
   616.85'27—dc21   99–040101

ISBN 0-06-095965-7 (pbk.)

08 09 10 WB/RRD 20 19 18 17 16

*To the millions of people who have been deprived of the
experience of feeling joyful, in love, and free:
May this book inspire them to heal on every level and
experience their birthright—the sacred joy of being alive.*

Acknowledgments

Much thanks to Lynn Sonberg, our friend and book packager, who was very important in the birthing of this book. We also owe a debt of gratitude to the staff of the Tree of Life Rejuvenation Center and the kitchen staff at the Tree of Life Cafe for their general support and help with the menus and recipes. Thanks as well to Nora Cousens, especially for her comments on our chapter on gender and depression.

Contents

Preface: My Odyssey from Ivy League Physician to
    Holistic Healer xi

Introduction: The Unique Approach of *Depression-Free*
    for Life xv

Part One: The Challenge of Depression

1. Natural Drugs of the Brain: A New Approach to
    Alleviating Depression 3

2. From Lithium to Prozac: The Limits of
    Antidepressant Drugs 20

3. The Gender Factor: Why More Women Than Men
    Are Depressed 43

4. Your Personal Biochemistry: The Customized Way to
    Defeat Depression 62

Part Two: Five Steps to Becoming Depression-Free for Life

5. Step One: Take Mood-Boosting Amino Acids 83

6. Step Two: Optimize Your Supplements 104

x   *Contents*

7. Step Three: Make the Fatty Acids Essential   139
8. Step Four: Diet for Mental Health   162
9. Step Five: Eight Lifestyle Choices You Can Make to   200
      Help Beat Depression
10. A New Approach to Alcoholism: Breaking Addictions   220
      and Cravings
11. A Plan in Full: Depression-Free for Life   235

Supplement Resources   252
References   255
Bibliography   277
About the Tree of Life Rejuvenation Center   281
Index   283

Preface

My Odyssey from Ivy League
Physician to Holistic Healer

Medicine has always fascinated me—when I was only four years old I told my parents I wanted to be a doctor. My friends in grade school liked to put together model cars and planes, but I preferred working on models of the human body and playing with chemistry kits. When I was in high school, I built a primitive heart-lung machine that won the top award in the state science fair. In my football career in high school and as captain of the football team at Amherst College, I served as the teams' unofficial physician and learned a great deal about bumps, bruises, sprains, and broken bones.

At Columbia Medical School in the late 1960s, I realized that I found broken minds and souls more fascinating than broken bones. The cultural trends at the time, such as the burgeoning interest in meditation, Far Eastern spirituality, and mind-body techniques, were slow to seep into medicine, but they offered intriguing insights into human health. Pioneering doctors like Hans Selye had begun to conclusively demonstrate that a person's inner experiences, particularly how he or she reacts to stress, could dramatically affect aspects of bodily health, such as the risk of suffering from heart disease.

I came to medical school having already co-authored a biochemistry research article and was all set to become a researcher-internist. I slowly came to the realization that many doctors had little idea about how to get from illness to health, or about what people should do to stay healthy in the first place. The focus seemed to be entirely on high-tech cures rather than on achieving and maintaining wellness.

As a third-year medical student doing medical rounds, it became clear to me that the best that modern medicine could offer was a graceful defeat. I found this extremely upsetting. The breakthrough for me was conducting an interview with a woman who had been to five leading medical centers in New York, none of which could figure out what her problem was. Their best guess was that she had some kind of pituitary problem. I interviewed her and quickly realized that she was psychotically depressed, yet no one at the various medical centers had apparently even asked her any questions about her personal life. I called in a well-respected psychiatrist from the psychosomatic consult service to interview her. The power and depth of his interview and treatment plan awed me. From that point on, I decided I wanted to pursue an approach to healing in accord with the understanding that people's moods and emotions greatly affect their health.

When I'd finished my psychiatry residency and moved to Petaluma, California, in 1973, I began working with patients and soon observed that not only does mind affect body but body affects mind in more ways than most psychiatrists were willing to admit. For example, I noticed that when people suffer from wild swings in blood sugar, they experience a great deal of depression and anxiety, and that with treatment of their glucose imbalance, their moods improve. This realization began to alter my basic medical approach. In fact, I wouldn't even begin psychotherapy with clients who were depressed or anxious until I did a full medical workup on them. I noticed many links between depression and various physical factors, including drug use, family history, hypoglycemia, and diet. Ever since, much of my focus has been on developing a natural, holistic approach to depression that truly unites mind and body.

The result is the *Depression-Free for Life* program, an individualized, five-step depression treatment that I believe embraces the best of both conventional and holistic medical techniques. I've worked with or talked to thousands of people with a variety of mood-related problems, the vast majority of whom have experienced tremendous success using these techniques. The program focuses on what you as an individual can do for yourself without resorting to expensive outside intervention and without exposing yourself to the dangers of prescription drugs. It shows you how you can adjust and correct your personal biochemistry and thereby regain the optimistic, energetic, and self-actuated condition that I believe is every person's birthright.

Depression-Free for Life can thus serve as an effective alternative for anyone whose affliction is not aching joints but rather the inability to fully enjoy life itself. It is available without a prescription to the estimated 40 million Americans who suffer from mild to moderate forms of depression. This includes people with common forms of depression such as seasonal affective disorder (SAD, the familiar "winter blues") and postpartum depression. It also addresses the estimated 10 million Americans who suffer from some form of anxiety disorder, including panic disorder and phobias. The program offers tangible benefits for the many people who are suffering from more serious mood disorders but who are dissatisfied with the conventional treatments their doctors routinely offer. Users of Prozac and other serotonin-boosting drugs who are unhappy with the results and side effects they are experiencing now have another option. The five steps can also help those who have not been diagnosed with depression but who nevertheless know the blues when they feel it.

Everyone who is interested in a natural, drug-free program for optimizing their mental health and increasing their ability to love themselves, friends and family, and society and nature can benefit from *Depression-Free for Life*. I believe that this natural way is more useful, less expensive, and much more enjoyable than conventional approaches, though it requires more of a sense of self-responsibility than is involved in merely taking a drug. The conventional treatments for major depression are not known for being especially effective, with some studies indicating that people who receive no treatment at all fare as well as those who receive the usual counseling and drugs. Furthermore, the increasing awareness of the adverse health effects tied to prescription antidepressants underscores the need for safe, nonaddictive alternatives.

What can people do that will make them more relaxed at bedtime, more alert in the morning, and more engaged during the day? What can depressed people do to reactivate the pleasure centers of the brain so that life becomes filled with joy again—or maybe filled with joy for the first time? I've written *Depression-Free for Life* to provide clear guidelines so that you can experience the answers for yourself.

Introduction

The Unique Approach of
Depression-Free for Life

If you're depressed, this is probably not the first book you've turned to for help. Perhaps in recent years you've *listened to* and *talked back to* and maybe even *gone beyond* Prozac, all of which were the subjects of popular books on depression. So why is this natural, five-step approach to depression an important treatment breakthrough, and what makes this book new and different? Let me immediately identify the key aspects of the *Depression-Free for Life* program:

The approach is customized for each individual. To adapt Tolstoy's famous line that opens *Anna Karenina,* happy individuals are all alike; every depressed person is depressed in his or her own way. Depression comes in many forms and for many reasons, and no single substance is ever going to address its many facets among diverse individuals. The first component in any successful treatment program must be to identify the characteristics—from dominant personality traits to diet to overall health—that shape and determine an individual's depression. To be successful, a depression treatment program needs to be structured enough to yield consistent results yet flexible enough to be customized for the individual.

Part One of this book, "The Challenge of Depression," directly addresses these issues. The first two chapters

- outline the key biochemicals that affect your brain and body in a way that can determine mood
- detail the surprising increase in depression-related conditions in modern society
- summarize the most common faces of depression
- describe the evolution—and the shortcomings—of conventional antidepressant drugs

The five-step treatment addresses the full range of potential biochemical imbalances in your brain and body that underlies the depression. The boom in serotonin-boosting drugs such as Prozac has focused public attention on that single neurotransmitter. Indeed, serotonin can have prominent effects on depression. But people's experiences and the latest research clearly suggest that serotonin is only one of almost a dozen biochemicals crucial for treating depression and maintaining positive mood. Granted, it would be much easier for depressed people and therapists alike if there were a simple Prozac-like solution to all forms of depression and for all individuals. Body, brain, and mind are more complex than that, however, and mood may be affected not only by serotonin but by dopamine, blood sugar, certain hormones, nutrient levels, blood pH (the balance of acid and alkaline substances in the blood), and other bodily chemicals.

Chapters 3 and 4 show you how to identify which factors, including hormonal and neurotransmitter activity, are most prominent in your condition. These chapters offer easy-to-follow recommendations and guidelines for determining which treatment options are most likely to offer long-term relief.

The natural methods used are safer and, over the long term, may be even more effective at relieving depression than conventional antidepressant drugs. Foremost among the natural treatment methods is the use of amino acids as precursors to activate the most important mind- and mood-altering neurotransmitters and therefore the brain's pleasure centers, the subject of Chapter 5. These increasingly popular supplements directly affect brain chemistry and can act as natural drugs with immediate beneficial effects on mood. I believe that amino acids are underused by health practitioners and that these supplements may well soon supplant herbs such as St. John's wort on the cutting edge of natural depression treatment.

Other chapters in Part Two, "Five Steps to Becoming Depression-Free for Life," present information on how and why to use nutritional supplements, essential fatty acids, diet, and lifestyle changes to prevent and treat depression. Each of these is a proven strategy for repairing and reactivating the brain's pleasure centers.

Nor are mood-related disorders the only conditions that the program successfully alleviates. Because it helps to balance chemicals in the body and brain that affect much more than mood, this five-step program may also benefit alcoholics, people who suffer from bulimia and other eating disorders, those with chronic pain or insomnia, victims of chronic fatigue syndrome, people with extreme levels of anger or hostility, children and adults with attention deficit disorder, and those who suffer from hypoglycemia, food allergies, candida infections, and a host of other common conditions. The two concluding chapters describe these additional benefits from the program and provide tips for making sure you can stick to the program and incorporate the recommendations into your busy life.

Although this holistic, five-step program works best when you incorporate all five steps—addressing amino acid, nutritional, and essential fatty acid supplements, as well as diet and lifestyle—into your life, even following any one step can provide significant help. Each step also works synergistically to bring about the program's extraordinary 90 percent success rate for defeating depression.

The *Depression-Free for Life* approach emphasizes the powerful effects that optimal body and brain function have in healing depression. This in no way diminishes the important role of psychospiritual growth in healing depression and increasing one's sacred joy of being alive.

Depression treatments that ignore the three commonsense yet frequently overlooked principles of customization, biochemical diversity, and long-term effectiveness may temporarily relieve a few symptoms, but all too often these programs fail in the long term. Many depressed people simply give up and attempt to live with their frequent bouts of depression. Compared to taking prescription antidepressants, the *Depression-Free for Life* program is both more effective and far less toxic. It doesn't require that readers go on a costly regimen of prescription drugs. The amino acids and other nutritional supplements described are inexpensive and are available at most health food stores. Even more important, *Depression-Free for Life* offers major advantages over Prozac and similar drugs in that it

- increases libido and sexual pleasure rather than deadens them
- promotes sharper, clearer thinking and better memory rather than confused thinking and learning problems
- helps control appetite and alleviate eating- and weight-related disorders rather than promoting weight gain
- encourages deeper, more natural sleep rather than disturbing the sleep cycle
- boosts energy rather than increasing daytime drowsiness and fatigue
- repairs and reactivates the brain's pleasure centers rather than merely supplying symptomatic relief
- Greatly enhances the mind-body's ability to heal on the psychospiritual level, and to recover from the unhealthy emotional scars caused by relationship patterns that may be at the root of the depression.

You'll find that this natural, drug-free program combines the best of the conventional and alternative approaches. It is solidly based on scientific studies that have been conducted over the past two decades on how natural chemicals in the body and brain intimately affect mind and mood. It shows you how to successfully fight off your bouts of depression and emerge with increased self-esteem, less despair, and a greater sense of control over your life. If you give this program a chance, you will enjoy life once again and reconnect with partners, family members, and friends. I encourage you to keep this vision of health and happiness in mind as the ultimate goal of *Depression-Free for Life*.

Part One

. . . .

The Challenge of Depression

1

Natural Drugs of the Brain: A New Approach to Alleviating Depression

By the time I was in the eighth grade I'd read all the books in the school library on anything to do with medicine. I didn't know at the time that I would eventually become a psychiatrist and holistic physician and that I would focus on the treatment of depression, but I do remember having the impression that the discussion of depression and other mental diseases seemed awfully vague. Some of the typical treatments, such as electroshock therapy and amphetamine drugs, seemed primitive. Most of the medical books I was reading at the time were no doubt published in the 1950s or even earlier, so it wasn't surprising that they waffled about the causes of depression and how best to treat it. The problem was simply that not enough was known about the functioning of the brain and the central nervous system. Doctors at the time were the proverbial researchers-in-the-dark, trying to describe an elephant when they were able to feel only its trunk.

Exactly how moods are generated is still being determined. Even so, since the 1950s, scientists have made a number of important inroads in the understanding of depression. The condition's biochemical underpinnings are being identified, especially with regard to the activity of brain biochemicals such as serotonin and dopamine, among the fifty or so known neurotransmitters. Unfortunately, the conventional drugs used for adjusting the activity of these neurotransmitters leave much to be desired. The first generation of antidepressants, potent drugs such as phenelzine (Nardil), developed in the 1950s, are notorious for their acute toxicity and adverse side effects, from headaches right up to sudden death.

Since the mid-1980s, pharmaceutical companies have responded by developing new and better antidepressants. Despite the initial hoopla surrounding fluoxetine (Prozac) and the rest of the new serotonin-boosting antidepressants, these drugs too are now being reevaluated with a more critical eye. Increasing numbers of both patients and doctors are acknowledging that these drugs don't work for everyone and that they can have adverse side effects, from anxiety to decreased sex drive.

More recently, the herb St. John's wort has been hailed as a natural, less toxic alternative to prescription antidepressants. I've found that it does help some people, although exactly how it works remains unclear. Because many factors no doubt contribute to depression, however, it is not possible for any single substance, whether natural herb or synthetic drug, to be a magic bullet that alleviates all depression. Although it may seem that a consensus has developed with regard to the cure for depression—increase serotonin activity—in many cases this approach provides no more than temporary relief of some of the symptoms.

The more holistic *Depression-Free for Life* approach, I believe, offers much greater potential for treating depression. It recognizes that a more diverse range of biochemicals than one or even a few neurotransmitters influences brain and nervous system activity. Recent studies have helped to confirm what many of my patients and thousands of other people have found out: that aspects of mood and behavior can be affected by the foods we eat, by the nutritional supplements we take (or fail to take), and by such everyday lifestyle choices as how much exercise or physical activity we get. This broader perspective is the basis for the natural five-step program described in Part Two of this book.

The coordinated five-step program is not only just as effective at alleviating depression as prescription drugs but is also safer and carries along with it a host of "side benefits." These include a reduction in cravings for alcohol and other drugs, increased alertness during the day and better sleep at night, and optimal control of appetite and weight. Although my depression-relief program has not yet made it into the medical books of the 1990s, I am convinced that no better alternative exists today.

A Modern Epidemic

Depression disrupts the lives of tens of millions Americans—and women in particular. It is a leading cause of disability and suicide in the United States. As many as 70 percent of the nation's 30,000 suicides annually can be attributed to untreated depression, and upward of 50 million Americans feel debilitated by some form of depression or anxiety every year. The costs—for medical care, lost work time, and loss of life—associated with depressive disorders are in the range of $40 billion annually. People who suffer from depression have much higher rates than average for various types of serious diseases, from heart ailments to alcoholism. People suffering from depression experience a worse quality of life than do people with such devastating conditions as diabetes, arthritis, and back pain. A recent study even concluded that longevity might be determined as much by your ability to avoid depression and maintain emotional stability as by what you eat or how much you exercise.

America is enjoying a sustained economic boom, but psychologically our current era may best be described as the second coming of the "great depression":

- Doctors estimate that as many as 8 million women and 4 million men in the United States are treated for major ("clinical") depression each year.
- Almost 40 million Americans frequently fall into chronic negative moods characterized by loneliness, boredom, and restlessness, according to a recent extensive survey of tens of thousands of adults.
- As few as one in ten people who could benefit from mood-elevating drugs or supplements are currently taking them, studies have found. In the United States alone, an estimated 12 million people suffer from depression without realizing it.
- Studies suggest that as few as one in twenty people suffering from depression receive a prompt and accurate diagnosis and an effective treatment.

This epidemic of depression in America and the widespread suffering associated with it is what ultimately inspired me to find a more natural program to treat it. Part of the challenge was to work with the body's own biochemicals, an approach that has a number of advantages compared to using prescription drugs:

- The human body has evolved over millions of years to successfully regulate and metabolize its own natural biochemicals.
- The techniques for adjusting the body's own chemicals are simple and easy for anyone to learn.
- The substances used, from amino acids to foods, are widely available and inexpensive.

Chief among the natural drugs of the brain are the neurotransmitters, substances such as serotonin that transmit nerve impulses. Let's first take a quick look at which neurotransmitters affect mood and how they can be adjusted to help alleviate depression.

The Brain's Own Antidepressants

Serotonin is the best known of the depression-relieving neurotransmitters, but a number of others also have direct effects on mind and mood by acting as the messenger between nerve cells, or neurons. Neurotransmitters are chemicals that cross the gap, or synapse, between the two ends of nerve fibers, or between neurons and muscle cells. At the target cell the neurotransmitter is received and binds to a protein receptor. When neurotransmitter molecules activate a critical mass of receptors, the receiving nerve initiates an electrical impulse. This impulse and its effects depend in part on which receptors are activated—the same neurotransmitter may bind to a dozen or more different types of receptors. The original neurotransmitter molecules then retreat back across the synapse. Those that aren't destroyed by enzymes or otherwise blocked (by the action of certain drugs, for example) can be reabsorbed at the original neuron. They can then be sent back across the synapse to help initiate another impulse.

This process allows messages to be transferred through nerves as electrical impulses and for information to be relayed throughout the body. These messages affect functions ranging from heartbeat to sleepiness to mood. Some neurotransmitters affect one type of bodily function more than another. Studies and clinical evidence suggest that the principal mood-related neurotransmitters are

- serotonin
- dopamine
- noradrenaline (most doctors refer to adrenaline as epinephrine, and noradrenaline as norepinephrine; I prefer to use the more familiar terms adrenaline and noradrenaline)
- glutamine
- gamma aminobutyric acid (GABA)

To understand each of these brain chemicals, as well as a related set of neurotransmitters that includes the endorphins (natural, opiate-like chemicals in the body that relieve pain and alter mood), we need to consider

- what it is and where it is concentrated in the brain
- how it is formed in the body, including which amino acids and dietary nutrients prescribed in Part Two are necessary to produce and activate it
- which moods and thinking patterns are associated with both its over-abundance in the brain and its deficiency

Subtle clues tell us which neurotransmitter or neurotransmitters may be most affecting a depressed individual. By learning to recognize your neurotransmitter connections, you can obtain valuable clues as to what types of foods, nutrients, and lifestyle habits are most likely to alleviate your depression.

Serotonin: Diverse and Complex Effects

Known to scientists as the chemical 5-hydroxytryptamine (5-HT), serotonin has notoriously diverse and complex effects on the heart, intestines, blood vessels, and other bodily organs. Serotonin may constrict or dilate blood vessels, or stimulate or depress heart output. Serotonin may raise blood pressure and stimulate the gut. Serotonin affects muscle contraction—the source of its name relates to muscles (sero for blood, tonin for muscle tone; the name was coined in the late 1940s when researchers in Italy and the United States independently discovered the chemical). Extra serotonin in the brain may help to alleviate pain.

Much is still being learned about this compound, but within recent years it has become clear that serotonin also plays a central role in mood and emotion. Along with dopamine, serotonin is one of the body's primary activators of pleasure centers in the brain. The right amounts of serotonin in the brain at the right time of day lead to feelings of emotional stability, well-being, personal security, relaxation, calmness, tranquility, and confidence. Low serotonin levels in the brain have been linked not only to depression but also to appetite (especially cravings for sweets and carbohydrates), anxiety, irritability, insomnia, and obsessive and compulsive actions. Low levels have also been tied to suicide, aggression, and violence.

Serotonin is found in various plants (including foods such as bananas and pineapples) and animals, but dietary sources are much less important than the serotonin manufactured within the body. The neurotransmitter is manufactured in special nerve cells within a part of the base of the brain known as the raphe nuclei. The bulk of your serotonin is a metabolic by-product of the amino acids tryptophan and 5-hydroxytryptophan (5-HTP). Along with various enzymes, the B-complex vitamin folic acid is an essential cofactor for the production of serotonin. The body synthesizes serotonin in the following manner:

$$\text{Tryptophan} \rightarrow \text{5-HTP} \rightarrow \text{Serotonin}$$

(Serotonin is further metabolized into an intermediate compound and then into the neurohormone melatonin, which has been shown to promote sleep and improve mood.)

Serotonin is circulated throughout the body, whereas other neurotransmitters have more limited areas of influence. The type of mood-related symptoms you experience may depend on which parts of the brain have a relative deficiency of serotonin. For example, researchers believe that too little serotonin in a part of the brain that controls voluntary movements may cause obsessive or compulsive behavior, while too little in the part that generates fear may lead to anxiety.

Taking serotonin orally doesn't have much effect on mind or mood. That's because the digestive and circulatory systems deactivate or reroute serotonin on its way to the brain. Prozac and other popular new "selective serotonin reuptake inhibitors" (SSRIs) are antidepressants that improve mood by promoting serotonin activity in the brain. These drugs work by preventing the neuron that emitted serotonin into the synapse from reabsorbing the molecules. Serotonin stays active in the gap longer and is able to bind with more receiving neurons, promoting and prolonging its positive effects.

Dietary supplements such as tryptophan and 5-HTP, on the other hand, work by providing nerve cells with more of the raw material they need to manufacture serotonin. When tryptophan is consumed in food or by supplements, some of it is used by the body to make proteins or stays in the blood. A significant amount, however, is transported to the brain, where it readily crosses the blood-brain barrier and is taken up by nerve cells for the production of serotonin. As we'll see, there is reason to believe that the serotonin-creating mechanism of tryptophan and 5-HTP is likely to be safer and more effective over the long term than SSRIs.

Studies find that serotonin levels and activity are reduced during aging, and that age-related changes in serotonin levels may predispose the elderly to depression. The loss of serotonin activity may combine with the decreased action of another neurotransmitter, acetylcholine, to play a role in the cognitive impairment of Alzheimer's disease. Stress may also cause neurotransmitter disturbances that may result in a serotonin deficiency and ultimately in depression.

Dopamine: Mood and Addiction

Along with serotonin, dopamine may be the only neurotransmitter afforded cover story status in the newsweeklies. A 1997 *Time* magazine cover story on dopamine described the neurotransmitter as "not just a chemical that transmits pleasure signals" but also possibly "the master

---

Your Personal Biochemistry:
Do You Have a Serotonin Deficiency?

Traits of the person whose depression may be caused by too little serotonin activity in the brain include

- anxiety
- low self-esteem
- lack of libido
- fatigue
- eating disorders
- cravings for carbohydrates and sweets
- impatience and impulsiveness

molecule of addiction." Dopamine is also increasingly being recognized as a brain chemical that plays a crucial role in elevating mood.

Scientists have used special imaging technology to determine where in the brain dopamine is concentrated. It turns out that dopamine is manufactured in nerve cells primarily in one section of the brain, and its activity is especially important in a primitive section of the brain called the nucleus accumbens. This is one of the key areas of the brain that helps to generate feelings of pleasure and euphoria. Dopamine can boost the libido, promote a sense of satisfaction, and encourage assertiveness.

Scientists are also finding that dopamine is vital for short-term memory, concentration, and learning. Like serotonin, it affects the body's appetite for food (possibly through an effect on secretion of the hormone prolactin) as well as muscle tone. A deficiency of dopamine in certain parts of the brain can cause problems with coordination and lead to spontaneous muscle movements or stiff muscles. These are symptoms of Parkinson's disease, which has been linked with the destruction of the brain cells that synthesize dopamine. Dopamine may boost secretion of growth hormone and promote the body's ability to repair damaged cells. An overabundance of dopamine in the brain may bring on hallucinations or the extreme behavior of schizophrenia.

Dopamine is derived from the amino acid phenylalanine in the following manner:

$$\text{Phenylalanine} \rightarrow \text{Tyrosine} \rightarrow \text{Dopa} \rightarrow \text{Dopamine}$$

Pleasurable experiences, whether it be receiving a compliment from a loved one or hitting a nice golf shot, tend to elevate dopamine levels in the brain. Various mind-altering drugs can also elevate dopamine levels, either by triggering a complex chemical cascade that results in dopamine release or by blocking dopamine absorption and letting it stay active in the synapse for a longer period of time. Drugs' effects are often complex and may involve other neurotransmitters, but dopamine action may account for much of the allure of cocaine, nicotine, alcohol, marijuana, heroin, amphetamines, and possibly caffeine. Addiction may be partly due to repeated use of a substance, causing a decrease in the number of dopamine receptors. (Other bodily systems, however, may also be damaged. For example, researchers have discovered that recovering cocaine addicts are much less able to process glucose in certain parts of the brain. Glucose is the brain's main source of fuel.)

Studies suggest that it is possible to repair dopamine pathways that have been harmed by drug addiction, poor nutrition, or stress and to thereby reactivate the brain's pleasure centers. This has been my clinical experience working at my health center with many recovered but not fully healed alcoholics and with people addicted to other drugs. I believe that the brain has the ability to rebuild itself with the help of proper nutrients, neurotransmitter precursors (especially the amino acids that can convert to mood-boosting biochemicals such as serotonin and dopamine), and a healthy diet.

Studies have confirmed that a decrease in dopamine activity is involved in depression, and that an increase can contribute to mania. One recent study found that exposure to a single "aversive experience" that is unavoidable or uncontrollable leads to inhibition of dopamine release in the pleasure-generating nucleus accumbens as well as to impaired response to "rewarding stimuli." The researchers suggested that this could be how for some people a worsening of depressive symptoms such as an inability to feel pleasure or feelings of helplessness is caused by life events. Researchers have also measured levels of dopamine metabolites, such as homovanillic acid, in cerebrospinal fluid and in various parts of the brains of suicide victims who were known to suffer from depression. The evidence suggests reduced dopamine activity in depressed suicides.

Too much dopamine activity in the brain can also cause problems, especially impulsive, irrational, or overly aggressive behavior; a tendency to form addictive relationships with pleasurable activities such as sex, eating (especially candy, chocolate, and other sweets), or gambling; and difficulty sleeping. This is more typical, however, of a manic than a depressive pattern.

Your Personal Biochemistry:
Do You Have a Dopamine Deficiency?

Traits of the person whose depression may be accompanied by too little dopamine activity in the brain include

- regular use of alcohol or other recreational drugs to get high
- apathy
- sleeping more than normal
- irritability

Noradrenaline: Adrenaline's Cousin

Noradrenaline acts on nerves that help to control heart rate and blood pressure. It's also a factor in how quickly glucose is converted to energy and how the body responds to stress and anxiety. Your body responds to a physical threat or a sense of danger with a surge of noradrenaline and adrenaline. This boosts your heart rate, increases your breathing, and sends extra blood to your major muscles. Whether you decide to take flight or stand and fight, your body is prepared for action.

Neurons synthesize noradrenaline in the body from the amino acid phenylalanine, with the following intermediate steps:

Phenylalanine → Tyrosine → Dopa → Dopamine → Noradrenaline

Noradrenaline can be further metabolized into adrenaline. Certain enzymes and cofactors, including some that are affected by nutrient levels in the blood, are necessary for these metabolic steps to take place. Also, some noradrenaline is produced by the adrenal glands.

Studies have confirmed a number of connections between noradrenaline function and depression. Noradrenaline may be more of a factor when depression is melancholic rather than manic. A major class of antidepressant drugs, the monoamine oxidase (MAO) inhibitors, is thought to work in part through effects on noradrenaline. Drug companies have also begun to develop selective noradrenaline reuptake inhibitors, like reboxetine. We'll look more closely at these in Chapter 2.

Too much noradrenaline activity in the brain causes symptoms that are similar to the pattern of mania we saw with excess dopamine, such as nervousness and restlessness, difficulty falling asleep, and weight loss. Much more frequently, depression results from a noradrenaline deficiency or inactivity.

Your Personal Biochemistry:
Do You Have a Noradrenaline Deficiency?

Traits of the person whose depression may be accompanied by too little noradrenaline activity in the brain include

- lack of energy
- reduced libido
- sluggish thinking
- lack of enthusiasm

Glutamine: Brain Fuel

Glutamine is an amino acid found in animal tissues as well as in the leaves of certain plants—cabbage juice is especially rich in glutamine. In plants glutamine plays an important role in protein metabolism. In humans glutamine is found in higher amounts than other amino acids in muscle tissue; it's also concentrated in the blood and spinal fluid. Along with a closely related amino acid (glutamic acid) that glutamine is converted into, glutamine is crucial for optimal brain function. Glutamine is a stimulating or "excitatory" neurotransmitter. It has a beneficial effect on mood and energy levels by helping to control brain levels of ammonia. Glutamine also plays an almost unique role as a brain fuel. Although the brain's main fuel is glucose, it doesn't store glucose in large quantities. Without sufficient glutamine, the brain can only shuffle along at a fraction of its remarkable capacity.

People report that glutamine, taken as a supplement (see Chapter 5), boosts mood and increases alertness.

Your Personal Biochemistry:
Do You Have a Glutamine Deficiency?

Traits of the person whose depression may be accompanied by too little glutamine activity in the brain include

- cravings for sweets
- a tendency toward alcoholism
- low sex drive

GABA: A Brake in the Brain

GABA is a nonessential amino acid that, like glutamine, acts as a neurotransmitter. GABA's effects, however, are more or less opposite to those of glutamine. GABA occurs in high concentrations in the brain and central nervous system, where it prevents nerve cells from firing too quickly. It thus slows the rate at which signals are transmitted from one nerve cell ending to another. Whereas other neurotransmitters, such as acetylcholine and noradrenaline, tend to speed things along in the brain, GABA acts like a brake to slow things down. Inhibiting message transmission causes you to feel calmer. It tends to reduce anxiety, relieve nervous tension, and relax muscles. It also promotes sleep.

GABA is formed in the body from the amino acid glutamate, with the help of cofactors such as pyridoxine and vitamin C. GABA breaks down into another compound with notable relaxant properties: gamma hydroxy butyrate (GHB). During the 1980s, a few supplement companies sold GHB as a nutritional supplement, but it can be very fast-acting and potent. A number of federal and state regulatory bodies have banned the sale of GHB in the United States, although it is still being studied as an experimental drug and is prescribed overseas.

It is possible to have too much GABA activity in the brain. This might be the case if the person shows sluggish thinking, poor physical coordination, extreme sleepiness, and memory problems. An anxiety depression is more likely from a GABA deficiency than from GABA overactivity.

Your Personal Biochemistry:
Do You Have a GABA Deficiency?

Traits of the person whose depression may be accompanied by too little GABA activity in the brain include

- frequently nervous and anxious
- panic attacks
- exhaustion from stress
- excessive stress reactions from normal stress situations

Endorphins: Natural Opiates

Morphine, one of the alkaloids that occurs naturally in the opium poppy plant, has been recognized for almost two centuries as one of the most effective pain-relieving substances known to humanity. Exactly how it affects the brain and central nervous system was a mystery to medical researchers until the mechanism of neurotransmission became clearer in the mid-twentieth century. Researchers then began to look for receptors that operated as specific binding sites for morphine and similar opium compounds in the brain.

It wasn't until the early 1970s that researchers at Johns Hopkins University discovered these long sought-after opiate receptors. Their discovery focused attention on a related issue: assuming that the brain didn't evolve specifically with opium use in mind, doesn't the presence of these receptors indicate that there must be natural, opium-like compounds in the body that act much like morphine to relieve pain?

Indeed, the body produces its own chemicals that are structured similarly to morphine and that fit into the same receptors as does morphine. These are now known as opioids, and include the better-known endorphins and enkephalins as well as other substances such as the dynorphins. The words *endorphin* and *enkephalin* were coined in the mid-1970s from the words *endogenous* (produced within the body), *morphine*, and *encephal-* (brain). Endorphins and enkephalins are both peptides (amino acid compounds), differing slightly in structure. These opiate-like chemicals are now known not only to relieve pain but also to affect mood and the body's response to stress. The endorphins also play a role in the following functions:

- timing of appetite
- cravings due to stress or starvation
- reproductive hormone cycles
- pregnancy and labor
- immunity
- circulation of blood
- aging

Researchers have identified twenty different types of endorphins, with beta-endorphin, a chain of thirty-one amino acids, being the most mood-elevating. Endorphins are short-lived in the body because of enzymes such as enkephalinase that break them down.

Much is still to be discovered about endorphins and enkephalins. Even after considerable research into their structure and functions, they remain somewhat mysterious. Scientists are not sure how opioids interact with each other and with other biochemicals to produce moods, pain relief, and other effects.

Among the factors that can increase the production of endorphins or their release into cerebrospinal fluid are

- exercise
- laughter
- sex (endorphins may be released during orgasm)
- certain foods and nutritional supplements
- overall well-being

Pain is not the only factor that causes the release of endorphins. Sustained muscular activity as from strenuous exercise affects endorphin levels. The body releases endorphins when you're sad in an attempt to alleviate the emotional pain. Normally the brain maintains enough endorphins to deal with emergencies—such as the pain from stubbing your toe or from running ten miles. If you're lacking these unique pain-relieving molecules, you may sink deeper into depression and inactivity.

Various diseases can reduce your supply of endorphins, as can stress. In the normal stress response, the anti-endorphin enzyme enkephalinase is released to break down endorphins and thus prepare your body for fight or flight. After the stress passes, enkephalinase levels decrease and endorphin levels return to normal. Under chronic stress, however, your ability to recover to normal endorphin levels diminishes. Several studies suggest that this leads to inner discomfort and fatigue. Drinking alcohol creates a type of false endorphin function and leads to a temporary sense of well-being, although over the long term it actually further diminishes the endorphins. Researchers have shown that chronic alcoholics have significantly fewer endorphins.

A number of studies have found that low levels of endorphins are correlated with depression as well as with anxiety, phobia, and obsessions and compulsions. Among the supplements that may be capable of increasing endorphin levels are phenylalanine and 5-HTP. One study found that subjects with major depression who took 5-HTP had significantly increased beta-endorphin concentrations when compared to subjects taking a placebo. The increased beta-endorphin levels were

---

Your Personal Biochemistry:
Do You Have an Endorphin Imbalance?

Traits of the person whose depression may be accompanied by too little endorphin activity in the brain include

- difficulty feeling pleasure
- inability to give or receive love
- tendency toward alcoholism or other forms of addictive behavior

---

correlated with improved scores on the Hamilton Depression Rating Scale, one of the standard tests used by doctors to diagnose depression.

Biochemicals to Rival the Neurotransmitters

Neurotransmitter activity in the brain has now become so widely recognized as a major factor in the biochemistry of mood that it threatens to overshadow all other possible factors. Yet recent research suggests that a number of other factors may come to rival the neurotransmitters for their importance in treating depression. Using a few reliable techniques, from questionnaires to simple self-diagnostic tests, it is possible to identify mood-altering imbalances in these other key areas:

The existence of underlying conditions, including other illnesses, drug reactions, nutritional deficiencies, and allergies to foods and chemicals. In the next chapter we'll take a look at these and other issues, particularly at the shortcomings of conventional prescription drugs that are becoming wildly popular for treating depression.

How the body handles sugars and complex carbohydrates. Anyone who has noticed the fatigue and irritability that follow an hour or so after a heavy lunch has experienced the direct connection between food and mood, a connection that has garnered increased scientific support in recent years. In Chapter 4 we'll see how blood sugar, the relative concentration of glucose in the blood, figures in a simple distinction—whether you are what I call a "fast oxidizer" of bodily sugar or a "slow oxidizer"—that can help you tailor your *Depression-Free for Life* program for quick and reliable results.

The balance of important hormones, such as estrogen, melatonin, thyroid hormones, and stress hormones. Sex-related hormones such as estrogen and season-related melatonin are the subject of Chapter 3. Melatonin is well-known for helping to regulate sleep, and it is now also being recognized for its ability to help treat mood disorders. People with low bodily melatonin levels are at greater risk for suffering from moderate depression and seasonal affective disorder (SAD, or the "winter blues") as well as greater risk for suicide. Additional hormones with potential mood-related effects are described in Chapter 4, including metabolic-related hormones such as thyroxine (the most important thyroid hormone), cortisone, and adrenaline.

Along with the previously mentioned neurotransmitters and the endorphins, these crucial factors form the basis for the *Depression-Free for Life* program. Much of the remainder of this book shows how these affect mood, how you can learn more about your unique condition as it relates to these biochemicals, and how amino acids, nutrients, herbs, diet, exercise, and lifestyle factors can help you to balance these biochemicals, rebuild neurotransmitter pathways, repair nerve cells, and reactivate the brain's pleasure centers, thereby alleviating depression.

In my experience at the Tree of Life Rejuvenation Center in Patagonia, Arizona, approximately nine out of every ten people can experience a relatively quick (many within a week, though others may take as long as two months) and dramatic relief of their depression from adhering to the following five-step program:

1. **Take mood-boosting amino acids.** Certain amino acids are used by the body to manufacture neurotransmitters (such as serotonin, dopamine, and noradrenaline) and neurohormones (such as melatonin) that have prominent effects on mood. These amino acids, with the exception of tryptophan, are readily available as dietary supplements in health food stores.
2. **Optimize your supplements.** A number of common vitamin, mineral, and other dietary supplements, including vitamins B-complex, C, and E, and the minerals calcium and magnesium, as well as a few herbs such as ginkgo, need to be taken in optimal amounts to support the body's depression-preventing system. Some of the latest supplements, such as NADH, address particular types of depression. These vitamins and minerals are specific for optimal brain cell function and metabolism.

3. **Make the fatty acids essential.** Surprising new research links depression to the balance of essential fatty acids in your diet and their effects on prostaglandins, fatty acids generated within the body. The essential fatty acids are found in certain foods and are widely available as dietary supplements. Chapter 7 describes the types of supplements on the market and details how to best take advantage of their mood-boosting effects.

4. **Eat for mental health.** Diet can affect mood-related biochemicals by boosting the action of certain neurotransmitters (from the amino acids in protein-containing foods, for example) and through effects on blood sugar balance as well. The diet connection also helps control appetite and weight.

5. **Live an uplifting lifestyle**. Exercise and other lifestyle factors— relationships, social network, sense of humor, relaxation—have prominent effects on mind and mood. Depression has psychological, social, and spiritual aspects that need to be addressed.

In the next chapter I'll talk about the causes of depression and the current crop of conventional antidepressant drugs. Most of these drugs work by affecting one or more of the neurotransmitters just detailed. Many depressed people are taking these prescription drugs, with varying degrees of success. We need to consider how and why these drugs work, what types of side effects they cause, and whether they truly get to the root of a person's depression.

2

From Lithium to Prozac:
The Limits of Antidepressant Drugs

When Martina first came to see me for depression, one of our immediate priorities was sorting out which of her symptoms related directly to her condition and which were resulting from the half-dozen drugs she was taking as treatment.

An urban-planning specialist in her early forties who had emigrated from Eastern Europe about a decade earlier, Martina was obviously bright and ambitious. About three years earlier she had begun to experience fatigue, lack of motivation, emotional and physical instability, severe insomnia, and anxiety. A series of doctors and psychiatrists had prescribed various drugs for Martina, and she had also undergone some group counseling. Unhappy with her progress, she eagerly followed up on a suggestion from a friend who knew about my natural approach to depression.

Dark-haired and somber, Martina quietly described to me her quite significant mood and mental problems. It turned out she was taking a codeine-containing prescription pain reliever for her headaches, an over-the-counter (OTC) sleep medication for insomnia, an antidepressant known as a tricyclic to elevate her mood, a prescription drug to counter the high blood pressure caused by the antidepressant, and OTC digestive aids to counter gastrointestinal problems (which may also have been tied to the tricyclic drug). At times she had also been prescribed various other antidepressants, including Prozac, lithium, and bupropion (Wellbutrin)—often in multiple combinations.

Martina's experience with these drugs was similar to that of many other patients I have seen: initial moderate success followed by a slow return of some symptoms of depression, frequently accompanied by annoying, even debilitating, side effects from the drugs. Over a period of months I slowly weaned her off the various drugs and put her on a regimen that included the amino acid tyrosine and 5-HTP early in the day along with tryptophan one hour before bedtime, and optimum doses of B-complex and other vitamins. Her high stress levels had resulted in a depletion in both serotonin and dopamine, and this regimen was designed to help her replenish her stores of these neurotransmitters. We also established that she felt best when she avoided certain foods, especially dairy (to which she was allergic), and when she could refrain from even her occasional alcohol intake.

Gradually, Marina's depression lifted, she slept soundly, and she began to work more productively. Moreover, her relief from depression, headaches, digestive problems, and the like seems permanent—she has successfully maintained the basics of her natural treatment for more than three years now while staying optimistic and confident. As she has stabilized, we've been able to slowly decrease the dosages of amino acids.

Martina's experience illustrates a number of common problems with the conventional drug approach to depression, including

- the tendency to lump all depressions together when in fact there are many forms of depression, each requiring variations in treatment approach
- the notable adverse effects and potential long-term toxicity from conventional antidepressants
- the diagnostic and treatment-related confusion that arises when a depressed person is given many different drugs at the same time

Perhaps most important, Martina's experience is an example of the underlying "magic bullet" theory that dominates much of modern medicine and psychiatry. In this view depression is solely a biochemical imbalance and thus can at least theoretically be treated by finding the right drug, or combination of drugs, to fine-tune the brain. To extend the magic bullet metaphor another step, conventional depression treatment has advanced from using "shotgun" drugs in the 1960s and

1970s—drugs that affect brain levels of numerous neurotransmitters—to somewhat less toxic "peashooters" in the 1980s and 1990s—drugs that more selectively affect only one or two neurotransmitters, such as serotonin or noradrenaline. As we'll see, depressed people have some reason to be thankful for this development. Drug-based therapy remains, however, a flawed and one-dimensional approach that often fails to provide the long-term solution depressed people need and deserve.

The Many Faces of Depression

Let's first take a quick look at the different types of depression. This diagnostic paradigm, although limiting in many ways, can help you recognize some aspects of your condition, understand the limits of the drug approach, and appreciate the significant advantages of a more holistic program that seeks to heal from the foundation upward.

Major or clinical depression. Everyone experiences feelings of sadness, emptiness, and self-reproach at some point in life. In many instances, however, these are normal responses to unfortunate events, such as the death of someone close or a disappointment in school or work. When these feelings are combined with other signs of depression, last continually for two weeks or longer, and are intense enough to be prominent all day and to disrupt all aspects of your life (including everyday activities such as eating, sleeping, and relaxing), then you may be suffering from a major depression.

A simple self-test for depression follows. Answer yes or no to each of the eight questions below, keeping in mind the factors that I just mentioned about duration and intensity.

1. Do you suffer from a loss of energy and from feelings of fatigue?
2. Do you have recurrent thoughts of death or suicide?
3. Have you lost your appetite or begun to overeat, or experienced rapid weight loss or gain?
4. Do you feel yourself withdrawing from normal activities and involvement, or have you had a noticeable decrease in your sex drive?
5. Do you find it unusually hard to think or concentrate?
6. Are you restless, irritable, or overly active or inactive?
7. Do you have trouble falling or staying asleep, or do you want to sleep all the time?
8. Do you have feelings of hopelessness, worthlessness, or inappropriate guilt?

Doctors diagnose major depression as one or more episodes character-ized by at least five of these eight criteria for two weeks. This is a some-what imprecise way to diagnose depression, given that people differ in their ability to truthfully and insightfully answer these questions. But depression is a complex condition with emotional, physical, and psy-chological aspects. No simple biochemical test exists for detecting depression, nor should we expect one to be developed.

Chronic mild depression or dysthymia. Major depression is a very debil-itating condition that typically affects work, relationships, and, of course, physical health. When a person's feelings of sadness, helpless-ness, withdrawal, fatigue, and so forth are frequent and prominent but less associated with obvious changes in activities and behavior, and when they last for most of the day more days than not, that person may be suffering from chronic mild depression, or dysthymia. (Literally an imbalance in mind or soul, its opposite is hyperthymia, which is charac-terized by optimism, energy, confidence, and cheerfulness.) Although less severe than major depression, this type of chronic discontent or long-term, low-grade depression nevertheless affects an extremely large group of people, perhaps as many as 40 to 50 million adult Americans.

Atypical depression. This is a controversial category—some doctors and psychiatrists find it useful while others dismiss it. Those who support it say that it provides a valid description of a unique type of depression. A person with atypical depression feels worse in the evening, is tired but can't fall asleep, has psychosomatic complaints, and may be at least tem-porarily cheered up by counseling or sympathy. The person seems to crave attention and is overly distraught by rejection and broken love affairs. Self-centered and impulsive people may be more likely to suffer from this type of depression, while passive and perfectionist types have the typical forms of depression. The condition may respond better to monoamine oxidase inhibitors, which I'll describe later in this chapter. Critics of this category say that studies have failed to substantiate a reli-able and valid diagnosis, and atypical depression is not included in the standard medical manual (the *Diagnostic and Statistical Manual of Mental Disorders*) for depression. In my practice, I've seen a number of patients who fit this pattern. I haven't noticed, however, a major difference in how they respond to any element of the natural treatment plan, so I think the diagnosis has limited value.

Manic depression. This is the most prominent of the mood swing disorders, which doctors often refer to as bipolar disorders. Manic depression is characterized by cycles of extreme highs and lows. The manic phase may find the person elated, energetic, and overly active. He or she may have an inflated sense of self-esteem, less apparent need for sleep, racing thoughts, and be easily distracted. The depressive phase finds the person fatigued, withdrawn, deeply sad, and disconnected. Studies indicate that manic depression has more of a genetic basis than most other mood disorders.

Just as major depression has a milder form, manic depression does as well. This is called cyclothymia, which may be more difficult to diagnose because the mood swings are less drastic and may be separated by longer periods of seemingly normal behavior. Also, the depressive phase is more like dysthymia than an episode of major depression.

Manic depression is one of the most difficult mood disorders to treat. The person's actual physiology changes according to the cycle. For example, in one phase he or she may be a slow oxidizer and in another phase a fast one. The treatment program needs to be dynamic and flexible for best results.

Seasonal Affective Disorder (SAD). This form of "winter blues" is not uncommon in climates that get little sunshine during the winter, such as much of Scandinavia and northern North America. An estimated one in twenty people who live in these sunlight-deprived areas experience some regular form of depression. Women are approximately four times as likely as men to suffer from SAD. People suffering from SAD tend to gain weight, lose their ability to concentrate, and show no interest in having sex during the winter months. Symptoms of depression including fatigue, sleeping problems, and lethargy are common. While scientists are not sure that they know the exact mechanism of SAD, it may be a hormonal malfunction. For example, the lack of daytime light may diminish release of melatonin during the night.

Postpartum depression. As many as seven out of every ten new mothers experience noticeable emotional problems in the period immediately after giving birth. Many new mothers feel inexplicably despondent, have trouble sleeping, cry without apparent reason, and even feel indifferent toward their new baby. This mild form of depression is usually very transient, although in some women it lingers or turns into a major postpartum depression and an ongoing fatigue. The condition is often underdiagnosed. In the following chapter on gender and depression, we'll take a closer look at the relative effects that such factors as sex and endocrine hormones, stress, and upbringing have on postpartum and other gender-related forms of depression.

Anxiety disorders. The main feature of a number of other common mood disorders is not depression but anxiety, an unreasonable level of uneasiness about one's situation or future. Anxiety may range in severity from mild apprehension to outright fear. The body responds to anxiety with increased sweating, raised pulse, and rapid or pounding heartbeats. The person may feel constriction in the chest area, dizziness, and fatigue. Another symptom I see in many of my patients is constant sighing. (Better breathing techniques, such as those I describe in Chapter 9, can help reduce anxiety.) Most people feel anxious at various times, but anxiety can be a major concern when it is so pervasive it interferes with your everyday activities, work, or sleep. An estimated one in twenty-five Americans suffers from a generalized anxiety disorder or more specialized forms, including

- obsessive-compulsive disorders, in which recurrent thoughts cause seemingly uncontrollable, repetitive behaviors (washing one's hands dozens of times per day, for example)
- post-traumatic stress disorder (PTSD), which is associated with a specific traumatic event, such as military combat, rape, or some type of disaster, and resulting nightmares, fear of the event returning, and feelings of detachment
- panic disorder, characterized by repeated panic attacks—the sudden appearance of severe fear and anxiety that is not reasonably connected to the person's situation
- phobia disorders, which result when irrational and exaggerated fears of objects (snakes, for example) or situations (such as heights or open places) become so pervasive as to disrupt the person's normal life

Diverse and Multiple Causes

People are sometimes reluctant to talk about depression, whether to other family members or to their doctor. A lingering prejudice exists that depression is a sign of personal weakness, of an inability to get

Your Personal Biochemistry:
Prescription Drugs That Cause Depression

Among the drugs with potential depression and mood disorder side effects are many common ones taken to control high blood pressure. The following table provides the chemical name first, followed by the more commonly known brand name.

- captopril (Capoten)
- propanolol (Inderal)
- metoprolol (Lopressor)
- clonidine (Catapres)
- methyldopa (Aldomet)
- reserpine (Diupres, Hydropres)

Other common drugs that may cause depression include the following:

- theophylline (Theophyl), for asthma
- triazolam (Halcion), for insomnia
- prednisone (Deltasone, Sterapred), a corticosteroid taken for the inflammation of arthritis and other conditions
- metoclopramide (Reglan), for heartburn
- cimetidine (Tagamet), for ulcers
- bupropion (Wellbutrin), for depression
- disulfiram (Antabuse), for alcoholism
- diazepam (Valium), for anxiety
- amantadine, for viral infections and Parkinson's disease
- levodopa (Sinemet, Atamet), for Parkinson's disease

along in the real world. Increasingly, doctors and the public alike are realizing that depression is an illness that may be caused by any number of factors, ranging from genetics to the side effects of prescription drugs.

A number of studies in recent years have tried to determine why a family history of depression increases an individual's risk. For example, scientists have identified potential genetic factors in blood type (though it is unclear whether it is type A, B, or O blood that may increase your risk) and in certain chromosomes (including genes on the X chromosome that affect blood clotting or color blindness, and in a genetic marker on chromosome 9). A notable recent study found that people with family histories of depression may be predisposed to depression but that in some cases an unfortunate life event is the actual trigger. Another large study involving 15,000 twins and an equal number of family members who answered a questionnaire on depression found that depressive symptoms were modestly influenced by heredity and almost not at all by common childhood environment (growing up in the same home with the same parents, school, and neighborhood). My consistent clinical observation is that children whose parents were alcoholics or were depressed often suffer from the same problem of having deficient levels of the precursors that form potentially mood-boosting neurotransmitters.

An often overlooked factor is that well over one hundred prescription drugs can cause depression or anxiety as side effects. This includes diverse types of drugs—birth control pills (estrogen and progesterone), antihistamines, sedatives, antibiotics, painkillers, corticosteroids, beta blockers, ulcer drugs, anticancer drugs, heart drugs, blood pressure drugs, and more. Even some antidepressants can cause anxiety and more extreme mental symptoms, such as hallucinations and paranoia.

Over-the-counter drugs may also cause or worsen depression and anxiety, including diet pills and common remedies for indigestion, asthma, and insomnia. I've seen many patients whose symptoms of depression could eventually be traced back to a drug taken for heartburn or for some other condition that should have been addressed with other treatments. Often these people end up being prescribed more potent drugs, including antidepressants, in an attempt to address the biochemical imbalance that is actually being caused by the original drug. Even worse, if this vicious cycle of heavy-duty drug taking goes on a long time, it can so disrupt the brain and body that merely tapering off the offending drugs does not restore full mental health.

Alcohol and tobacco are the most prominent and the most widely used of the recreational drugs that can predispose a person to depression.

> **Your Personal Biochemistry:**
> **Depression Linked to Overindulgence**
> **in Recreational Drugs**
>
> Habitual use of the following recreational drugs may also lead to depression:
>
> - alcohol
> - tobacco
> - cocaine
> - caffeine
> - marijuana

Many people who suffer from serious diseases often become depressed. This should not be surprising. Conditions such as heart disease, cancer, and diabetes are debilitating to mind and body. They sap your energy, disrupt your sleep, and break up relationships. Perhaps most dramatically, they cause you to ponder the likelihood of your imminent death. The ensuing depression can further complicate the underlying disease and make it even more difficult to recover.

It is not uncommon for people with painful and chronic diseases eventually to accept their depressed state as normal or typical for their condition. They assume that when the underlying condition is cured or addressed, the depression will naturally disappear. This may or may not be the case. I've seen plenty of patients who had seemed successfully recovered from some type of major surgery, for example, but who continued to suffer from lingering symptoms of depression.

Allergies to Foods, Chemicals, and Metals

As many as three out of every five persons may suffer from food allergies, resulting in some of the same symptoms (such as fatigue and sleeping problems) typical of depression. For example, one study found that undigested grain particles can attach themselves to morphine receptors in the brain, suggesting a direct link between food allergies and mood.

Perhaps the most controversial food allergy studies were conducted by Dr. Benjamin Feingold in the 1970s. His research determined that many children were adversely affected by eating foods containing artificial colors, flavors, and preservatives, and foods such as grapes and oranges high in the natural compound salicylate. Subsequent studies have yielded conflicting results, but it's clear that at least some children are sensitive to such compounds and benefit from avoiding them.

In recent years, nutrition-oriented health practitioners have extended Feingold's findings and recognized the existence of a broad range of food and chemical allergies. These foods, chemical pollutants, and heavy metals may cause not only depression, anxiety, and mental confusion but also headaches, fatigue, hyperactivity, runny nose, dark circles under the eyes, sneezing, gastric upset, and various other symptoms. The allergic reaction itself may range from a mild sensitivity to an extreme, whole-body response (as in an anaphylactic shock from an allergy to shellfish, for example).

Our industrialized society has also contributed greatly to an increase in average exposure to chemical and metal contaminants. These enter your body from a wide range of sources, including air pollution (lead), water (lead), dental fillings (mercury), the home (formaldehyde, benzene), cookware (aluminum), and cigarette smoke (lead, cadmium).

Your Personal Biochemistry:
Underlying Ailments That May Cause Depression

The following physical illnesses may predispose or precipitate depression among some people:

- diabetes
- schizophrenia
- infectious hepatitis
- cerebrovascular disease
- heart or lung disease
- chronic pain
- cancer
- arthritis
- premenstrual syndrome
- thyroid conditions, especially hypothyroidism
- attention deficit hyperactivity disorder (ADHD)
- bulimia
- post-viral flu syndrome
- chronic fatigue syndrome

**Your Personal Biochemistry:
Foods, Chemicals, and Heavy Metals That May Cause
Allergic Reactions and Depression**

The following foods and substances are among those that often cause allergic reactions and depression:

FOODS
- milk and dairy products
- chocolate
- peanuts
- wheat
- corn
- tomatoes
- apples
- shellfish
- soy

CHEMICALS
- paints
- formaldehyde, as from particleboard, carpets
- household cleaners
- benzene
- pesticide

HEAVY METALS
- lead
- mercury
- arsenic
- cadmium
- aluminum

Another important and often overlooked cause of depression is nutritional deficiencies. I'll look at this issue in more detail in Chapter 6, where I detail the top twenty nutrients that you can take to help prevent or treat your depression. Here let me simply list the many nutrients that may lead to depression if not taken in optimal amounts.

Your Personal Biochemistry:
Nutrient Deficiencies That May Lead to Depression

If blood levels of the following nutrients shrink below a critical point, depression may result:

- thiamine (B_1)
- niacin (B_3)
- folic acid
- NADH
- vitamin B_{12}
- pyridoxine (B_6)
- choline
- vitamin C
- vitamin D
- vitamin E
- chromium
- iron

Illnesses, licit and illicit drugs, allergic reactions, and nutritional deficiencies are not the only causes of depression that are too frequently overlooked. As I'll show in subsequent chapters, many factors can either trigger a depression or predispose a person to depression over time. These include extreme or prolonged stress or grief, as from loss of a job, a death in the family, a divorce, or some other major life event. (Admittedly, how a person responds to such adversity determines whether a major depression follows or a more minor type of adjustment disorder.) Early life experiences, such as sexual abuse or the loss of a parent, can be factors. Physical inactivity, social isolation, and an inability to relax in a mindful manner are among the prominent lifestyle factors. I've seen many cases of depression that were caused or worsened by

- gender and seasonal factors (we'll look at why women are diagnosed with depression more frequently than men in Chapter 3)

- a poor diet, especially one containing excessive amounts of sugar, caffeine, and refined carbohydrates leading to rapidly swinging blood sugar levels (see Chapter 4), or one with an imbalance in the type and quantity of amino acids or essential fatty acids
- imbalances in hormones, including those produced by endocrine glands such as thyroid hormone, sex hormones, stress hormones, melatonin, and others (more on these in Chapter 4)

Clearly, your depression may be due to biochemical, genetic, psychological, and emotional components. Its ultimate cause may never be fully known. Each person's depression is unique, even if its onset is similarly affected and can be addressed by brain neurotransmitters or by other biochemicals.

The Pharmaceutical Approach: Shotguns and Peashooters

Until about the 1940s, doctors didn't really have any drugs they could prescribe for depressed patients. Talk therapies were recognized as useful, but also difficult to do well, time consuming, and not totally effective. Doctors knew that some drugs did promote better mood, but at a stiff price. For example, stimulants such as cocaine and amphetamines can definitely brighten mood. Sigmund Freud and other influential psychiatrists of the late nineteenth and early twentieth centuries had initially embraced cocaine, but it didn't take long before the drug's addictiveness and side effects caused it to be rejected. Amphetamines went through a similar evolution.

In the 1950s researchers began to test what they thought might be a nonstimulating antidepressant. This was lithium, a natural metallic salt that could apparently dampen the mood swings of mania and manic depression. Pharmaceutical companies weren't enthusiastic, perhaps because they couldn't patent a natural substance (thus limiting potential profits) and maybe also because lithium was known to be somewhat toxic. It wasn't until 1970 that the FDA approved lithium for mood disorders. It remains in use today, with varying degrees of acceptance, primarily to prevent the manic phase of manic depression. Critics of lithium dismiss it as a toxic metal without any curative value. They say that yes, lithium can reduce mania, but mainly because it deadens the mind and makes the person lethargic, even stupefied. The specific biochemical mechanism by which lithium affects manic depression is not completely understood even today. Among lithium's acknowledged side effects are blurred vision, nausea, and drowsiness. Its toxic dosage levels (where it is especially damaging to the nervous system, heart, and kidneys) are close to its therapeutic levels.

A more promising development from the point of view of depression researchers and pharmaceutical companies ensued from studies done in the late 1950s demonstrating that moods could be altered and depression lifted by small changes in the levels of certain chemicals in the brain, especially the neurotransmitters serotonin, noradrenaline, and dopamine. These brain chemicals play an important role in the process by which neighboring nerve cells relay electrical impulses and can directly influence mood. When neurotransmitters such as noradrenaline and serotonin go on strike, in effect, and don't do their impulse-relaying job, brain chemistry is affected in a way that leads to lethargy, irritability, and other symptoms of depressed mood. Researchers have also determined that certain drugs can help neurotransmitters to loiter in the synapse, the gap between the outer terminals of two nerve cells, giving the neurotransmitters more time and opportunity to take effect. Other drugs can destroy the enzyme that inactivates neurotransmitters. The effect is the same: more mood-elevating neurotransmitting.

The neurotransmitter revolution has inspired pharmaceutical companies to develop dozens of new prescription drugs, though most fall within three classes:

- MAO inhibitors
- tricyclics
- selective serotonin reuptake inhibitors (SSRIs)

Researchers developed the first monoamine oxidase inhibitor (MAOI), iproniazid, in the early 1950s. At that time it was being used as a treatment for tuberculosis. It became more popular, however, when doctors discovered later in the decade that patients taking it enjoyed improved mood and more energy. MAOIs are now thought to accomplish this by increasing the effective life of neurotransmitters such as serotonin, dopamine, and noradrenaline in the brain. An enzyme found in nerve cells, MAO inactivates these brain biochemicals by oxidizing them. Therefore, a drug that neutralizes MAO or otherwise inhibits its action has the effect of limiting the enzyme's ability to destroy neurotransmitters. Less enzyme thus means more neurotransmitter action and an increased sense of well-being.

Many doctors at first welcomed this new class of antidepressants. It wasn't long, however, before it became apparent that MAOIs caused some serious side effects. When MAOIs in the body encounter the chemical tyramine, they can cause an extreme reaction, including sudden high blood pressure, headaches, and even (occasionally) strokes. This means people taking MAOIs must avoid a long list of relatively common tyramine-containing foods, drinks, and nutrients (especially the amino acids tryptophan or tyrosine). Restricted foods include certain cheeses, beer and wine, coffee, yogurt, and chocolate. Various drugs can also cause this toxic reaction, including nasal decongestants, cold remedies, and hay fever medications. A wide variety of prescription drugs are similarly contraindicated when a person is taking MAOIs, including beta blockers and SSRIs such as Prozac.

Although the so-called cheese effect is the most serious potential side effect from using MAOIs, users have also been known to experience headaches, insomnia, constipation, fatigue, restlessness, blurred vision, and confusion. Less frequently these drugs may also cause liver damage, convulsions, schizophrenia, or coma. An overdose can be lethal, which is an important consideration for use with depressed patients who may be suicidal.

Iproniazid and a number of other MAOIs are no longer on the market. Others remain, such as phenelzine (Nardil) and tranylcypromine (Parnate). To some extent, the advent of the SSRIs since the mid-1980s has cut into MAOI use. Doctors almost always try other drugs first, but they do still prescribe MAOIs and patients often suffer the consequences of these drugs' adverse side effects.

A more popular class of antidepressants is the tricyclics, the first of which were synthesized in the 1940s. As was the case with the first MAOIs, doctors initially used tricyclics to treat a condition other than depression (in this case schizophrenia). Studies conducted on the tricyclic imipramine in the late 1950s showed it could alleviate depression, especially among lethargic, inactive people. (Imipramine often worsened the depression in people who were manic or agitated.) Today, doctors widely prescribe imipramine and other closely related tricyclics such as amitriptyline, doxepin, and desipramine.

Researchers have found that tricyclics affect a number of neurotransmitters, including acetylcholine and histamine, as well as noradrenaline and serotonin. Tricyclics may improve mood by allowing neurotransmitters to remain active in the nerve synapse, rather than being grabbed back by the transmitting cell. Scientists are unsure, however, whether this is the tricyclics' main depression-relieving action. The drugs must be taken for several weeks before the person taking them notices any effects on mood. Studies have yielded conflicting results. Some have found that tricyclics help a significant percentage of patients, while others have found that benefits on mood are minimal or that tricyclics are not much more effective than placebos at elevating mood.

Though tricyclics don't cause potentially fatal increases in blood pressure as the MAOIs do, they do have numerous unwanted side effects. These include drowsiness, dry mouth, sweating, blurred vision, weight gain, and constipation. Instead of noticing a brightening of mood, some people may feel detached and lethargic while others react as if overstressed. Tricyclics make some depressed people become manic. Patients can get addicted to tricyclics and they can die from taking too high a dose. Antidepressant drugs are among the most likely to cause fatal poisonings, and tricyclics are especially dangerous.

Researchers now refer to the first generation of psychiatric drugs, the MAOIs and the tricyclics, as "shotguns" and "dirty drugs." The problem was that some target neurotransmitters were hit but so also were many other biochemicals that affected (often adversely) not only mood but energy levels, alertness, and overall health. Despite the tendency of these drugs to cause potentially dangerous side effects, at least five million Americans are currently taking forms of these now outmoded antidepressant drugs.

The "Prozac Revolution"

An avalanche of publicity, including best-selling books and endless articles in the mass media, has generated a surprising popularity for Prozac. Upward of 20 million Americans have now tried Prozac. In 1998, more than 60 million prescriptions for Prozac were written. An estimated three quarters of a million prescriptions for children aged six to eighteen were written in 1996, almost double the number of such prescriptions doctors wrote two years earlier. According to Peter Breggin, M.D., author of *Talking Back to Prozac* and *Your Drug May Be Your Problem*, there is no evidence that Prozac is any more effective than an active placebo for children.

Defenders of Prozac and other SSRIs claim that these new psychiatric drugs are not stimulants, nor do they cause euphoria. According to Dr. Kapit, the FDA psychiatrist who wrote the official "safety review" of adverse reactions, Prozac has the "profile of adverse effects that more closely resembles that of a stimulant drug," but his review of the Prozac research was ignored. Contrary to the U.S. whitewash, the European labels on Prozac do contain warnings of high suicidality and agitation.

Dr. Breggin reports that after extensive analysis of the fourteen Prozac studies submitted to the FDA, he found only three studies showed that it was better than placebo, six of seven studies showed Tofranil, an older tricyclic antidepressant, was more effective, and eight studies showed Prozac had no effect. He points out that the minor tranquillizers, sleep medications, and sedatives such as Benzodiazepines, chloral hydrate, and Dalmane, were allowed to be given, along with Prozac, during the studies. When the patients receiving these drugs were filtered out of the statistics, Prozac itself was not found to be more effective than placebo. What the FDA in reality approved was Prozac in conjunction with sedatives. This suggests that through incredible public relations and press, we are having a national placebo effect, but it is not a benign effect when we look at the seriousness of the side effects.

The pharmaceutical companies claim the SSRIs are safer than earlier classes of antidepressants, but recent independent studies give a much different picture that suggests that SSRIs are hardly benign. Adverse effects can vary and long-term safety is still being assessed. Actually, according to Dr. Breggin, only 63 people had taken Prozac for as long as two years before it was released to the public. The various side effects and contraindications for SSRIs are serious enough to cause at least as many as one in four users to discontinue the drug.

Analysis of the original FDA data by Dr. Breggin and of other studies by two Harvard psychiatrists, Martin Teicher and Jonathon Cole, one of my mentors, reported in the 1990 American Journal of Psychiatry, found Prozac to have a suicidality rate three times greater than older antidepressants and to be associated with "intense, violent, suicidal preoccupation" and severe anxiety and agitation within two to seven weeks of use. Joseph Glen Mullen, M.D., and Peter Breggin, M.D., in their respective books, Prozac Backlash and Talking Back to Prozac, both outline the extent of the side effects. According to these two authorities, Prozac interferes with the function of every part of the brain. Research independent from that of Eli Lilly suggests at least 60 percent of users experience sexual dysfunctions with decreased or absent libido, loss of capacity to orgasm, and ejaculatory problems. (I shudder at the ramifications of this effect on the 750,000 six- to eighteen-year-olds who are using Prozac during their adolescent psychosexual development.) It may affect the frontal lobes with a loss of empathy and social judgment, the temporal lobes with a loss of long- and short-term memory, the cerebral cortex with a decrease in mental acuity, the hypothalamus with dysregulation of temperature control and weight gain or loss, and may create apathy or hypomania by its effects on the limbic system and the basal ganglion, causing asthma, tics, spasms, and dyskinesias.

In addition to all of these side effects, there seems to be a further disruption of the biologically altered brain from SSRI use. A potentially more serious alteration is pointed out in both *Prozac Backlash* and *Talking Back to Prozac*. This is a down regulation of the brain's serotonin nervous system in response to the hyperserotonin stimulation caused by the SSRI. According to animal studies, this down regulation includes a decrease in natural serotonin production and the loss of up to 40 to 60 percent of the serotonin receptor sites. This down regulation sets people up for a 50 percent rate of withdrawal symptoms from Prozac, including: 1. sensoral disturbances, including electric-shock sensations, 2. disequilibrium, with dizziness and spinning sensations, 3. depression, 4. flulike symptoms, including lethargy, fatigue, and muscle pain, 5. sleep disturbances, including insomnia and vivid dreams, 6. gastrointestinal symptoms, including nausea and vomiting, and 7. anger and irritability.

Associated with this is a "Prozac poop-out" in which, as the brain down-regulates, more Prozac is needed to get the same effect. One of the hardest things about the withdrawal, because patients are not warned about this, is the mistaken belief that their depression is returning. With careful withdrawal and timely application of my five-step *Depression-Free for Life* program, I am able to successfully help people withdraw from Prozac and other SSRIs, and succeed with this natural five-step program to heal their depression.

When we look at the Prozac phenomenon from a larger perspective, we are looking at two competing paradigms in our society. One is the myth of "better living through chemistry" paradigm exemplified by the use of central nervous system stimulants to create the illusory "personality plus" mentality given to us by the use of "ecstasy" (MDMA), cocaine, and amphetamines, the latter of which reached its peak in 1967 with 23 million prescriptions, and now Prozac. The other paradigm is to restore fully integrated brain function naturally in a way that builds our natural joy and helps us grow physically, emotionally, mentally, and spiritually. The *Depression-Free for Life* program is designed to help you achieve this extraordinary state of physical, mental, and spiritual health.

From an even larger perspective, the choice is about the quality and meaning of our lives. Do we choose the myth of "better living through chemistry" and take on the debilitating effect of pesticides, herbicides, synthetic fertilizers, junk food, genetically engineered foods, and Prozac as a way of life which speeds up the deterioration of the planet and our own minds and bodies, or do we return to a natural, organic approach that heals our bodies, our brains, and ultimately the whole planet?

Psychotropic Drugs and Their Effects on Neurotransmitters

Within the past few years drug manufacturers and research scientists have been working on developing further generations of antidepressants, including drugs that selectively affect noradrenaline, dopamine, or serotonin or some combination of these. The theory behind these new drugs is that controlling specific neurotransmitters lets doctors fine-tune depression treatment and possibly treat patients for shorter periods of depression. Thus, for example, people who are depressed and who have an obvious lack of drive or inability to motivate themselves may benefit from enhancement of noradrenaline function.

Clinical experience with these drugs is still very preliminary. The accompanying box lists common psychotropic drugs that have well-known effects on neurotransmitters.

Selective serotonin reuptake inhibitors
(enhance serotonin levels and stimulate adrenergic neurotransmitter system; lower dopamine levels)

- fluoxetine (Prozac)
- sertraline (Zoloft)
- paroxetine (Paxil)
- fluvoxamine (Luvox)

MAO inhibitors
(varied effects on serotonin, noradrenaline, and dopamine)

- phenelzine (Nardil)
- tranylcypromine (Parnate)
- isocarboxazid (Marplan)

Selective noradrenaline reuptake inhibitors
(enhance noradrenaline function)

- reboxetine (Edronax)

Tricyclics
(varied effects on noradrenaline and serotonin)

- clomipramine (Anafranil)
- amitriptyline (Elavil)
- imipramine (Tofranil)
- desipramine (Norpramin)
- chlordiazepoxide and amitriptyline (Limbitrol)
- doxepin (Sinequan)
- perphenazine and amitriptyline (Triavil)
- protriptyline (Vivactil)
- trimipramine (Surmontil)

Atypical antidepressants
(varied effects on dopamine and noradrenaline)

- bupropion (Wellbutrin)

Atypical antidepressants
(varied effects on serotonin)

- trazodone (Desyrel)

Atypical antidepressants
(varied effects on noradrenaline and serotonin)

- venlafaxine (Effexor)
- mirtazapine (Remeron)
- nefazodone (Serzone)

Selective dopamine reuptake inhibitors
(enhance dopamine function)

- amineptine (Survector)

GABA promoters

- chlordiazepoxide (Librium)
- diazepam (Valium)
- clorazepate (Tranxene)
- alprazolam (Xanax)
- lorazepam (Ativan)
- flurazepam (Dalmane)
- temazepam (Restoril)

Doctors are also now trying combinations of antidepressants. Some are known to be dangerous, such as using MAOIs simultaneously with SSRIs. Others are still being evaluated, although the simultaneous use of SSRIs and tricyclics seems to have become commonplace (one recent study found that approximately two thirds of antidepressant users were taking more than one antidepressant drug). There's even a name for this approach: augmentation drug therapy. One primary antidepressant may be used, with a half dozen or more other drugs for balancing effects, treatment of side effects, and so forth. Like Martina, whom you met earlier in the chapter, you might be prescribed Prozac or one of the other SSRIs, a tricyclic such as desipramine, Viagra to counter the sex-deadening effects of the SSRI, atenolol or some other beta blocker to balance the tricyclic's noradrenaline boost, and an antacid for digestive side effects. Researchers have conducted very few studies on the risks and benefits of using multiple antidepressants and other drugs at the same time. In my experience, I've noticed that as a general rule, the more drugs you take, the more varied and worrisome become the side effects.

Toward a More Natural Treatment Program

Pharmaceutical companies spend more than $10 billion promoting and advertising drugs to Americans each year. Whereas at one time almost all of this marketing was directed at physicians, nowadays much of it is directed at you, the potential consumer. Who hasn't noticed the glossy, four-page ads for Prozac in *Time*, *Newsweek*, and similar magazines? Mostly favorable cover stories on Prozac, Ritalin, and other drugs are among the newsweeklies' bestselling issues. Some promotional efforts border on the outrageous—in 1995 Eli Lilly was taken to task for allowing its salespeople to turn a "National Depression Awareness Day" at a Maryland high school into a virtual pep rally for Prozac.

Not surprisingly, the result is that drugs are now exceedingly popular for treating depression and anxiety. Patients read about the wonders of Prozac and ask their doctors to prescribe it. Most doctors are more than willing to support the drug approach. Many have neither the time nor the inclination to talk with a patient, learn about her problems, or counsel her about dietary and lifestyle factors. Because prescription drugs are often not a covered benefit, managed care plans find it cheaper to dispense antidepressants than to provide long-term talk therapy. Pharmaceutical companies court doctors by advertising in medical journals and by organizing seminars and lectures to which they attract doctors with lush dinners and comfy vacation packages. The bottom line is that doctors give prescriptions for one or more antidepressant drugs to approximately four out of every five patients who are diagnosed with depression. More than 60 percent of prescriptions for the new generations of antidepressants come from general practitioners, not from psychiatrists. Patients who do see an outpatient psychiatrist, a recent study found, were more than twice as likely to have an antidepressant drug prescribed to them in 1993–1994 than in 1985.

But the question remains: Does all this medication actually get at the root of a person's depression? Depression rates are high, especially among women and young people, as are rates of suicide, especially among men. Studies show that of those who seek medical help and receive prescriptions for depression, only one in ten manage to get the right combination of proper dose and duration of treatment. And the long-term effects of taking SSRIs over many years are mostly unknown. The person's fundamental imbalance is not being addressed if, as is often the case, he or she quickly sinks back into depression when the SSRI is stopped. People do not suffer from a deficiency of Prozac. The answer for meaningful healing is not lifelong treatment with Prozac, but rather a more comprehensive program. What is needed is the five-step program described in this book, which holistically addresses mind and body.

While the SSRIs are more like peashooters than the shotguns of the tricyclics and MAOIs, their very design limits their potential: they can alter the activity of only one or two of numerous biochemicals—including not only neurotransmitters but hormones, blood sugar, and nutrients—that have now been shown to contribute to depression. This fatal shortcoming of conventional drug approaches to depression sharply contrasts with the natural, five-step approach, which acts synergistically to provide long-term relief from depression by actually healing the preconditions that cause biochemical imbalances, which play such an important role in depression in the first place.

3

The Gender Factor:
Why More Women Than Men
Are Depressed

If you talk to practically any medical researcher who has advertised for subjects for a forthcoming depression-related study, he or she is likely to confirm an unusual pattern: many more women than men will respond to the request. This reflects a central mystery about depression: in various societies around the world, women are two to three times as likely as men to suffer from major depression, from chronic low mood, or from seasonal affective disorder. In some parts of the developed world, as many as one in five women may suffer from depression at some point in her life. Many researchers believe that among women worldwide, depression is now the leading cause of "disease burden," a composite measure of both illness and death. Nor is women's proclivity to depression necessarily limited to modern times—the ancient Greeks believed that emotional excitability and excessive fear were peculiar to women, caused by disturbances of the womb. (The Greek word for womb, *hystera*, serves as the root for both hysteria and hysterectomy.)

A number of population studies performed within the past two decades have documented women's increased susceptibility to depression. One of the first was done in the mid-1970s by a wife and husband team of psychiatrists, Myrna Weissman and Gerald Klerman. Their landmark study, published in *Archives of General Psychiatry* in 1977, documented an approximately twofold greater risk of depression in women in the United States and elsewhere during the previous forty years. Weissman and Klerman noted the need for more research into such possible explanations as biological susceptibility, psychosocial factors such as social discrimination, and "female-learned helplessness."

Over the ensuing two decades Weissman and Klerman continued to publish surveys that show notable gender differences in the rate of depression. In a 1989 review article they described not only "a persistent gender effect" but also an increase in the depression rate in cohorts born after World War II. They also found that people were experiencing their first bout of depression at younger and younger ages. The risk of depression was "consistently two to three times higher among women than men across all adult ages," they said. These trends were evident in the United States, Sweden, Germany, Canada, and New Zealand, though not in Korea or Puerto Rico.

In 1996 a team of researchers led by Weissman published an even wider-ranging study in the *Journal of the American Medical Association*. It included data from population-based studies that totaled 38,000 subjects. The researchers found that the lifetime rates for major depression varied among the ten countries included (the United States, Canada, Puerto Rico, France, West Germany, Italy, Lebanon, Taiwan, Korea, and New Zealand). The low was 1.5 cases of major depression per 100 adults in Taiwan and the high was 19.0 in Beirut. "In every country, the rates of major depression were higher for women than men," the researchers found. Overall, the lifetime rate for major depression was 7.4 percent for women and 2.8 percent for men. Little gender difference existed, on the other hand, for incidence of manic depression. Many smaller studies done by other researchers in developing countries and among various social and ethnic groups have also found higher rates of depression in women. For example, a recent study of depression in some 1,100 elderly citizens of Leganes, Spain, found depressive symptoms in 20 percent of the men but 46 percent of the women.

Researchers have been busy investigating the reasons why women suffer from higher rates of depression, with some of the most prominent theories relating to sociocultural, psychological, and biochemical factors. Other roads have been explored but deemed unpromising. For example, genetics appears not to be much of a factor. Studies of families with a history of depression show that women and men are more or less equally affected, and data from a 1985 family/genetic study led researchers to conclude that "the excess of females with major depression cannot be attributed to increased genetic loading for depression in women."

Many researchers now believe that in all likelihood a combination of factors is responsible for higher rates of depression in women. Late in 1993 the *Journal of Affective Disorders* published a series of studies on the issue and concluded that the causes were likely to be "many and intertwined, involving cultural roles, differing styles of reactions to stress, sex hormones, and perhaps even male-female variations in the brain." The complex and fascinating roles that neurotransmitters and other biochemicals, such as serotonin, melatonin, the sex hormones estrogen and progesterone, the stress hormone cortisol, and thyroid hormones, may play in gender and depression has been the impetus for an explosion of interest in the new field of "psychobiology." In 1992 the National Institute of Mental Health (NIMH) even sponsored a conference, "Toward a New Psychobiology of Depression in Women."

Before we examine the potential biochemical distinctions between men and women that may account for much of the difference in depression rates, let's first consider sociocultural factors. As we'll see, these two approaches are not necessarily mutually exclusive. In fact, they can and do affect each other.

The Role of Sociocultural Factors in Depression

Like many doctors who treat depression, I've noticed in my own practice that women outnumber men. The gender factor sometimes comes up during counseling, as it did when I was talking to a bright young schoolteacher recently. She said that she often felt overwhelmed by all that was expected of her as a woman. "There are so many different stresses," she said, "so many places that I feel as a woman I don't measure up to current cultural norms, even though I recognize that those norms—being model-thin, always made up, able to talk to men about sports or cars—are divorced from what is really important for me as a woman."

Cultural expectations of women differ dramatically from one society to the next. A few of the studies that have actually failed to establish gender differences in the rate of depression were conducted in societies where cultural norms and gender roles are relatively straightforward. For example, a 1995 study found similar rates of depression among men and women in a sample of 339 Jews affiliated with orthodox synagogues. Researchers credited the lack of gender disparity to "specific cultural-religious values." They said, "These values included the esteem attached to women's central role in family management and the low use of alcohol and suicide as escape routes from depression." Another study found little difference in the depression rates among a group of Amish in Pennsylvania, possibly because of fewer role differences between men and women.

Obviously, conditions for women differ widely in different societies, and pressures on them range from subtle discrimination to widespread physical abuse. The following are some of the most obvious factors relating to cultural inequalities and social oppression that may account for higher rates of depression among women.

Women are exposed to negative life events, including rape and sexual abuse, more frequently than men. In some societies, as many as one in three women has experienced significant sexual or physical abuse by age twenty-one, and as many as one in two women are physically abused by partners at some point in life. Sexual and other forms of abuse early in life can damage self-esteem and create negative self-images, which can later lead to depression. I have certainly observed in my clinical practice over the last thirty years that many of my female patients were seriously damaged psychologically by early sex experiences. A 1997 study found that women are more frequently victimized as children, and that childhood sexual abuse accounted for a significant proportion of the sex difference in depression. The researchers determined that women are also victimized as adults more often than men, although adult victimization was not associated with higher depression levels. Other evidence (and common sense), however, indicates that adult women's negative experiences can in fact lead to depression. In addition to abuse, these experiences may include such misfortunes as miscarriage, workplace discrimination, and poverty (women and children account for much of the poor). For example, the psychologists who conducted a 1996 study determined that "depressed women were more likely to have experienced a negative severe event before the onset of depression and had a greater frequency of negative interpersonal events."

Being married protects men but not women from depression. Why is it that married men have a lower rate of depression than single men, and the depression rate for single women and female college students is close to that for men? In other words, why is marriage more of a bummer for women than men? One reason probably relates to the fact that women are more often at home raising the children. Some societies recognize this as the noble and meaningful endeavor it is, but other cultures devalue it. Women who have children and whose main identity is as a housewife may suffer from poor self-image. They may also feel isolated and unappreciated. Not having their own source of income can be frustrating and a source of insecurity. Among the elderly citizens of Leganes, Spain, in the study mentioned earlier, women's higher rate of depression was tied to lack of a confidant, few social activities, and a sense that women lack control of their lives—all factors that may more notably affect married women than married men.

Young girls may be taught behaviors that encourage later depression. More so than young boys, girls are encouraged to be nurturing, to develop empathy, and to value relationships and social activities. Yet an overemphasis on the feelings of others can undermine one's own self-actualization and self-esteem, especially when friends or partners are critical (or abruptly leave). This can lead to passivity, dependency, undue self-sacrifice, or feelings of powerlessness and helplessness—the seeds of depression. A study of patients at a psychiatric hospital in Sweden indicated significant gender differences with regard to "eliciting factors"—what brought on the bout of depression. The eliciting factor in female depression was most commonly "threat to social bonds," whereas in male depression it was "threat to self-esteem" or "threat to self-respect." In addition, the emphasis on physical beauty that modern societies ingrain in young girls can set the stage for erosion of self-worth later in life as looks fade and partners may abandon them for younger and more attractive women.

Women may respond to stress, disappointment, or adversity differently from men. A number of studies have suggested that men are more likely to respond to potentially depression-related factors such as stress, disappointment, or adversity by active (or distractive) behaviors, which in the extreme can include excessive drinking and even violence. For example, a 1995 study found that men with depression tend to have higher scores than women on trait measures of hostility, "suggesting that men may be at greater risk than women of developing patterns of pathologic aggression and hostile behavior." Some psychologists believe that women, by focusing more on their feelings and acknowledging their negative emotions, are more likely to experience longer and more severe episodes of depression.

It is worth noting that a minority of researchers disagree with the contention that sociocultural factors cause depression to be vastly more prevalent among women. From these researchers' perspective, an overlooked factor may be that women are just more willing than men to seek treatment for their depression. Studies have shown that divorce and the death of a loved one are just as likely to depress men as they are women. The apparent unwillingness of men to seek professional help at such times has been referred to as the "stiff-upper-lip syndrome." Some studies, however, have been designed to take into account this factor yet have still found higher rates of depression among women.

A related argument for more equal rates of depression hinges on men's much higher rate of alcoholism and other forms of substance abuse. Psychologists have noted that if you include alcoholism as a form or a symptom of depression, men and women's rates are almost equal. My experience with treating both men and women for depression is consistent with these findings—the overall rate seems to be similar, but the symptomatic expression is different for men and women.

Underdiagnosing of male depression may be more of an issue than some are willing to admit. A 1991 study showed that doctors miss 67 percent of depression in men because they're looking for what one observer has called "feminized" symptoms, like crying. Depressed men, however, may be more likely to exhibit hostility or anger.

Male depression is more often covert, say researchers such as Terrence Real, a Boston-area social worker who has written about men and depression in his book *I Don't Want to Talk About It*. Real says that men hide their depression in an "unholy triad" of destructive behavior: drinking, addictive work, and other forms of self-medication, isolation, and lashing out, which may range from verbal abuse of partners to murder. Men are also more than four times as likely as women to commit suicide. Real contends that "the cure for covert depression is overt depression," and then learning intimacy.

Toward a Biochemical Understanding of Women and Depression

Scientists and others continue to debate the relative importance of sociocultural factors in gender and depression. I've known patients who've insisted that their condition was wholly due to an early childhood experience or to gender discrimination. It is possible to acknowledge, however, that these play a role while also recognizing that biochemical factors are influential. In fact, a number of new findings are suggesting that these factors affect each other; that sociocultural factors such as experiences and perceptions can alter brain chemistry. For example, studies have found that an animal's social rank—where it stands in the dominance hierarchy—affects its blood and brain serotonin levels. On the other hand, biochemical factors such as hormonal changes can produce different emotional responses in women than men. High-tech brain imaging, according to one researcher, "reveals that psychological phenomena such as anger and sadness have biological underpinnings; we can now see circuits of brain cells becoming activated when these emotions arise."

A recent groundbreaking study, conducted by researchers at the NIMH, involved comparative brain scans of men and women. The researchers found that blood flow to a certain part of the brain is markedly different in depressed men compared to depressed women. The researchers first asked ten men and ten women to feel sad while having their brains examined by a positron-emission tomography (PET) scan, a sophisticated imaging technique. The women and men reported similar subjective feelings of sadness, but the researchers found that "the brain activity of the two groups looked very different." Blood flow in the anterior limbic system in the brains of the women was eight times greater than in the same area of men's brains. Such major differences were not in evidence for other emotions, such as anger and happiness. The researchers speculated that women were more likely to suffer from an imbalance in regions of the brain that malfunction during clinical depression.

Other depression researchers have focused on gender and serotonin, the neurotransmitter that, in the right amounts and at the right times of day, is associated with a brightening of mood and feelings of self-assurance. In a provocative recent study that suggests an important gender factor may be at work, researchers at McGill University in Montreal found that women's brains are much less efficient at synthesizing serotonin in comparison to men's brains. The researchers gave tryptophan-deficient solutions to eight men and seven women, aged eighteen to thirty-five. Drinking a tryptophan-deficient solution is a reliable way to reduce a person's brain serotonin levels, because serotonin is produced in the body from the breakdown of tryptophan. If you provide a solution containing much higher levels of other amino acids that compete with tryptophan for uptake in the brain, the result relatively quickly will be very low levels of serotonin in the brain. After drinking the tryptophan-deficient solution, men were found to have 79 percent lower levels of serotonin. Women experienced an even greater reduction, of 89 percent. Moreover, serotonin synthesis was reduced by 40 times in women and only 9.5 times in men. The researchers also measured rates of serotonin synthesis in the brain using PET scanning. They concluded, "The mean rate of synthesis in normal males was found to be 52 percent higher than in normal females; this marked difference may be a factor relevant to the lower incidence of major unipolar depression in males."

Some brain researchers now believe that women have more difficulty than men adjusting to lower levels of tryptophan. That's because although men and women start off with similar stores of serotonin, women produce it at a slower rate, allowing stress or other factors to lead to a low-serotonin state of depression. It is interesting to note that low-serotonin brain levels in men have also been linked to what we might call "male depression"—alcoholism, hostility, aggression, and suicide.

The Depression Season

One of the subtle consequences of technological innovation has been a lack of awareness about how the body is affected by natural rhythms. Electric lights create artificial day at any time of the night. Our homes, autos, workplaces, malls, and even sports stadiums now provide year-round constant temperatures, allowing us to feel cool in the midday desert sun and warm in the middle of a New England winter. Women's menstrual cycles, however, remind them of the ebb and flow of biochemicals within their bodies, and how these substances can affect not only levels of sexual desire but also appetite, mind, and mood. Beyond that many men and women barely give a second thought to how the body is affected by and responds to daily and seasonal changes.

This is unfortunate because a surprising number of people, and women in particular, suffer from depression primarily during the winter. As I mentioned in the previous chapter, SAD is a major seasonal depressive episode, often accompanied by sleep disorders (sleeping too much in particular), cravings for carbohydrates, and unusual weight gain. The lack of natural light in northern areas during the winter is a major factor in causing seasonal affective disorder, but scientists are still investigating exactly how light interacts with bodily organs and chemicals to regulate sleep, mood, and other functions, and to cause SAD. Melatonin function seems to be closely connected in some way. The pineal gland, a tiny endocrine organ located in the center of brain, produces melatonin. Melatonin secretion, of course, is a crucial factor in sleep patterns, which themselves are often closely tied to depression. Melatonin also plays a central role in controlling the body's daily clock.

The pineal gland responds to a wide variety of changes in your environment, constantly adjusting levels of melatonin in your body. These factors include:

Time of the day. Scientists think that the pineal gland is linked to the eyes either by nerves or through the action of the part of the brain known as the hypothalamus. Thus melatonin secretion patterns are intimately affected by exposure of the eyes to sunlight and to changes in light and dark.

Age. Blood levels of melatonin tend to decrease progressively with advancing age, especially after age seventy.

Exercise levels. Female athletes who exercise to the point that their menstrual cycles shut down have melatonin levels twice as high as normal.

Electromagnetic fields. Exposure to electromagnetic fields, such as from sleeping under an electric blanket, can lower melatonin levels in some people and has been linked to increased rates of depression.

One additional factor is gender. Studies have found that women are overwhelmingly more likely to suffer from SAD than men. A common ratio is that of three to four women with SAD to every man—that is, 75 to 80 percent of those with SAD are women. New findings suggest that melatonin may be a prominent biochemical factor in depression among women. Some intriguing recent research has looked into how and why women seem to be more susceptible than men to fluctuations in daily melatonin production. At least indirectly, melatonin levels have been linked in a number of ways not only to SAD but also to depression, manic depression, and other mood disorders. For example:

- Women taking high doses of melatonin (75 mg per day) as part of a long-term study of its effectiveness as a birth control agent have reported improvements in mood as a side effect.
- Certain antidepressants (MAOIs, lithium, some SSRIs, for example) apparently work, at least in part, by increasing melatonin levels, and some other (nonantidepressant) drugs that increase melatonin levels at night or decrease them in the morning (as beta blockers do) seem to improve mood or relieve depression as a side effect.
- Scientists have found lower levels of melatonin in the pineal glands and brains of suicide victims when compared to persons who died by accidental (though also violent) means. Also, reduced melatonin secretion leading to "low-melatonin syndrome" has been demonstrated in patients suffering from a major depressive episode.
- One study that used psychological profiles found that melatonin benefited a half-dozen mood-scale categories, including tension/anxiety, depression/dejection, and fatigue/inertia.
- When manic-depressive patients are in the depressive phase, they tend to have lower levels of melatonin; they also experience lower nighttime levels of melatonin during episodes of suicidal behavior, according to studies.
- Children suffering from some kinds of depression have been found to have low levels of melatonin, and traumatic events early in life may cause low melatonin levels.
- Studies have found that melatonin can increase GABA levels and that melatonin reduces anxiety and stress by interacting with the same brain receptors acted upon by antianxiety benzodiazepine drugs such as Valium.
- One of the endorphins, destyr gamma endorphin, seems to have antidepressant effects that may be linked to its ability to significantly increase melatonin levels.

Some of the most dramatic connections between melatonin and depression, however, also involve gender:

- A 1998 study looked at the effect of gender on hospital admission statistics for mood disorders in Birmingham, Great Britain (which is approximately as far north of the equator as Calgary, Canada). The study demonstrated a significant seasonal pattern for depression, with the incidence highest in winter. Admissions for conditions not related to mood disorders did not show significant seasonal variations. The statistics also confirmed a gender effect, with women but not men experiencing a significant winter peak for depression and a summer peak for manic depression.

- Researchers recently found that during the winter, women increase their nightly production of melatonin and during the summer they decrease it. In contrast, the nightly secretions of melatonin in men don't change from winter to summer. This suggests that women are more sensitive to natural light than men.

- A study done on Siberian hamsters had a similar finding—the animals were shown to experience gender-related differences in melatonin response to prenatal light exposure. There was also a gender-related difference in another hormone, follicle-stimulating hormone (FSH).

- A recent study also found gender-related differences in sleep between depressed men (who had less slow-wave sleep, the deep sleep phase that precedes the period of dreaming) and depressed women. Melatonin, of course, intimately affects sleep.

- Studies have found that women's melatonin levels drop right around ovulation, and that very high levels actually cause infertility (which is why melatonin is being tested as a form of birth control). Melatonin secretion increases with menstrual flow.

One proposed cause of SAD is an overproduction of melatonin during the long winter nights. Ideally, your pineal gland secretes a spike of melatonin between about midnight to three A.M., and then begins to produce less. When daylight hours dwindle, the pineal gland may never effectively shut down, causing higher-than-optimal levels during the day and depressed mood. Another possibility is that the lack of daytime light may diminish release of melatonin during the night, causing lower-than-optimal levels at nighttime and depressed mood the next day.

What we do know is that people suffering from SAD become happier and more energetic when they are exposed to especially bright, full-spectrum lights for extended periods (such as three hours in the morning and three more hours in the early evening). I've used this therapy myself successfully with a number of patients with SAD. The SAD-busting lights, however, are expensive and the need to be exposed to them for many hours per day can be a problem.

Melatonin supplements are also being tested for their potential mood-elevating effects. Unlike serotonin, for example, melatonin from supplements enters the bloodstream and easily passes through the blood-brain barrier. Studies using melatonin to treat SAD have reported mixed results. Some have reported subjects improving. Others have found subjects stay the same or even get worse. Clearly, too much melatonin (or taking it at the wrong time of the day) can cause adverse effects, including symptoms often associated with depression. Most nutritional advisors recommend that you consult a physician before taking melatonin supplements if you suffer from major depression, or are taking conventional antidepressant drugs.

Like most other hormones, melatonin has varied and diverse effects on the body. It also interacts with other bodily compounds, from drugs to the sex hormones. Studies done on animals, for example, have found links between melatonin secretion and reproductive function. Other studies have looked at the effect of stress hormones on melatonin. All this complicates the treatment of SAD and gender-related depression, but recognizing the potential effects of melatonin on mind and mood is an important first step.

Depression and Hormones

The fact that many women seem to experience depression at specific times in their reproductive cycle—immediately after giving birth (postpartum), and in the year or two of perimenopause (just before menstrual cycles cease)—suggests a role for estrogen or other sex hormones in depression. There are five periods in many women's lives when they undergo hormonal changes that may affect their moods.

In early adolescence at the onset of menstruation. Menarche is the term used to describe the onset of menstruation in girls of age thirteen or so, due to increased production of the sex hormones estrogen and progesterone. The onset of puberty has attracted the attention of depression researchers because boys and girls seem to have similar rates of depression until roughly this age, when the depression rate increases for adolescent girls. It is very difficult, however, to separate hormonal influences from the various other factors that may account for emotional differences between boys and girls at this age. Puberty can be a difficult age for both

Your Personal Biochemistry:
Are You a Seasonal Depressive?

The following are signs of balanced melatonin function:

- relaxed
- calm
- tranquil
- mild euphoria/moderate elation
- contentment
- improved mood

Too little melatonin activity may cause the following signs and symptoms:

- insomnia
- depression
- anxiety

Too much melatonin activity may cause the following signs and symptoms:

- depression
- morning grogginess
- lethargy

sexes, but as we mentioned earlier we can see that in many ways young girls today face greater psychosocial challenges than boys do. The unfortunate overemphasis our society places on personal appearance, body weight, and sexual attractiveness challenges girls' self-identity and self-worth, as is seen in the tremendous disparity in eating disorders between young girls and boys. Young girls are also more likely to be sexually abused, to have their natural talents ignored, and to suffer from conflicting social expectations.

At different points in the menstrual cycle. During the twenty-eight days or so of most menstrual cycles, women experience a number of hormonal changes. Pituitary hormones, such as luteinizing hormone (LH) and follicle-stimulating hormone (FSH), affect ovulation, as do estrogen and progesterone. Estrogen peaks around mid-cycle, shortly before ovulation, while progesterone is at its highest a few days after ovulation. The most common time for women to experience mood changes is before menstruation. Premenstrual syndrome (PMS) may affect as many as 90 percent of fertile women at some point in their lives. Symptoms include the usual depression-related suspects: problems sleeping, nervousness and anxiety, irritability, tension, and fatigue. These typically occur in the week or two before menstruation. Hormonal changes are probably factors but other considerations, from diet to nutrient levels to stress, may be equally important in PMS.

When taking birth control pills. Oral contraceptives have major effects on the levels of various sex hormones. Studies have shown that taking birth control pills is linked to an increased rate of depression—as many as one in three women on birth control pills suffers from depression. Whether this association is mainly due to hormone levels, however, is unknown. Taking birth control pills is also associated with nutritional deficiencies that may affect mood.

One of the first things I do when a woman comes in with depression is find out whether she is taking birth control pills and, if so, suggest that she use an alternative method. The results can be dramatic. I remember one twenty-year-old woman who was hypersensitive and depressed to the point of being suicidal. It turned out that the only treatment she needed was to stop taking birth control pills. Within a few weeks her mood and emotions returned to normal.

During pregnancy and the postpartum period. Hormonal changes during and immediately after pregnancy can be dramatic. Pregnant women develop a new, hormone-generating organ in the uterus: the placenta. It produces estrogen (estradiol, the most important of the estrogen hormones, increases by some 130 times during pregnancy), progesterone (seven times as much as when a woman is not pregnant), and human chorionic gonadotropin (the hormone measured in home pregnancy kits). Pregnancy also prompts the pituitary gland to produce hormones, such as prolactin and oxytocin. Estrogen and progesterone levels fall quickly when the baby is delivered and the placenta is expelled.

These precipitous hormonal changes may be related to the widespread emotional problems associated with the post-birth period. Postpartum depression is very common, affecting perhaps seven out of ten new mothers. Instead of (or sometimes in addition to) the expected joy of new motherhood, many women experience a short period of indifference, despondency, insomnia, and emotional instability. This may resolve itself within a week or so with counseling and support, although postpartum endocrine exhaustion is a common finding of mine. I often see postpartum depression lasting for years, only to be resolved within a month or two with proper endocrine support and nutritional adjustments. A case in point is Sue, a thirty-eight-year-old school administrator who had this syndrome for a number of years after giving birth to her second child. Her adrenals and pituitary were exhausted. She was deficient in vitamin B_{12} and low in B-complex vitamins in general. Treatment included supporting her endocrine function with tonic herbs such as Siberian ginseng (see Chapter 6) and taking optimal levels of vitamin B_{12} and other nutrients. Sue was glad to find that after only six weeks of treatment her depression cleared and her energy returned. She couldn't believe that after so many years, seeing various therapists, and taking Prozac and other drugs, it could be so easy.

As we'll see in Chapter 7 on essential fatty acids, recent studies suggest another nutritional factor in postpartum depression: a deficiency of docosahexaenoic acid (DHA), one of the omega-3 fatty acids. Since becoming aware of this connection, I've noticed the deficiency in a few of my female patients and have used supplemental DHA with success.

As many as one in ten women experiences more worrisome effects that linger for weeks or months postpartum, a condition called "nonpsychotic major postpartum depressive disorder." Doctors often prescribe antidepressants, although this treatment presents obvious problems relating to side effects and safety for breastfeeding infants. Cases of postpartum psychosis, in which the mother becomes delusional and possibly dangerous to herself or to her child, are relatively rare. Some evidence suggests, however, that women with a previous history of manic depression have a much greater risk for developing postpartum psychosis (1 in 5 against the norm of 1 in 500).

Before and during the time of menopause. In the year or two before menstruation ceases (perimenopause), for most women in their mid-forties, estrogen and progesterone levels begin to fall. During menopause other hormones, including FSH, increase. For some women, the perimenopausal period can be a time when they experience not only hot flashes, sleep difficulties, and memory lapses, but also depression. Although results have been mixed, estrogen has worked as an antidepressant (or boosted the effectiveness of antidepressant drugs) for some perimenopausal women. On the other hand, for most women menopause itself does not seem to be a period when they experience depression. A number of studies have also borne this out—the gender factor is less evident in depression rates of fifty- and sixty-year-olds.

Many researchers in the field believe that the female sex hormones probably play a role in depression and other mood disorders, but that the effect in most women is not strong and direct. Much more research is needed to help us answer such questions as how sexual hormones affect depression (and vice versa) and how hormonal changes affect the action of antidepressant drugs (which are prescribed much more frequently to women than to men). The point to keep in mind is that women are more exposed to causes of depression from menstrual cycles, postpartum depletion, and menopause. I am not surprised at the high numbers of women with depression. Rather than consider women more susceptible to depression, however, maybe we should consider that women are more exposed to depression-causing stresses.

The Stress Connection

As we can see, the evidence for direct hormonal effects on depression in women is intriguing but still not conclusive. Hormonal influences may also operate through more subtle and elusive channels. No one is really sure about the long-term effects of early hormonal experiences, for example. Sex hormones can also have indirect effects. Estrogen and progesterone seem to extend the effects of cortisol, one of the hormones secreted by the adrenals in response to stress. The action may be through an increased production of adrenocorticotropic hormone (ACTH), which the pituitary secretes and which is the trigger for the adrenals to produce cortisol. (See Chapter 4 for more on the stress-depression connection.) Estrogen might also inhibit the body's stress-feedback mechanism, whereby circulating cortisol sends the message to cut back on ACTH production.

Studies have begun to confirm some of these links between gender, stress, and depression. For example, a rat study found that cortisol's negative feedback effects were weaker in females compared to males or to spayed females. A study done on normal humans found that older women in particular experienced significantly larger cortisol responses than men. A study of ACTH and cortisol response in depressed and normal adolescents found that boys had higher measures of ACTH than girls, regardless of depression status, possibly due to gender-related differences in how ACTH is metabolized.

Just as seasonal factors may affect women's melatonin levels more than men's, seasonal factors may play a role in how women respond to stress. This is suggested by two recent studies. One compared the results of a stress-related test given to depressed and schizophrenic patients during two periods, from November to February and from March to October. Depressed females and depressed males showed different responses, suggesting a gender/seasonality effect. The other study demonstrated that in healthy men corticotropin-releasing hormone (CRH, the substance secreted by the hypothalamus that then stimulates the pituitary to release ACTH) has an inhibitory effect on the pineal's secretion of melatonin. The researchers concluded that the action of CRH on melatonin secretion as well as the mutual feedback among various hormones may be how stress eventually causes depression.

Gender was also a factor in a 1995 study. Researchers gave subjects a dose of a drug meant to induce a stress response. The researchers found that ACTH and cortisol response diminished with age in male subjects but increased with age in females. The cortisol response of older females was significantly larger than that of all the other subjects.

Scientists have speculated that sex hormones may thus make women more susceptible than men to severe and extended bouts of stress, setting the stage for depression. According to Dr. Frederick Goodwin, former director of the NIMH, "If there is chronic, repeated stress and if it involves helplessness, there may be an overshoot of the arousal that stress causes, and you then shift from an arousal state to a despair state that has now taken on a life of its own."

Finally, I should mention a further source of hormonal effects on mood: the thyroid. This is another area where gender research is still in its infancy, but a number of studies have suggested that thyroid imbalances in women are more likely to cause or aggravate depression than in men. According to one researcher, "Such abnormalities are more highly prevalent in women than in men and so may play a role in gender differences in clinical depression." We'll take a closer look at the thyroid's effects on mood in the next chapter.

Your Personal Biochemistry:
Is Gender Contributing to Your Depression?

If you answer yes to any of the following questions, it is quite possible that gender is contributing to your depression.

- Were you sexually abused as a child?
- Is your current husband or partner abusive?
- If you live in a northern climate, is your depression more prominent in the winter?
- Does your depression regularly worsen at some point in your menstrual cycle?
- Do you constantly face high levels of stress and have no regular method (such as mindful relaxation; see Chapter 9) for dealing with it?
- Are you taking birth control pills?
- Are you postpartum?
- Are you menopausal?

Gender and Depression Treatment

Given the uncertainties and the complexities involved, it is difficult to recommend radically different approaches to alleviating depression in women than men. For the most part, healthful and effective steps for beating depression work in men's and women's bodies for similar reasons. Yet I've found that some steps are especially important for women to keep in mind:

- Many women gain tremendous benefits from a regular exercise or physical activity program. The benefits are both physical (more energy, greater strength and endurance), psychological (more self-confidence, better body image), and social (the health club can be a way to meet people and make friends). The exercise and physical activity recommendations I make in Chapter 9 can really help women.
- Because multiple roles are associated with less depression, I encourage women who are mostly housebound with kids to find other activities. Have Dad take the kids on a regular basis so you can volunteer, run a book group, or take a class. Follow your heart in creat-

ing multiple meaningful life activities. Of course, taking on too much can also present problems, and many women today are finding themselves overextended due to demanding jobs and a busy life at home. Living in balance is the key to preventing depression.

- Women are often more open and in touch with their feelings than men, and thus in a better position to benefit from counseling. Therapies that help them recognize negative thoughts and take positive steps toward a goal are especially worthwhile.

- Women who are susceptible to SAD may benefit by reducing their melatonin supplementation (to 750 mcg, for example, or even to zero) during the winter months, when they may naturally produce more of it. On the other hand, they can increase their nighttime calcium or magnesium intake for its slight relaxing effect.

- Women who are depressed are more likely than men to develop eating disorders. Researchers have found, for example, gender differences in vulnerability to depression among obese persons. Also, factors such as binge-purge behaviors may be prominent predictors of depression. Making the kind of dietary adjustments I describe in Chapter 8 is crucial for women who may become depressed.

- Natural sunlight is especially important for the stimulation of all the organs and most specifically for the pineal and the pituitary glands. Sunlight is needed for the proper functioning of the whole endocrine system and for the production of vitamin D. If you live in a northern climate with limited sunlight, three hours per day or more of exposure to full spectrum light is helpful. In areas where, due to daylight savings time, it gets dark by mid to late afternoon but is light very early in the morning, women may benefit by going to bed earlier and arising earlier, so that they are exposed to as much natural light during their waking hours as possible. Keep your blinds and curtains open during the winter, and if you work at a desk, try to situate it so that you are exposed to lots of light.

- Most important, don't accept as a necessary and unavoidable burden a depression related to postpartum, menopause, or menses. Actions such as those outlined above, as well as the information included in chapters 5 through 9, can help any woman overcome gender-related depression and become depression-free for life.

4

Your Personal Biochemistry: The Customized Way to Defeat Depression

I can't begin to tell you how many patients have come to me over the years with a very similar complaint. It runs something like this: "I've been to see several physicians. All my lab tests are normal. They say I'm fine, that there's nothing wrong with me. But I feel terrible. I have half the energy I used to have, my sleeping patterns are erratic, I suffer from anxiety attacks at weird times, and sometimes I don't even seem to think straight. Why can't anybody tell me what's ailing me?"

My answer to these patients goes to the heart of the difference between the conventional and my natural, five-step treatment program for depression. Essentially, modern medicine focuses on only a few of the many factors that can contribute to depression. Recently, the action of a single neurotransmitter—serotonin—has gained such prominence in conventional treatments that little else seems to matter. Yet in my experience, serotonin or any other single neurotransmitter is only one piece of a complex puzzle, a puzzle that moreover fits together differently for each individual.

In this chapter we'll consider four diet- and hormone-related factors that determine your unique biochemical balance, and thus your emotional well-being. Only then can you gain practical knowledge about the state of your own biochemical balance as it relates to mood and depression. The main questions you need to consider are:

- How rapidly and efficiently does your body handle sugar?
- Is your thyroid gland and the various hormones that affect it working properly?
- Is an inability to handle stress or an imbalance in related hormones contributing to your depression?
- Do you suffer from an imbalance in the types of fat you need?

For each of these I'll offer insights and practical techniques for assessing your status.

Sugar, Metabolism, and Depression

I have found in my practice that how a person metabolizes not only simple sugars and complex carbohydrates but also proteins and fats is a crucial factor in as many as three out of every five cases of depression. Barbara, a thirty-three-year-old psychotherapist, was typical of many cases I've seen. She had become very unhappy with her work and was chronically tired and depressed. She also suffered from such wild swings in her blood sugar levels that she was constantly reaching for sweets to temporarily bolster her energy levels. She said that at times her sugar cravings were severe—"I drop whatever I'm doing to run out and wolf down some donuts or candy," she told me. The program we developed for her featured changes in her diet, nutritional supplements, and lifestyle, focusing not so much on adjusting neurotransmitter levels as on balancing her blood levels of glucose. Within five months she felt as good mentally as she ever had in her life. She told me she was much more emotionally steady and physically energetic. Not surprisingly, she no longer suffered from depression or hypoglycemia.

One of the first things I tried to do for Barbara was to demystify the mechanisms by which the body processes major nutrients. This gave her a better understanding of the direct effects that foods and supplements can have on energy levels, moods, and emotions. I also took the time to describe the diagnosis and treatment of sugar-metabolism-related ailments, particularly the much misunderstood condition of low blood sugar or hypoglycemia. This set the stage for an important distinction I make among all my depressed patients: *Are they fast or slow oxidizers?* Fast oxidizers are people whose bodies are relatively quick and efficient at breaking down or oxidizing glucose—blood sugar—into the simplest energy compounds necessary to fuel the brain's processes. Slow oxidizers are people whose systems metabolize glucose at a much less rapid rate.

In the mid-twentieth century a researcher named George Watson pioneered the study of oxidation rates and their effects on mind and mood. His research showed that many mood disorders involve impaired nervous system and brain function due to abnormalities in metabolism. Watson found that in order to reestablish metabolic balance, you must provide the body with an adequate supply of the right nutrients and food. Watson's research showed that when proper brain energy metabolism was reestablished, many mental states such as anxiety, depression, obsessive-compulsive disorders, and paranoia faded away.

I am finding the same results in my work. If the brain's cellular metabolism is producing optimal energy, and if the acid/alkaline balance of the blood supplying the brain is correct (which can be accomplished by following the dietary guidelines in Chapter 8 to adjust the ratio of your carbohydrates, fats, and proteins), mental and emotional imbalances are more likely to be alleviated.

One of the principal factors in this process is blood sugar. The glucose transported in the blood is the basic food for all the muscles and organs as well as for the brain and central nervous system. All of the energy used by the brain is derived from the process of cellular respiration, which uses glucose as its primary fuel. Cellular respiration is the process by which complex foods—proteins, fats, and carbohydrates (starches and sugars)—are broken down into simple substances. These are then oxidized at the cellular level to make energy for the body and mind. The brain needs optimal levels of glucose in order to function well, and a dysfunction in glucose metabolism quickly affects your mental state.

During oxidation, glucose is transformed by the action of enzymes into a series of intermediate substances. These substances then drive complex metabolic cycles that create the basic biological energy molecules for the body and brain cells. This molecular compound is called adenosine triphosphate (ATP). Two main biochemical energy cycles at the cellular level produce ATP. One is called glycolysis and the other is called the citric acid cycle. Glycolysis produces approximately 30 percent of our cellular energy and the citric acid cycle, when operating optimally, produces approximately 70 percent. To make each of these cycles work at their peak, you need to provide your body with an optimal ratio of fats, protein, and complex carbohydrates in the diet, as well as certain vitamins and minerals.

The key to understanding the fast and slow oxidizer concept lies in how the body produces ATP from glucose. In the two primary cellular respiration cycles just described, any interference with the step-by-step breakdown of the glucose to ATP—such as from the incomplete oxidation of glucose intermediates in the brain—may result in impaired mental functioning. An example of this might be a deficiency in niacin, which participates in the enzymatic breakdown of sugar at several places in the energy production cycles. A deficiency of niacin slows brain metabolism and therefore affects the creation of energy for brain/mind function.

Fast Versus Slow Oxidizers

Although glucose metabolism is primary in brain metabolism, the adequate use of protein and fat breakdown products in the citric acid cycle strongly affects the amount of ATP used for brain metabolism. A proper mix of the intermediates from both glucose metabolism and from fat and protein metabolism is necessary to produce optimal amounts of energy for proper functioning. Either too much or too little glucose and its breakdown products interferes with the proper functioning of the citric acid cycle, which produces most of the ATP. When you have a correct mix of these intermediaries, the citric acid cycle has the right fuel mix to work perfectly and produce optimal amounts of ATP.

A person with slow oxidation metabolizes glucose too slowly. A slow oxidizer thus needs more carbohydrates in his or her diet to compensate for the slower metabolism and lower production of glucose and its metabolic products. Higher amounts of carbohydrate will supply more glucose to drive the slow oxidizer system to produce more of the relevant intermediates needed to make ATP. A slow oxidizer consequently needs a high-complex-carbohydrate, low-fat, and moderately low-protein diet.

A fast oxidizer is one whose glycolysis cycle is working too rapidly. Fast oxidizers are people whose metabolism burns glucose quickly and produces too much of the intermediates. To get the correct mix of intermediaries, fast oxidizers need to eat more protein and fat to balance the high glucose metabolism.

Fast oxidizers who go on a low-fat, low-protein, and high-complex-carbohydrate diet experience a significant disruption of energy production in their nervous system. Severe personality changes may result, such as social withdrawal, anxiety, depression, violent tendencies, and even paranoid delusions. I have seen this happen in fast oxidizers who have tried to convert to the stereotypical vegetarian diet that is high in complex carbohydrates and limited in fat and protein. This does not mean that fast oxidizers cannot be successful vegetarians. I have known many fast oxidizers who have done well as vegetarians when they switched to a higher-protein, moderate-fat, and low-carbohydrate diet.

There is a third type of oxidizer that I call a mixed oxidizer. These are people who are balanced between slow and fast oxidizer metabolism. In general, when you eat a healthy, primarily vegetarian diet, your oxidation rate becomes more balanced and your mood benefits.

Clearly, fast and slow oxidizers require different diets to optimize brain cell energy production, and being on the wrong diet can be a major factor in causing their depression. Thus, the dietary adjustments covered in Chapter 8 can indirectly relieve depression. For example, the relatively high-protein, high-fat diet popularized by Barry Sears's best-selling book *The Zone* generally works well for fast oxidizers because their systems need a higher percentage of protein and fat intake to balance their speedy glucose metabolism. When fast oxidizers try to stay on a high-complex-carbohydrate diet, however, the result may be depression. Conversely, a slow oxidizer who tries a high-protein, high-fat, and low-carbohydrate diet will also have difficulties with energy and brain metabolism.

Your Personal Biochemistry:
Are You a Fast or Slow Oxidizer?

The following is a self-assessment questionnaire based on the physiological characteristics of fast and slow oxidizers. Answer yes or no to each question.

SLOW OXIDIZER QUESTIONNAIRE

1. Do you "eat to live" as opposed to "live to eat"?
2. Is it easy for you to skip meals and maintain energy and a sense of well-being?
3. Are you generally not concerned at all with eating?
4. Do you have a minimal appetite for lunch or dinner?
5. Does eating before bedtime worsen your sleep?
6. Does eating fatty foods like lots of cheese, pastries, chips, and butter make you feel lethargic?
7. Does eating a high-protein meal or lots of nuts, seeds, beans, meat, fish, or tofu drop your energy afterward?

8. Does eating sweets, grains, or fruits restore lasting energy and give you a sense of well-being?

9. Does a serving of apple or orange juice energize and satisfy you for a long time?

10. Does a high-carbohydrate, low-protein, low-fat vegetarian meal like a salad, grains, vegetables, or just fruits make you generally feel satisfied and energized?

11. If you could eat anything you want (what you like, not what you think is good for you) at a buffet, would you sample all the salads and leave room for the desserts?

12. Do you handle juice or water fasts without many headaches, extreme hunger, nausea, or shakiness?

13. If you feel low energy, does eating sweets or fruits restore lasting energy?

14. Are you particularly fond of potatoes?

15. Do you have a sense of sustained well-being after eating sweet foods?

16. Do foods taste too salty?

17. Does eating red meat reduce your sense of energy and well-being? (If you're a vegetarian, recall your experiences when you used to eat red meat.)

18. Do you get sleepy or lethargic eating a high-protein, high-fat meal, such as one rich in meat, cheese, and beans?

19. Do you not particularly care for sour foods such as lemons?

20. Do you rarely want snacks?

21. Is it easy for you to go more than four hours without food?

22. Is a low-protein, high-carbohydrate diet easy and natural for you?

23. Do you feel good and energetically sustained after eating grains?

24. Has your general health and well-being improved since you became vegetarian or minimized high-protein foods?

25. Did you grow up having any aversions to flesh or fatty foods?

FAST OXIDIZER QUESTIONNAIRE

1. Do you "live to eat" as opposed to "eat to live"?

2. Do you have a strong appetite for breakfast?

3. Do you have a strong appetite for lunch?

4. Do you have a strong appetite for dinner?
5. Do you need to snack frequently?
6. Does a high-carbohydrate diet with lots of fruits, vegetables, and sweets make you feel worse or not satisfy you?
7. Do you feel satisfied after a high-protein meal rich in meat, beans, tofu, nuts, or seeds?
8. Do you crave flesh foods?
9. Does going four hours without food make you feel jittery or weak?
10. Do you need to snack often to feel okay?
11. Does eating sweets throw you out of balance or deplete your energy within an hour or so?
12. Does eating before bedtime help you to sleep through the night?
13. Does having orange or apple juice alone make you feel light-headed or hungry?
14. Does eating a high-protein or high-fat lunch such as lots of seeds and nuts restore lasting energy and feelings of well-being?
15. Do you like to eat potatoes?
16. If you are a vegetarian, can you remember if eating red meats used to give you energy?
17. Does eating fruit, pastries, or candy make you feel worse?
18. Is it hard for you to fast on juice or water?
19. Do you really not care for sweet desserts, preferring something fatty or salty?
20. Do you feel worse after eating grains?
21. Do you like sour foods?
22. Do sweet foods seem too sweet?
23. Do you get a quick lift and then a sudden drop of energy from eating sweet foods?
24. If you skip a meal, does it cause you to feel weak, jittery, low in energy, and unbalanced?
25. Do you love or crave salty foods?

If you answer yes to more questions on the slow oxidizer profile than the fast oxidizer one, you are a slow oxidizer. If you answer yes to more questions on the fast oxidizer profile, you are a fast oxidizer. If your scores for slow or fast oxidizer are about the same, then you fit into the mixed metabolism.

A glucose tolerance test can also help to assess whether you are a slow or fast oxidizer. This is a blood test done at your doctor's office. You'll need to fast overnight before the test, which involves drinking a glucose-rich solution and then testing your blood at various intervals for glucose levels. A gentle, rolling curve for the three-hour glucose tolerance test, in which there is not a rapid drop back to the fasting glucose level, suggests a slow oxidizer. A curve with a large and rapid spike suggests a fast oxidizer.

By learning how to recognize the signs and symptoms of a sugar-metabolism imbalance, you can take the necessary steps to reduce its role in your depression. By devising and following a regimen of amino acids (particularly glutamine; see Chapter 5) and nutritional supplements (such as the B-complex vitamins and the mineral chromium; see Chapter 6), it is possible to balance sugar metabolism. Thus, the sugar metabolism of a fast oxidizer is slowed down to normal and that of a slow oxidizer speeded up to normal.

Thyroid Depression: A Hidden Epidemic?

Carla was a mother and homemaker in her late twenties when she first visited me. She described a number of fairly common symptoms of depression, including fatigue, lack of initiative, loss of interest in sex, and weight gain. In the course of talking to her, however, I noticed some physical symptoms that suggested an underlying hormonal imbalance. Carla's long brown hair and her unpolished nails seemed to be brittle and lackluster. I also noticed that although it was a fairly balmy day, with the temperature in the low sixties, Carla was dressed like she was ready for an expedition to the North Pole. She was wearing a hat and a scarf, which she didn't take off during the almost two hours she spent in my office. When I asked her about her tolerance for cold, she readily admitted that she often felt cold and was constantly playing "thermostat tag" with her husband.

A week later, after Carla had performed a simple home test for thyroid function and I'd run some lab tests, my suspicion was confirmed. Carla suffered from an underactive thyroid, or hypothyroidism. Insufficient levels of thyroid hormones circulating in her blood were causing her overall metabolism to be artificially low. Her cells were just not producing the energy she needed to function optimally. This left her always feeling too cold, as her body tried to conserve heat (or energy) by restricting blood flow to her hands, feet, and skin.

Thyroid hormones control diverse functions in the body and affect the metabolism of every cell. They also affect the development and function of every major organ in the body. Too much thyroid hormone can speed up metabolism and oxygen consumption and too little can slow these processes down. Thyroid hormones directly affect protein synthesis, sex hormone secretion, absorption of nutrients, night sight, and the action of nucleic acids, among other functions. Thyroid hormones' effects on mind and mood are also substantial. Brain cells that produce depression-busting neurotransmitters can be inhibited by lack of thyroid hormones. Thyroid hormones affect blood glucose levels and the release of stress hormones, both of which can have myriad mood-related effects.

These profound effects are remarkable, coming as they do from an approximately one-ounce, U-shaped gland located below the larynx in the front of the neck. As small as it is, the thyroid is the largest endocrine gland and its hormones are potent enough to cause effects even at one part per every ten billion parts of blood plasma.

The thyroid gland produces a number of hormones. We'll consider here only two of the most active: thyroxine, also known as T4, and triiodothyronine, or T3. They are formed from the amino acid tyrosine and the mineral iodine.

The thyroid secretes much more (about sixty times as much) T4 than T3. One of T4's functions, however, is to serve as a precursor for T3, which is faster acting and more potent compared to T4. On the other hand, T3 has a shorter duration of action. The pituitary gland also plays an important role because it synthesizes and releases another hormone, called thyroid stimulating hormone (TSH), that uses a feedback mechanism to control the production and secretion of thyroxine. The relationship is inverse. That is, when the blood levels of T4 and T3 rise, the pituitary (under influence itself from the hypothalamus) responds by secreting less TSH. This causes the thyroid to produce less T4 and T3, bringing the system back toward a balance. The opposite occurs when blood levels of T4 and T3 are too low—the pituitary secretes more TSH, causing the thyroid to increase production of T4 and T3. As noted, thyroid hormones are very potent—only tiny amounts are needed to regulate the body's functions—so this constant feedback system helps to keep these hormones within relatively narrow margins.

Too much and too little thyroid hormone being produced or secreted by the thyroid gland accounts for the two main types of thyroid dysfunction. (How active the hormone itself is in the body is usually a lesser factor.) Hypothyroidism is an underactive thyroid, characterized by low hormone production. Hyperthyroidism is an overactive thyroid, as from too much hormone being produced. Depression and anxiety can result from either too much or too little circulating thyroid hormone. T3 seems more important than T4 in adult brains, where it may act as a neurotransmitter. T3 may enhance the effects of noradrenaline, serotonin, and GABA.

Hypothyroidism may result from any number of factors. An autoimmune condition called Hashimoto's thyroiditis, in which the body attacks its own thyroid gland, is a common cause. Various conventional drugs, such as sulfonamides, antidiabetic drugs, and corticosteroids can reduce thyroid function. Nicotine has a very adverse effect on thyroid function and certain antidepressant drugs can alter it. The element lithium, a popular treatment for manic depression, is widely recognized as suppressing the release of thyroid hormones. Thyroid function typically declines with advancing age. Women are more prone to thyroid imbalances, especially hypothyroidism, than men, for reasons that researchers are still investigating. Seasonality may be a factor, according to a 1993 study done on 250 normal women in the Boston area. Researchers found that subjects' blood levels of thyroxine were positively associated with scores for depression and dejection in August through November and with better scores for vigor and activity in February through May.

Dozens of symptoms may suggest hypothyroidism. Symptoms may come on slowly, with mental symptoms often being among the first to appear. Depression in particular is a common symptom of a thyroid imbalance. People suffering from thyroid ailments may also experience apathy, reduced initiative, social withdrawal, and impaired memory. They may experience major disruptions in energy, immunity, sleeping, mood, and attitude. One of the reasons hypothyroidism is often underdiagnosed is that doctors and patients are constantly addressing the fatigue or the recurrent infections as separate problems without realizing that the underlying condition is a thyroid imbalance.

Your Personal Biochemistry:
Is Your Depression Thyroid-Related?

The following include some of the most common symptoms of an overactive thyroid:

- fatigue
- anxiety
- nervousness
- irritability
- sensitivity to heat
- increased sweating
- weight loss
- rapid heartbeat
- diarrhea
- protruding eyeballs
- hand tremors

The following include some of the most common symptoms of an underactive thyroid:

- fatigue
- cold hands and feet
- dry skin (which becomes thick and puffy as the condition advances)
- chronic constipation
- difficulty breaking into a sweat
- sensitivity to cold and dampness
- weakness
- slowed speech
- weight gain
- muscle cramps
- easy bruising
- loss of hair
- loss of appetite
- weak and brittle nails
- low blood pressure
- recurrent infections
- loss of interest in sex
- irregular menstrual periods

If any of these symptom patterns suggest a thyroid imbalance, a simple home test can also help to diagnose it. Your resting or basal body temperature can signify thyroid function, because too little thyroid slows metabolism and slightly reduces body temperature. The late physician Broda Barnes, author of *Hypothyroidism: The Unsuspected Illness*, published in the mid-1970s, popularized this connection between body temperature and thyroid function. Barnes was a noted thyroid researcher who determined that body temperature was an even better indicator of an underactive thyroid than blood tests, symptoms, or medical history, although he said all four of these indicators can and should be used.

Barnes's recommendation for taking your temperature was to shake a thermometer and leave it by your bed before falling asleep at night. Immediately upon wakening in the morning, before getting up or even moving much, shake the thermometer again and place it in your armpit. After ten minutes, read the thermometer and record the temperature. This is your resting or basal temperature. Do this for three consecutive days. Most people's resting temperature is approximately 0.4 to 0.8 degrees F. lower than their normal temperature. (Normal temperature averages 98.6, but yours may be slightly higher or lower.) Thus, most people's basal temperature is between 97.8 and 98.2 degrees. If your normal temperature is 98.6, a three-day average reading of lower than 97.8 may be an indication of hypothyroidism. Women who are menstruating may not get an accurate reading, so they should take their resting temperature when they are not menstruating.

If you suspect you have a thyroid imbalance, ask your doctor to check the gland. He or she will probably first look and feel for signs of enlargement, a condition called goiter. A number of blood tests can also help to diagnose an imbalance. The most popular measure blood levels of T4, T3, and TSH.

Many doctors nowadays rely exclusively on these blood tests to diagnose a thyroid imbalance. They may even discount symptoms if the tests don't suggest an imbalance. In my experience, however, this is a mistake. Blood tests should be only one of several considerations. One reason is that the normal range for these blood tests is broad. If your scores are in either the high or low end of "normal," you may have a marginal thyroid imbalance. Thyroid researchers are currently debating the importance and prevalence of "hypothyroidism with normal blood tests," or "subclinical hypthyroidism." An array of studies has suggested that significant numbers of people, especially women, may have various symptoms of hypothyroidism but still have normal blood tests. For example, a 1993 study found a 56 percent lifetime prevalence of major depression in nonelderly females with subclinical hypothyroidism. Another found that 15 to 20 percent of depressed subjects show some degree of subclinical hypothyroidism

Your doctor should also consider the results of other tests that can indicate a thyroid imbalance, including a number of cholesterol-related scores (such as a total cholesterol higher than 250 and an LDH, low-density lipoprotein level higher than 40).

In Part Two we'll take a look at various strategies, including taking over-the-counter glandular products such as those available at natural food stores (see Chapter 6), that can help to balance thyroid hormones and thus reduce the symptoms of depression.

The Stress Factor

Stress refers to various types of bodily or mental tension. It may come from many sources: physical (work, exercise), chemical (food poisoning), or emotional (relationships). Stress that is extreme or long-lasting can overwhelm the body's control mechanisms and increase the risk of disease. How your body reacts physically to stress is more or less the same whether the source of the stress is a pending divorce or an armed robber in your bedroom. The stress in itself is not necessarily harmful, and indeed it would be a dull life for all of us if we tried to eliminate all stress. Some stress is good—it can push us to do better, or alert us to possibilities. In the case of exercise it benefits body and mind and promotes longevity.

How you deal with the stress you face is the crucial question. A region of the brain, the hypothalamus, and two neuroendocrine organs—the pituitary, located just under the hypothalamus in the forebrain, and the adrenals, located just above the kidneys—are the principal biochemical actors in handling stress.

The hypothalamus helps to control various bodily organs. When the hypothalamus receives signals of stress or alarm from other regions of the brain and from elsewhere in the body, its specialized nerve cells respond by producing corticotropin-releasing hormone (CRH). Nerves and blood vessels connect the hypothalamus to the pituitary, allowing CRH to stimulate the pituitary to produce adrenocorticotropic hormone (ACTH). This hormone then travels through the bloodstream to the adrenals.

The adrenals consist of two distinct parts. The outer layer, or adrenal cortex, secretes hormones known as corticosteroids. Formed from cholesterol, these include cortisone, cortisol, and corticosterone. The inner layer, or medulla, secretes adrenaline and noradrenaline. All of these hormones are involved in an elaborate feedback loop that helps to control the body's response to stress. For example, if cortisol levels in the blood become too high, the pituitary responds by producing less ACTH.

Fear, injury, and other forms of stress promote the release of ACTH and cortisol. Adrenaline pumps into the bloodstream and travels quickly to the heart, lungs, and major muscles. Adrenaline signals the heart to beat faster and the lungs to process more oxygen. The hormone also helps to divert blood from the inner organs to large skeletal muscles. All this bodily action better prepares your body either to fight or take flight in response to the perceived stress.

Stress-related hormones can be harmful to overall health when your body is constantly producing them. They can elevate blood sugar, suppress immunity, and weaken the heart. Various studies have also closely tied excessive or insignificant amounts of the stress hormones to causing depression or aggravating an existing depression. Cortisol secretion in depressed persons, for example, is often higher than normal or is timed differently than in normal subjects. When synthetic corticosteroid drugs are administered to nondepressed persons (to relieve inflammation, for example), depression, anxiety, and sleeping problems are common side effects. As mentioned in Chapter 3, sex hormones may have subtle interactions with stress hormones to promote higher rates of depression among women. Chronic stress decreases the ability of the pineal gland to make melatonin, with further potential adverse effects on mood. Finally, corticosteroids' need for tryptophan may detract from the brain's supply of mood-boosting serotonin.

> **Your Personal Biochemistry:**
> **Do You Have a Stress-Hormone Imbalance?**
>
> Some of the most common symptoms of an imbalance in the hypo-thalamus, pituitary, and adrenal system are the following:
>
> - anxiety
> - fatigue
> - headache
> - weakness
> - poor memory
> - slow healing of wounds
> - weight gain
> - muscle pains

It is possible to have your physician order blood and urine tests that measure the levels of cortisol, ACTH, adrenaline, DHEA, or other hormones. Lab tests must take into account daily rhythms in stress-related hormones. For example, ACTH levels are usually lowest around midnight and highest around six A.M. A new test measures the levels of hormones such as DHEA and cortisol in your saliva. You need to take four salivary samples at different times of the day. A few mail-order companies (see Supplement Resources) now offer this test, and it may soon become more widely available.

Many aspects of the five-step program described in Part Two help to balance stress hormones and alleviate stress-related depression. Nutritional supplements, diet, exercise, and mindful relaxation in particular help to stabilize blood sugar and promote better hormone function.

The Fat Factor

Most people today have a negative perception of anything pertaining to fats. Food manufacturers go to great lengths to market products that are "low-fat," "no-fat," or "fat-free." Procter & Gamble has even developed a fake fat, which supposedly has the smooth taste and feel of real fat when you eat it but glides through the body without being absorbed (and presumably added onto your thighs and buttocks) like real fat.

Much of this modern-day aversion to fat is well founded. Industrialized societies that have adopted diets dominated by certain types of fatty foods suffer from high rates of diet-related conditions, especially heart disease. Yet dietary fats are not the complete evil they've become in many people's minds. Even beyond their obvious roles as a source of energy, a protective cushion for vital organs, and keeping the body heated, fats literally allow our hearts, brains, and other organs to function. Some fats, in fact, are quite like antidepressant drugs or nutrients—they promote the optimal functioning of the mind in a way that prevents or even alleviates depression. Indeed, it may come as a surprise to some that certain fats not only are not harmful but are actually *essential* to optimal health.

These are the essential fatty acids (EFAs), various long-chain fats composed of molecules of carbon, hydrogen, and oxygen. The molecules in essential fatty acids are arranged so that there is more than one double-bond of carbon-to-carbon. Another way of characterizing this bonding is to say that essential fatty acids are polyunsaturated, and thus mostly liquid at room temperature. (Saturated fats like lard and butter are more likely to be semisolid at room temperature.) Because the body cannot produce these nutrients, you must consume them in foods or supplement your diet with essential fatty acid products. As I'll show in Chapter 7, your body needs relatively large amounts (compared to vitamins and minerals, for example) of these nutrients in order to stay healthy.

The recent demonization of fat and cholesterol that has swept the American food industry has no doubt had some salutary effects. People are much more aware today than they were ten years ago that a diet overloaded with fatty meats and dairy products is not healthful over the long run. Yet a disturbing question has arisen in recent years related to this dietary trend. While Americans seemingly embrace "lite" versions of everything from beer to yogurt, why are they on average fatter and apparently more depressed than ever?

A number of experts on essential fatty acids now think that the answer to this question may well be related to the types of fats that Americans eat, and perhaps even to a spreading pattern of essential fatty acid deficiencies. A growing body of evidence suggests that the basic American diet has in recent years become increasingly imbalanced in the amounts and types of fat it provides. Moreover, this fat imbalance may alter crucial neurotransmitters such as serotonin and certain biochemicals known as prostaglandins that can increase the risk of depression. It's possible that Americans are eating the lowest essential-fatty-acid diet in the world, and that the majority of Americans are already suffering the consequences, including more depression, of eating too little of the right fats.

Your Personal Biochemistry:
Signs of a Dietary Fat-Related Depression

Depression accompanied by the following symptoms may be due to an imbalance in the types of fat you're consuming:

- fatigue
- overall weakness
- minor skin problems
- headaches
- nervousness
- fingernails that break easily
- constipation
- lack of appetite
- low metabolic rate
- frequent colds or other indications of a weak immune system
- arthritis or other inflammatory conditions
- hair loss
- problems with vision
- tingling in arms or legs

These symptoms may be the direct result of dietary patterns that over the long term can create an essential fatty acid imbalance. Consider whether you have any of the following eating habits:

- You regularly consume foods rich in sugars, saturated fats, and hydrogenated vegetable oils (this includes a wide variety of processed foods such as cookies, donuts, cakes, and crackers).
- You strictly avoid nuts, seeds, fish, butter, eggs, whole milk, and other sources of natural fats, and prefer "lite" and low-fat versions of mostly processed and refined foods.
- You regularly use safflower or sunflower oil for cooking.
- You are always dieting to try to lose weight.
- You follow a strict, extremely low-fat vegetarian diet.
- You are a fast oxidizer who eats very little fat.
- You are a slow oxidizer who eats lots of fat.

If you suffer from a number of symptoms mentioned above and follow the eating patterns just outlined, some simple but fundamental changes in what you eat and what supplements you take (see Chapter 7) may help provide quick and dramatic relief from your depression.

Unfortunately, symptoms and dietary patterns are an inexact barometer of essential fatty acid status. In the near future, it may be possible to use blood tests or other lab results to monitor the body's essential fatty acid levels. Currently, this technology is in its infancy and is not widely available. The necessary lab work is relatively complex because some of the most important essential fatty acids represent tiny percentages (less than one percent) of the body's total fatty acid content. You'd also have to monitor EFA blood levels for weeks or months to determine what kinds of supplements and what dosages are optimal. Moreover, the field is so new that researchers are still developing ranges for what is normal. For now, watching for the symptoms of a deficiency and analyzing your diet for an imbalance is the best route to take.

The Web of Cause and Effect

By now you have gained a much deeper understanding of the many physiological causes of depression, and which parts of the mind and body are most involved in its cause and cure. You are in a much better position than ever to benefit from the five-step program that follows. Imbalances among neurotransmitters, blood sugar, hormones, and other biochemicals are crucial to depression and less serious mood disorders as well as varied conditions such as overeating and other eating disorders, insomnia and sleeping patterns, anger and violence, obsessive-compulsive actions, pathological gambling, attention-deficit disorder, panic attacks, and more.

This would be a good time for you to review the various "Your Personal Biochemistry" profiles and questionnaires in this chapter and the others in Part One of this book. We've seen that depression may result from a variety of factors. Some of these, such as early childhood experiences and the side effects of prescription drugs, may play major or minor roles. My focus in chapters 1 through 4 has been on a half-dozen factors that, in my experience, every depressed person needs to consider, including neurotransmitter dominance, underlying conditions, hormonal balance, how your body handles blood sugar, and stress. Here are the ten major factors of your personal biochemistry that can help you personalize your depression-busting program:

1. a deficiency in the neurotransmitter/brain chemicals serotonin, dopamine, noradrenaline, glutamine, GABA, or endorphins
2. use of prescription, over-the-counter, and recreational drugs
3. underlying ailments, nutritional deficiencies, and allergies to foods, chemicals, and metals
4. seasonal/melatonin imbalance
5. gender-related factors
6. blood sugar imbalance/fast oxidizer
7. blood sugar imbalance/slow oxidizer
8. thyroid deficiency
9. stress hormone imbalance
10. dietary fat/essential fatty acid imbalance

In Part Two we will focus on how you can better balance these aspects of your personal biochemistry and become depression-free for life. The five crucial steps are:

1. Adjust your amino acid intake, primarily to balance neurotransmitter activity in the brain.
2. Take nutritional, herbal, and hormonal supplements to help optimize virtually all of the depression-related factors, from neurotransmitter activity to hormone balance.
3. Make essential fatty acids an essential part of your life because of their stabilizing effects on hormones, blood sugar, fat balance, and other factors.
4. Eat a diet optimal for mental health and brain cell function.
5. Make healthful lifestyle choices day to day that can integrate all aspects of the depression-free program, more easily heal psycho-spiritual thought patterns associated with depression, and elevate you physically, emotionally, mentally, and spiritually.

For each step, one of my main concerns has been to keep the information practical. I've seen the vast majority of my depressed clients benefit tremendously from following this simple plan. They gain new insights into why they feel withdrawn, tired, lonely, or sad, and what they need to do day-to-day to once again be joyful, self-activated, and involved with friends and family. This is my hope for you.

Part Two

. . . .

Five Steps to Becoming Depression-Free for Life

5

Step One: Take Mood-Boosting Amino Acids

I'll open this chapter with an admission: treating depression would be much easier if the condition could be reduced to the activity of one neurotransmitter such as serotonin. As we have just seen in the previous chapters, however, some people's systems are more dominated not by serotonin but by dopamine, noradrenaline, glutamine, or GABA, or by such hormones as melatonin, insulin, thyroxine, or cortisol. Using "Your Personal Biochemistry" questionnaires and self-tests in Part One, readers can make the sometimes complex connections between their moods and the various neurotransmitters and hormones. Now comes the comparatively easy part—using any of a half-dozen amino acids to alter the brain's balance of serotonin, dopamine, noradrenaline, glutamine, GABA, or the endorphins and rebuild the neurotransmitter pathways and nerve cell connections to the brain's key pleasure centers.

Why is this the easy part? Because biochemists know that certain amino acids, whether they are taken as nutritional supplements or as elements of the protein in foods, are *precursors* to certain neurotransmitters. That is, the body breaks down these amino acids to form neurotransmitters. In fact, two of these amino acids—glutamine and GABA—are now thought to have neurotransmitter-like effects in the brain without being metabolized.

In many cases I've found that amino acids, by altering neurotransmitter levels in the brain, play the most important role in defeating depression. An example from my practice is the case of Janice, who at fifty was a busy mother of two teenage girls when she first came to see me. Normally quiet and serious, she often surprised me with her dry wit during casual conversations, as when she described one member of her book-reading group as "a closet books-on-taper." In addition to being a soccer mom whose road time rivaled that of a cabbie's, Janice held a part-time administrative job in her small city's parks department. She was an avid gardener, a regular walker, and an occasional tennis player. She had also been following a spiritual path for many years, meditating regularly and staying active in her church.

About a year earlier, Janice had suddenly begun to feel overwhelmed by stress, anxiety, and depression. Over a period of about three months, her sleeping patterns became irregular, she suffered from severe swings in her blood sugar levels, and she began to develop compulsions that disrupted all aspects of her life. By the time she consulted me, she was almost at the point where she couldn't leave her home or function at all at work.

After examining Janice and talking to her extensively about her diet and lifestyle, I suspected that the neurotransmitter dopamine had become overly depleted in her system. We made some dietary adjustments to address a coexisting sugar metabolism imbalance that was sapping her energy, but I think even more important, she began to take the amino acid supplement phenylalanine to help balance her brain biochemistry. The effects were positive and pronounced. Within a matter of weeks, she pulled out of her depression, experienced fewer compulsions, and reacquired her zest for life. She took on new projects at work and reconnected emotionally with her family.

Janice's experiences with an amino acid supplement should come as no surprise to anyone who has studied the role of amino acids in reducing insomnia, relieving anxiety, treating depression, and promoting various other positive effects. Recent scientific studies have demonstrated conclusively that bodily levels of a half-dozen major amino acids can increase or decrease the body's supply of brain neurotransmitters, thus altering mood, sleeping patterns, sexual arousal, immunity, and other bodily functions. These neurotransmitter-affecting amino acids include two "essential" amino acids (meaning they must be obtained through diet or supplements):

- tryptophan
- phenylalanine

Four nonessential amino acids, which are formed in the body, often from the metabolism of other amino acids, also can affect neurotransmitters:

- 5-hydroxytryptophan (5-HTP)
- tyrosine
- glutamine
- gamma aminobutyric acid (GABA)

Another substance, a metabolite of the amino acid methionine, is also beginning to attract scientific attention for its reliable antidepressant properties. We'll take a closer look at this compound, S-adenosylmethionine (SAM), later in this chapter as well. But first, let's consider what amino acids are and how they affect mind and mood.

The Amazing Aminos

Most people know of amino acids as the building blocks of protein. A few amino acids found in the body, such as taurine, are not used by the body to build protein but have other potential therapeutic effects. The body makes protein molecules from twenty amino acids. The current scientific consensus is that eight of these are essential amino acids. I say "current scientific consensus" because the criteria that distinguish essential from nonessential amino acids are not hard and fast. For example, for most people arginine is a nonessential amino acid, but during childhood, when it is needed in greater amounts to promote growth, arginine may be considered an essential amino acid.

Among those amino acids that help to relieve depression, phenylalanine and tryptophan are the essential amino acids. 5-HTP is not essential because it is derived from the metabolism of tryptophan. Tyrosine is not essential because it is derived from the metabolism of phenylalanine. Glutamine is considered a nonessential amino acid, although it is possible that under certain conditions it is like arginine in that it can become essential. GABA is nonessential, although as we'll see, the body needs certain nutrients to form it. S-adenosylmethionine is nonessential because it is derived from the metabolism of methionine.

The effects of these amino acids on mind and mood and the benefits from their selective use as supplements to alleviate depression are closely linked to how each breaks down in the body. In essence:

- Tryptophan and 5-HTP are metabolized into serotonin and then eventually into melatonin. These amino acids thus work best for people with major depression, suicidal feelings, anxiety, insomnia, obsessive or compulsive thinking, SAD, and sleep problems.
- Phenylalanine and tyrosine break down into dopamine and noradrenaline. These amino acids are especially effective against generalized depression and problems related to an inability to experience life's pleasures to the fullest. Phenylalanine also elevates endorphin levels and thus is particularly useful for chronic pain, depression, and alcoholic depression, conditions in which endorphins are often depleted.
- Glutamine seems to be especially effective for people who crave sweets or who are addicted to alcohol.
- GABA works at the same sites in the brain as the conventional anxiety-reducing benzodiazepine drugs (such as Valium) to promote relaxation.
- Researchers are still trying to determine which neurotransmitters are most affected by SAM. Most likely, it promotes primarily serotonin action, much like tryptophan and 5-HTP. It may also help convert noradrenaline to adrenaline. SAM's benefits may be due to activating a number of components of brain metabolism and enhancing overall brain function.

In the discussion of amino acids that follows, I'll mention scientific studies that indicate their safety and effectiveness in treating mood-related disorders, as well as other potential beneficial effects they may have. How best to take amino acids is a major concern for most people, so I'll offer advice on how to ingest these substances through foods as well as through supplements.

Finally, I should note that scientists refer to amino acids by using the prefixes L- (for levorotatory or "left-handed") or D- (for dextrorotatory or "right-handed"). These letters designate slight differences in a given amino acid's molecular structure; thus, for example, L-tryptophan or D-phenylalanine. For most amino acid supplements, the naturally occurring L-forms are much more common than either the D- form or the mixed DL- form. For simplicity's sake, I'll drop the prefix L- except when it is necessary to distinguish specific forms, as is sometimes the case with phenylalanine.

Tryptophan: The Banned Amino Acid

Until the FDA banned it in 1989, tryptophan was a wildly popular nutritional supplement. Millions of people who felt anxious and tense, or who needed to promote sleep late at night, would reach for their jar of tryptophan. British pharmaceutical companies even included tryptophan as an ingredient in two antidepressant products. Most tryptophan users were not disappointed—tryptophan is an effective agent for increasing brain biochemicals that boost mood and, eventually, cause drowsiness.

We know this because tryptophan has been the subject of numerous scientific studies conducted since the 1970s. The bulk of these studies showed that tryptophan does indeed elevate mood and promote relaxation. For example, clinical studies have shown that tryptophan can reduce the fatigue, irritability, and sadness associated with forms of depression, in some cases as effectively as conventional antidepressants that have much higher levels of toxicity and side effects. And population studies have linked low tryptophan intakes with increased suicide rates.

In some of the studies that most dramatically demonstrated tryptophan's effect on mood, test subjects ingested a tryptophan-deficient amino acid drink. This soon caused very low levels of serotonin in the brain. Many subjects subsequently felt depressed, irritable, agitated, and even violent. In one such study, male subjects experienced marked increases in anger, aggression, annoyance, quarrelsome tendencies, and hostility. Supplying the subjects with a source of tryptophan reversed these feelings.

In a study published in 1997, researchers demonstrated that tryptophan can successfully augment light therapy in patients suffering from SAD. Subjects who had only partial or no response to light therapy were given one gram of tryptophan three times daily. After two weeks, 64 percent of the patients had very good clinical responses (based on two depression scales) and minimal side effects. This study involved only sixteen patients and was not placebo-controlled, so it needs to be followed up by better studies. It nevertheless suggests that tryptophan is a promising anti-SAD remedy.

Tryptophan doesn't work for everybody, but until the late 1980s it was probably one of the most promising antidepressant substances on the market, pharmaceutical or natural. Unfortunately, from my perspective, much has changed since then. In 1987 Eli Lilly introduced Prozac, which soon became the most successful antidepressant drug ever. In 1989 tryptophan, a natural, unpatented substance, experienced a serious contamination episode.

By the mid-1980s, almost all of the tryptophan being sold in supplements in the United States was being supplied by a half-dozen nutrient manufacturers. These producers distributed tryptophan powder to hundreds of smaller companies who encapsulated it and sold it under various brands. Tryptophan was cheap—twenty cents for a 500 mg capsule—and widely available. One of these large producers, a Japanese pharmaceutical company, decided to experiment with a new manufacturing process. It was seriously flawed (the company reduced filtering and introduced a genetically engineered strain of bacteria) and resulted in a flood of contaminated tryptophan hitting the worldwide market. The tryptophan contained a new, human-made amino acid that, when consumed regularly, caused a rare blood disorder called eosinophilia-myalgia syndrome (EMS). In 1989 medical investigators tied the contaminated tryptophan to dozens of deaths from EMS and some 1,500 cases of serious illness.

The Food and Drug Administration (FDA), no friend of nutritional supplements even in the best of times, quickly stepped in and banned the sale of supplemental tryptophan. Even though a number of scientific investigations in the early 1990s, including one by the federal Centers for Disease Control, linked the EMS episode not to tryptophan itself but to the contaminant, the FDA has not withdrawn its ban. Unfortunately, the issue is now more political than scientific. I agree with those who think that if the scientific issues were paramount, tryptophan would be treated like other substances, from hamburgers to Perrier water, that experienced contamination episodes but were allowed back on the market when the source of the toxicity was identified. I think it is revealing, and sad, that the FDA has allowed thalidomide back on the market (admittedly for very restricted use) but not tryptophan. Various European countries have allowed tryptophan back onto the market, and overseas orders now account for much of Americans' tryptophan consumption. Fortunately, in recent years the tryptophan-related compound 5-HTP has come onto the nutritional supplement market and can be used in much the same manner as tryptophan.

Prime candidates for tryptophan use: You may gain special benefit from taking tryptophan if your depression is related to
- too little serotonin activity in the brain
- seasonal rhythms

Safety concerns: Pregnant women should not take tryptophan supplements, nor should anyone who is taking MAO-inhibiting drugs, has bronchial asthma, or has the autoimmune condition lupus. Taking tryptophan supplements at the same time as taking SSRIs could cause headaches or other symptoms of excess serotonin levels. Tryptophan may also cause side effects such as nausea, headaches, gastric discomfort, or constipation in some people. Large daily doses, such as 6 to 10 g, should be taken only with professional supervision, as it is possible such amounts may reduce rather than increase serotonin availability. (Some researchers believe that tryptophan's mixed record in scientific studies is due to dosage levels that are either too high or too low.)

With my patients, I have seen minimal side effects at moderate doses. It continues to be highly effective for increasing serotonin levels in a natural way. I've found it particularly safe and effective for serotonin-deficient insomnia.

How to use it: You can get tryptophan from compounding pharmacies (which specialize in mixing or altering drugs for a patient, at the direction of a physician; they're not as tightly regulated by the FDA as regular pharmacies), but you'll need a prescription. An average daily starting dose is 500 mg, taken before bed.

You might think that the best way to maximize tryptophan would be to eat foods containing high levels, such as eggs, poultry, meat, and other protein-containing foods. Unfortunately, these foods are also rich in other amino acids, like phenylalanine, that compete with (and mostly defeat) tryptophan for uptake by the brain and that have different effects.

Two better strategies exist. One is to eat foods with a high ratio of tryptophan to other amino acids, while avoiding other sources of protein. Foods with a good tryptophan ratio include pumpkin and sunflower seeds, bananas, milk, peanuts, and lentils. Still, you must eat relatively large amounts of these foods to approach the levels of tryptophan once widely available in supplements. For example, you would have to eat 100 g, or about 3.5 ounces, of pumpkin seeds in order to ingest about 500 mg of tryptophan.

Another way to maximize the tryptophan content of protein-containing foods is to consume them with foods rich in complex carbohydrates, such as grain dishes, bread, or cereal. The carbohydrates promote the secretion of insulin, which helps amino acids cross from the blood into cells.

Insulin has less effect, however, on tryptophan than on the other amino acids. This leaves more tryptophan in the blood to cause a gradual rise in levels of mood-elevating serotonin in the brain.

5-HTP: Tryptophan's Legal Cousin

5-hydroxytryptophan is a natural amino acid found in high amounts in seeds and other foods. In the body, 5-HTP is formed from tryptophan, with the help of an enzyme and certain cofactors. 5-HTP is the immediate precursor of serotonin in the process that eventually produces melatonin. 5-HTP has begun to garner increased attention as a potential serotonin-enhancing supplement, probably both because tryptophan is banned as a dietary supplement and because 5-HTP is about ten times as potent per dose as tryptophan.

A number of studies have confirmed that oral doses of 5-HTP result in increased brain levels of serotonin as well as beta-endorphins, the body's natural painkillers. Studies have also begun to confirm its notable antidepressant properties.

- A study of patients with anxiety syndromes found that 5-HTP significantly reduced anxiety as measured by three separate scales.
- A Japanese study of twenty-four patients hospitalized for depression found a "marked amelioration of depressive symptoms" in seven patients after two weeks of treatment with 5-HTP.
- A number of studies have determined that 5-HTP is comparable to conventional tricyclic antidepressants in effectiveness while being much safer and better tolerated.
- A study showed that 5-HTP supplements elevated levels of endorphins, the body's pleasure-generating chemicals, among patients with major depression.

Unlike SSRIs, 5-HTP doesn't recycle serotonin; it actually increases its synthesis. More can then be released into the synapses, where it imparts its mood-boosting effects. The possibility that 5-HTP may help address a serotonin deficiency syndrome was supported by a 1991 study done by a team of Swiss and German psychiatric researchers. Using as subjects a group of sixty-three patients between the ages of eighteen and seventy-five with clinical depression, the researchers compared the effects of 5-HTP to the SSRI fluvoxamine (Luvox). Subjects' responses to the drugs were evaluated according to the Hamilton Rating Scale for Depression, a standard psychiatric test, as well as through self-assessments. The researchers determined that 5-HTP was as effective as fluvoxamine in reducing the symptoms of depression (after six weeks, both substances averaged better than 50 percent reductions in depression scores). The dietary supplement, however, caused fewer and less severe side effects than the prescription drug.

Prime candidates for 5-HTP use: You may gain special benefit from taking 5-HTP if your depression is related to
- too little serotonin activity in the brain
- seasonal rhythms

Safety concerns: Most researchers report that adverse effects from taking 5-HTP are relatively few and benign, the most common being digestive problems such as nausea and diarrhea. Taking 5-HTP with food may help prevent gastric upset. Daytime grogginess may also be a problem; many people take 5-HTP only at night, with their melatonin supplements. Extremely high doses of 5-HTP (such as 600 to 800 mg) may decrease libido, much as the serotonin-boosting SSRIs are known to do.

Anyone who wants to take 5-HTP and is already taking an SSRI or any other antidepressant drug should proceed with caution. Even more so than tryptophan, taking 5-HTP supplements at the same time as taking SSRIs may lead to nausea or other adverse effects from excessively high serotonin levels.

People with the rare condition known as carcinoid syndrome should not take 5-HTP. This disease is characterized by tumors of serotonin-forming cells usually in the gut or lungs and is associated with extremely high levels of serotonin in the blood. Anyone with gastrointestinal diseases such as ulcers or Crohn's disease should also avoid 5-HTP supplements.

Recent research has led to the speculation that a 5-HTP serotonin overload in the blood could cause fibrosis of the aortic valve and deterioration of the heart muscle. This has not been verified in the literature, but I feel anyone with existing cardiovascular disease, including arterial fibrillation, coronary artery disease, congestive heart failure, cardiomyopathy, valvular disease, or pulmonary hypertension should completely avoid 5-HTP.

How to use it: 5-HTP comes in capsules and powders. It is not as widely available in health food stores as some other supplements, but a number of mail-order companies offer it (see Supplement Resources). An average dose for depression is 100 mg, taken before bed. Some people may need to take higher levels in divided doses, such as 100 mg three times per day, and 5-HTP's antidepressant effects may not be evident until you have taken it daily for two to three weeks.

People who take melatonin supplements at night and want to add 5-HTP to their supplement regimen may need to reduce their dosage of one or the other supplement in order to avoid morning grogginess.

Supplement manufacturers often use 5-HTP extracted from the seed of an African legume (*Griffonia simplicifolia*), but 5-HTP does not occur in significant amounts in common foods and at this time I know of no way to obtain it through diet.

I often use 5-HTP in conjunction with tryptophan. I suggest taking moderate doses of 5-HTP during the day and tryptophan one hour before bedtime. Most of the people I've treated who've taken 5-HTP have reported that taking it during the day for its antidepressant effects does not cause unwanted drowsiness. In my experience, 5-HTP causes much less drowsiness than tryptophan. As is the case with tryptophan, taking 5-HTP when your stomach is empty of other proteins or with foods high in carbohydrates may somewhat improve its delivery to the brain.

Phenylalanine: The Stimulating Amino

Phenylalanine is found in common protein foods including poultry, meats, soybeans, fish, dairy products, nuts, and seeds, as well as the synthetic sweetener Aspartame. Such sources supply the average person with an estimated 500 to 2,000 mg of phenylalanine from diet alone. In the body it is able to cross the blood/brain barrier.

· In supplement form, phenylalanine is one of the most widely used single amino acids. The minor molecular differences between L-phenylalanine, D-phenylalanine, and DL-phenylalanine (half L- and half D-phenylalanine; also known as DLPA) account for slightly different effects on the body. L-phenylalanine is a nervous system stimulant, mood and cognition enhancer, and appetite suppressant. While D-phenylalanine also apparently has antidepressant properties, it and DLPA are taken primarily to control chronic pain and to enhance the pain-relieving effects of acupuncture.

Researchers have identified a number of possible mechanisms that may account for the mood-elevating properties of L-phenylalanine or DLPA. Phenylalanine is a precursor of tyrosine, which can raise brain levels of the neurotransmitters dopamine and noradrenaline. These play important roles in various brain functions that relate to memory, alertness, and mood. The antidepressant action of noradrenaline has attracted the attention of a number of pharmaceutical companies, which have recently begun to market prescription antidepressants that have the same mechanism of action as phenylalanine. The so-called selective noradrenaline reuptake inhibitors boost noradrenaline function. In addition, D-phenylalanine acts to discourage the breakdown of endorphins, the body's natural opiates that reduce pain and encourage mild euphoria.

Phenylalanine may also have other antidepressant mechanisms. Researchers have found that phenylalanine can be converted to the related compound phenylethyamine, PEA. Abundant in chocolate (which may account for chocolate's reputation as a love- and romance-inducer), PEA has stimulating and antidepressive effects in humans.

In an uncontrolled study of twenty-three depressed patients, phenylalanine caused a positive response in seventeen patients previously unresponsive to major, conventional tricyclic or MAOI antidepressants. Some studies show a beneficial effect on people with Parkinson's disease, a condition associated with dopamine deficits in the brain.

Phenylalanine has worked successfully on a number of my patients, even including one who had a seven-year history of manic depression. A fifty-two-year-old teacher, Lisa had not been able to improve much by adjusting her diet or taking homeopathic remedies. She got better almost immediately, however, on a regimen that included phenylalanine and another amino acid, glutamine, to enhance her overall brain metabolism. It led to fewer mood swings, less craving for sweets, and more physical energy. Her severe depressive episodes are now completely gone.

Prime candidates for phenylalanine use: You may gain special benefit from taking phenylalanine if your depression is related to
- too little noradrenaline activity in the brain
- too little dopamine activity in the brain
- too little endorphin activity in the brain

Safety concerns: Phenylalanine is relatively benign and is certainly safe enough to deserve its current status as a dietary supplement. The L-form can, however, cause side effects typical of nervous system stimulants, such as high blood pressure, agitation, anxiety, and insomnia. If this is a problem, reducing the dosage, using DLPA, or taking supplements only once in the morning may work. You could also try tyrosine instead. On occasion people report headaches or nausea from taking phenylalanine.

Certain people should avoid phenylalanine supplements. People with high blood pressure and those taking MAO inhibitor antidepressants, which can lead to dangerously high blood pressure, should avoid using L-phenylalanine or DLPA. Children, pregnant and breastfeeding women, and anyone with psychosis should also avoid taking phenylalanine supplements. Both L- and D- forms should be avoided by people with phenylketonuria, a genetic disorder of phenylalanine metabolism. Because tyrosine helps to produce melanin, the pigment that colors skin and hair, phenylalanine and tyrosine should be avoided by anyone suffering from malignant melanoma.

How to use it: Phenylalanine typically comes in powders and capsules. My usual recommendation to boost mood is to take 375 to 500 mg of L-phenylalanine up to three times per day. Taking it half an hour before a meal maximizes its effects. Users should take optimal levels of vitamin B-complex (see Chapter 6) to promote phenylalanine's activity. It may start to elevate your mood within a few days, or it may take longer.

Tyrosine: An Offspring of Phenylalanine

Tyrosine is similar to phenylalanine in its uses and effects. This should not be surprising, since tyrosine is derived from the metabolism of phenylalanine in the body. (Tyrosine also occurs in many protein foods.) Tyrosine's antidepressant action is thought to relate primarily to its ability to increase brain levels of dopamine and noradrenaline. When it is administered to the right candidate in large doses, its mood-boosting powers can be quite dramatic. One patient I treated, a divorced woman in her early thirties who worked as a hospital administrator, had been suffering from periodic bouts of depression. She was finding it increasingly hard to work at her job and felt unable to cope with the demands of raising two young children. She also complained that "nothing was fun anymore" and that she had no libido. I helped her make gradual adjustments in her diet and she began to take B vitamins and other nutrients, but nothing was working fast. Clearly she needed an emergency adjustment, something to pull her out of her depression. Within two days of her starting to take 1,000 mg of tyrosine three times per day, her depression lifted. She told me, "I feel like the real me now. I'm more alert and taking an interest in new things. I'm also having fun being with my son and daughter again."

Scientists have conducted a number of studies on tyrosine's ability to relieve depression and anxiety. Early findings confirmed that taking oral doses of tyrosine can increase the levels and activity of noradrenaline in the brain. Some studies have found tyrosine to be as effective against mild depression as conventional antidepressants, with fewer serious adverse side effects. Researchers have also tested tyrosine's effectiveness against more serious conditions such as major depression and manic depression. Results have been mixed. A well-controlled 1990 study of sixty-five outpatients with major depression found "no evidence that tyrosine had antidepressant activity." A notable French study, however, found that tyrosine reliably cured immediate and long-term "dopamine-dependent depressions." The researchers noted that "this treatment is ineffective in other types of depression." I think that this is the key finding to keep in mind: tyrosine is much more likely to alleviate your depression if you've taken the time to determine that your biochemical imbalance is in noradrenaline or dopamine, rather than, for example, serotonin. Making this distinction is a key aspect of my depression evaluation of patients.

People who take tyrosine often report increased energy levels and alertness. Some women find that tyrosine helps to alleviate symptoms of premenstrual syndrome, such as fatigue and irritability. Tyrosine tends to suppress appetite and increase metabolism and thus can play a role in a weight-loss program. Because cocaine and many other drugs cause euphoria by increasing dopamine activity in the brain, tyrosine can help people addicted to these drugs overcome their condition. I often use either phenylalanine or tyrosine in helping people repair the neurotransmitter damage caused by cocaine or alcohol.

Choosing between phenylalanine and tyrosine is often a matter of trying each and seeing which works better. Phenylalanine may be better absorbed by most people and cause fewer headaches, but some people find that tyrosine is less stimulating to the nervous system and less likely to increase blood pressure compared to phenylalanine. If a patient has chronic pain I will use DL-phenylalanine because it indirectly affects the endorphins, which help with pain. I tend to use tyrosine with patients who have hypothyroid-related depression, because as we saw in Chapter 4, tyrosine (along with iodine) is necessary for the production of thyroid hormone.

Prime candidates for tyrosine use: You may gain special benefit from taking phenylalanine if your depression is related to
- too little noradrenaline activity in the brain
- too little dopamine activity in the brain
- underlying conditions, especially overindulgence in recreational drugs or alcohol
- a thyroid imbalance

Safety concerns: Tyrosine causes few side effects even at fairly high doses. Overstimulation and insomnia are possibilities, although taking tyrosine early in the day usually avoids these problems. The potential adverse effects cited above for phenylalanine also apply to tyrosine, with the exception of the warning to phenylketonurics, since tyrosine can't be converted back into phenylalanine. Thus, users need to proceed with caution if they suffer from insomnia or high blood pressure. Those who shouldn't take tyrosine at all include women who are pregnant or breast-feeding, children, anyone taking MAO inhibitors, and those who suffer from psychosis or have malignant melanoma.

How to use it: Tyrosine comes in capsules and powders. N-acetyl L-tyrosine is a new form that has recently come onto the market (see Supplement Resources) and may be more readily processed in the body.

I usually start a mildly depressed person on 500 mg two to three times per day. It is best to take tyrosine on an empty stomach (although this sometimes causes mild gastric upset) or with carbohydrate-rich meals. Taking it with protein foods will increase competition from other amino acids for uptake by the brain. You can increase tyrosine's effectiveness by also taking optimal levels of vitamin B-complex (see Chapter 6).

Although I have not seen any problems in patients taking as much as 1,000 mg of tyrosine three times per day, if you are going to be taking the kinds of therapeutic doses used in some of the depression studies, such as 2,000 to 4,000 mg up to three times daily, it is best to work closely with a physician or with a knowledgeable nutritionist or naturopath. Taking large doses over an extended time may cause the brain to adjust by inhibiting the action of an enzyme necessary for tyrosine to be transformed into neurotransmitters.

Glutamine: When Cravings Strike

Taking glutamine helps to energize the mind and boost the spirits, without leading to the depleted feeling caused by overuse of central nervous system stimulants such as caffeine and ephedrine. Many healthy people now take glutamine because it is a nontoxic mental and physical stimulant. Users report that glutamine promotes clear thinking, increases alertness, and alleviates fatigue. People feel livelier, more confident, and mentally sharper.

Glutamine has been the subject of a number of studies, though only a few that I know of have focused directly on glutamine's mood-boosting and mind-stimulating effects. For example, on the basis of animal studies, researchers in the mid-1950s first suggested that glutamine (but not glutamic acid) supplements could help to control alcoholics' desire to drink and could reduce their alcohol intake. Well-controlled, long-term studies on humans haven't been done, but the therapy has been used with some success in alcohol rehabilitation clinics. Other studies, also predominantly done in the 1950s, found that daily doses of glutamine in the range of 1.5 to 2 grams are more effective than conventional therapies (restricting diet and taking antacids) in the treatment of peptic ulcers. Additional studies have suggested a possible role for glutamine in promoting cognitive function in the elderly and in mentally handicapped children. Glutamine's effects on the intestines may help prevent allergic reactions to some foods. It seems to be helpful in treating permeable bowel syndrome.

Two recent studies have examined the effects of a MAO inhibitor antidepressant and two antimanic drugs (lithium and valproic acid) on glutamine levels in the cerebrospinal fluids of rats. The MAO inhibitor decreased brain levels of glutamine while increasing GABA levels. Lithium and valproic acid both significantly increased GABA levels, while only the latter increased glutamine concentration.

A nonessential amino acid, glutamine is structurally similar although functionally different from the related compound glutamic acid. Like glutamine, glutamic acid is also widely distributed in plant and animal proteins and can be found in the form of supplements. Glutamine, however, has the advantage of more readily crossing the blood-brain barrier compared to glutamic acid, and is thus the preferred form of the nutrient for increased stimulation.

Prime candidates for glutamine use: You may gain special benefit from taking glutamine if your depression is related to
- too little glutamine activity in the brain
- underlying conditions, especially overindulgence in recreational drugs or allergic reactions to foods
- an imbalance in blood sugar

Safety concerns: High doses of glutamine, such as 2,000 to 4,000 mg per day, may cause overstimulation, including anxiety, restlessness, and insomnia. Also, some people seem to be especially sensitive to certain salts of glutamic acid, such as glutamate or monosodium glutamate (MSG), a compound added to foods as a flavor enhancer. Glutamine may cause headache, chest pain, and other side effects in these people.

How to use it: Glutamine comes in tablets and capsules (usually 500 or 1,000 mg) and in powders from a number of "smart drug" and amino acid producers. Glutamine is also included in some energy- or brain-boosting nutritional formulations, with names such as Neuro Nutrients, Brain Alert, Ultra Energy Plus, and Higher Mind. I usually suggest that patients try 500 mg once or twice daily. For increased effect, you can combine glutamine with choline, DMAE, or other nutrients that enhance acetylcholine production.

GABA: Relief from Anxiety

Gamma aminobutyric acid is an amino acid that works much like a neurotransmitter in the brain. It can be a lifesaver for people like Tom, a retired airline pilot I treated in the early 1990s. He came to me with depression as well as fatigue, a decreased sex drive, high blood pressure, and headaches. Within a month of being put on GABA (he also needed to change to a fast oxidizer diet and take some supplements for adrenal support), he reported a remarkable lifting of his depression. Tom's sex drive and energy levels also returned to normal.

Studies have found that levels of GABA in the blood, brain, and cerebrospinal fluid are significantly lower than normal in depressed persons. Studies have also shown that drugs and other substances that promote the activity of GABA in the brain have antidepressant effects, while conversely agents that decrease GABA function tend to promote depression. Researchers have suggested that people who have low GABA function may have their depression triggered by long-term alcoholism or poor dietary habits. Scientists have established that the anxiety-reducing and slight antidepressant effects of benzodiazepines such as Valium are due to their effects on GABA receptors in the brain. Some research has suggested that the use of GABA in recovering alcoholics may increase a desire for alcohol. So I am now using it cautiously with post-alcoholics.

In the near future I hope researchers take the next step and perform well-controlled clinical trials on supplemental GABA for depression. Although such research has yet to be done, I've found that GABA is a safe and effective mood-booster and anxiety-reliever.

Prime candidates for GABA use: You may gain special benefit from taking GABA if your depression is related to
- too little GABA activity in the brain
- stress

Safety concerns: GABA has mildly relaxing effects, so it is a good idea to avoid using it when drinking alcohol or taking conventional relaxants. High doses may cause daytime sluggishness. Few people report any other side effects from taking GABA.

How to use it: Supplement producers offer GABA as a powder, tablets, and capsules. I usually recommend a starting dose of 500 to 750 mg of GABA two to three times per day to elevate mood and reduce anxiety. Some people are more sensitive to GABA than others. I had one patient who had been depressed and anxious for several years. She also had trouble sleeping. When she took 750 mg per day of GABA, she slept much better and her spirits improved, but she felt so tranquil that she couldn't work! When we reduced her GABA dosage to 250 mg per day, the antidepressant effects remained, but she was not overly tranquilized.

In some people, even low doses may cause a deep relaxation and sleepiness. Although you may welcome this effect, I warn people to initially try it in situations where relaxation and sleepiness are not a problem.

Although GABA is a nonessential amino acid (that is, it is formed in the body), it is useful to take optimal doses of niacinamide (B_3), pyridoxine (B_6), and vitamin C (see Chapter 6) to help form GABA in the body, enhance its metabolism, and deliver it to the appropriate receptors in the brain.

SAM: A Depression-Busting Amino Acid Metabolite

One final supplement is worth mentioning for its potential mood-boosting effects. S-adenosylmethionine (SAM; also known as SAMe) is not an amino acid, but rather a naturally occurring metabolite that the body forms from the addition of the energy-carrying compound adenosine triphosphate (ATP) to the amino acid methionine. SAM is found in cells throughout the body, helping to keep cell membranes fluid and promoting the activity of enzymes. It also protects the liver and stimulates cartilage growth. Among its most important jobs is to transfer a part of its structure, the methyl group, to other molecules. This process of "methylation" is prominent in the formation of many brain chemicals as well as liver compounds.

SAM's multiple effects have led nutritionally oriented healers to use it to help treat cirrhosis and other liver disorders, arthritis, multiple sclerosis, fibromyalgia, migraine headaches, and other conditions. One of the substance's most promising applications is in the treatment of depression. In fact, some researchers suggest that it is the most effective antidepressant substance available, surpassing Prozac in the percentage of users who benefit from taking it. Studies have determined that levels of SAM are significantly lower in the cerebrospinal fluid of severely depressed persons than in persons in a control group. Women suffering postpartum depression have been shown to benefit from taking SAM.

A number of double-blind studies, many done in Italy (where SAM was first identified in the early 1950s), confirm antidepressant action for SAM. A 1988 study compared SAM (administered intravenously) to the conventional tricyclic antidepressant imipramine in eighteen persons with major depression. After two weeks six of the nine people being administered SAM had clinically significant improvements in depressive symptoms compared to only two taking the tricyclic. A meta-analysis (a study that analyzes the results from a whole group of related studies) of clinical studies done on SAM conducted by Italian researchers and published in 1994 concluded that SAM showed a greater response rate than placebo and was comparable in its antidepressant effect to standard tricyclic antidepressants. The researchers also noted that SAM causes relatively few side effects.

In most of the studies conducted on SAM, researchers have administered SAM intravenously. Recent studies confirm that oral doses are also mood-boosting. For example, a randomized, double-blind, placebo-controlled study published in 1990 in the *American Journal of Psychiatry* involving fifteen inpatients with major depression characterized oral SAM as a "safe, effective antidepressant with few side effects and a rapid onset of action." A clinical trial conducted by researchers at Massachusetts General Hospital, also published in 1990, found that nine out of twenty outpatients with major depression significantly improved by taking oral doses of SAM. Scientists have also found that oral doses of SAM raise its levels in cerebrospinal fluid, indicating that SAM crosses the blood-brain barrier.

Exactly how SAM helps to alleviate depression has not yet been determined. Italian researchers have speculated that "at least some major mood disorders are due to abnormalities affecting the [SAM]-dependent methylation of a substance in the central nervous system." SAM promotes the body's use of healthy fat compounds such as phosphatidylcholine and phosphatidylserine. SAM may also promote the production of neurotransmitters such as serotonin or allow the brain to use neurotransmitters more efficiently. SAM's effects on dopamine are unclear, however. One recent study suggested SAM may reduce dopamine availability in the frontal lobe of the cerebrum in persons with Parkinson's disease, potentially actually increasing depression rather than relieving it. Further studies should help to clarify SAM's mechanism of action.

SAM has been an important supplement for a number of my patients. One in particular was Kathleen, a mother and part-time interior decorator. In her mid-forties when she came to see me, she had been experiencing depression, hypoglycemia, and chronic fatigue for several years. She said that she often experienced strong cravings for sweets. Kathleen began to take approximately 400 mg of SAM four times per day, along with glutamine, vitamin B-complex, and other nutrients. I also suggested that Kathleen avoid chocolate, wheat, corn, and dairy, and eat more foods consistent with her fast-oxidizer system. Within three weeks her depression began to lift and she reported more energy and enthusiasm for life. She told me she was developing a clarity of direction that she'd been missing for many years, and felt confident that she could once again take the life steps she needed to attain greater personal happiness.

Prime candidates for SAM use: You may gain special benefit from taking SAM if your depression is related to too little serotonin activity in the brain.

Safety concerns: SAM appears to be relatively nontoxic, especially compared to conventional antidepressant drugs. The most common minor side effects that people report are nausea, dry mouth, and restlessness. Some evidence suggests that large doses may induce mania in some persons.

Although SAM contains a form of the amino acid methionine, taking methionine directly is not a healthful shortcut to increasing SAM availability in the body. Methionine breaks down to form homocysteine, and excessive blood levels of homocysteine have recently been shown to increase the risk of heart disease. A number of B-complex vitamins play important roles in allowing methionine to produce SAM and keeping homocysteine levels down; thus, people who take SAM for help with their depression should complement it with optimal levels of B-complex, especially folic acid, pyridoxine, B_{12}, and NADH. (See Chapter 6 for optimal supplement recommendations.)

How to use it: SAM remains a hard-to-find supplement in U.S. health food stores, although it is offered by mail-order companies (see Supplement Resources). I usually start patients at 200 mg four times per day, which can be increased up to 400 mg four times per day if larger doses are more effective and don't cause any side effects.

The Mood-Boosting Amino Acids in a Nutshell

The following table summarizes the chief properties of each of the six mood-elevating amino acids:

	NEUROTRANSMITTER AFFECTED	PREDOMINANT ACTION	CONDITIONS TREATED
Tryptophan	serotonin	calming	depression, anxiety, insomnia; suicidal feelings, obsessive-compulsive disorder
5-HTP	serotonin	calming	depression, anxiety, insomnia

Phenylalanine	dopamine, noradrenaline	stimulating	depression, fatigue, lack of pleasure
Tyrosine	dopamine, noradrenaline	stimulating	depression, fatigue, lack of pleasure
Glutamine	glutamine	stimulating	depression, fatigue
GABA	GABA	calming	depression, anxiety
SAM	serotonin	stimulating	depression

Beyond the Amino Acids

Amino acids can often have almost miraculous effects. In many cases I've seen them transform a person's condition within a week or two. Yet, I want to emphasize that amino acids are not magic bullets. Ideally, they should be used to support and enhance other supplements as well as lifestyle adjustments. Moreover, optimal amounts of certain vitamins and nutrients can help to maximize the effectiveness of the amino acids. I've identified what I consider to be the top twenty depression-relieving nutrients. Along with a trio of herbs and a couple of hormones, these will be the subject of the next chapter.

6

Step Two: Optimize Your Supplements

I've long been in the habit of immediately checking young women who regularly take birth control pills for deficiencies in the B vitamins. That's partially because of a dramatic study conducted in the late 1960s and published in the respected British medical journal *Lancet*. This study was among the first to make the vital connection between B vitamin status (in this case, B_6, usually taken in supplement form as pyridoxine) and mood. Conducted by researchers in Madison, Wisconsin, the study was one of those rare ones that offered such a clear-cut benefit that subjects eventually rebelled against the protocol.

Here's what happened. Some fifty-eight depressed women, all of whom were on the pill, were administered 25 mg of B_6 twice a day at the first signs of low mood. The response rate after three months was remarkable, with more than 75 percent of the women reporting partial or full relief from their symptoms. Researchers wanted to confirm the beneficial effects of the B vitamin by taking these forty-four positive responders off B_6. But the relief from depression was so pronounced and the prospect of a return to their gloom so unappealing that these subjects refused to stop taking their new vitamins!

Numerous better controlled and more tightly designed studies done over the past three decades, on B_6 as well as various other vitamins, minerals, and nutrients, have confirmed that nutritional and herbal supplements can play an important dual role by both preventing and treating depression. First, by preventing outright deficiencies, nutrients can head off symptoms of depression such as sadness, irritability, and fatigue. Depressed mood, for example, is an early symptom of scurvy, the condition caused by a vitamin C deficiency. Perhaps equally important, recent studies have determined that optimal doses of certain nutrients can actually aid in the treatment of depression not directly related to deficiency conditions. This is true both for individual nutrients and for a balanced program of optimal supplementation. For example, one recent long-term study done by British scientists demonstrated a significant improvement in mood, especially among female subjects, from taking a daily multivitamin supplement over the course of one year.

Many vitamins and minerals are involved in the complex interplay between the nervous system and the brain. Certain nutrients are crucial for hormone secretion, neurotransmitter production, nerve transmission, and cellular metabolism. A long-term deficiency in one or more of these nutrients thus can contribute to imbalances in neurotransmitters such as noradrenaline, serotonin, and dopamine, possibly leading to depression or other mood disorders because of the disruption in brain cell metabolism. Such symptoms as confusion, loss of energy and sex drive, fatigue, restlessness, and sadness on occasion can be alleviated by simple nutritional supplementation. Nutrients can help prevent damage from the stress hormone cortisol, which has various adverse effects on brain and nervous system function, including disrupting the brain's fuel supply of glucose, interfering with neurotransmitters, and creating free radicals. Antioxidant nutrients can neutralize these harmful molecules and prevent their adverse effects.

Your optimal supplement program may also include in some instances herbs, particularly St. John's wort or ginkgo, and hormonal supplements such as thyroid "glandulars" or melatonin. (I'll discuss the essential fatty acid supplements in the following chapter.) Natural food stores and supplement catalogs are chock-full of choices, often to a confusing degree. This chapter will steer you toward what you need and show you how and why to use supplements to alleviate your depression.

Optimizing the Nutrients

Before I summarize the evidence for individual nutrients, I want to emphasize the importance of customizing a nutritional supplement program for each reader's unique type of depression, psychophysical constitution, and biochemical balance, as determined from previous chapters. No standard prescription exists for the average person—and there is no average person. You are unique and will gain the greatest benefit by tailoring your supplement program according to your personal biochemistry. Don't expect to find one magic supplement that will turn your life around, although this is certainly possible in selected cases, for example, where depression is a direct result of a deficiency of a single nutrient. Much more frequently, you must look for patterns of imbalance that will be improved by various nutrients.

In the following discussions of nutrients, I provide an "optimal" range for each supplement that is typical of what provides the most healthful results for most people. Consider these recommendations as starting points for determining what works best for your condition, age, body weight, gender, metabolism and absorption rates, alcohol or other drug usage, diet, exercise and stress levels, psychophysical balance, and overall health. In general, taking optimal daily doses of these nutrients can not only help prevent or treat depression, but is also one of the safest methods for ensuring your overall long-term health.

Let's first take a closer look at the most important vitamins and minerals with the potential to either prevent or relieve depression. I will pay particular attention to how the nutrient may benefit depression, the best food sources of the nutrient, its overall safety, and finally its optimal daily dose for average adults. Note that with the exception of melatonin, the suggested dosage levels should be spread out over the day, for example by taking one third of an optimal level at each meal.

Vitamin A and Mixed Carotenoids

Vitamin A is a fat-soluble, animal-derived nutrient that is essential for healthy vision, cell reproduction, immune function, wound healing, and other crucial bodily functions. Various predominantly plant-based carotenoids, especially beta-carotene, act as precursors to vitamin A and possess additional health benefits unrelated to their vitamin A activity. Vitamin A and carotenoids have mostly indirect impacts on depression. For example, they help to protect the body from the adverse effects—including depression—of stress, damage from free radicals (molecules that are highly reactive and, when oxidized, potentially harmful to bodily cells) or from toxic chemicals, and immune dysfunction. These nutrients may also benefit people with various debilitating conditions that often cause low mood, from AIDS to alcoholism to premenstrual syndrome. Vitamin A is a cofactor in the metabolism of essential fatty acids.

Preformed vitamin A is found in animal foods, such as milk and butter. The body, however, is able to convert plant-derived beta-carotene (as well as dozens of other carotenoids) into vitamin A. Various carotenoids occur in dark-green leafy vegetables as well as in orange-yellow fruits and vegetables such as cantaloupes, carrots, sweet potatoes, and squash. Concentrated green foods, such as spirulina and blue-green algae, and the dried juice of young shoots of cereal plants such as barley and wheat grass, are rich in beta-carotene as well as other carotenoids. Such natural sources are preferable to supplements. Eating a diverse, carotenoid-rich diet supplies an estimated 5 to 10 mg of beta-carotene daily; average adult consumption of beta-carotene on the standard American diet is much lower at 1 to 2 mg daily.

Prime candidates for vitamin A/mixed carotenoid use: You may gain special benefit from taking vitamin A/mixed carotenoids if your depression is related to

- an underlying condition, especially degenerative ailments and reactions to toxic chemicals
- an imbalance or deficiency in essential fatty acids
- an imbalance in blood sugar, and you are a fast oxidizer

Safety concerns: High doses of preformed A can accumulate in the body (especially the liver) and cause serious adverse health effects. Mixed carotenoids have much less potential toxicity. Taking very high doses of beta-carotene (more than 100,000 IU, or 60 mg per day) may cause a slight orange tinge to the skin. This condition, however, is considered benign and is easily reversible by decreasing your intake of beta-carotene.

How to use it: Vitamin A and mixed carotenoid supplements come in capsules, tablets, softgels, and powders. Potency typically ranges from 10,000 to 50,000 International Units (IUs), with the most popular potency probably being 25,000 IU. Many supplements contain only beta-carotene (derived either synthetically or from carrots or algae), though others have added preformed vitamin A (usually derived from cold-water fish liver oil), alpha and gamma carotene, and such carotenoids as lycopene, lutein, and cryptoxanthin.

An optimal daily dose for an adult is 5,000 to 10,000 IU of preformed vita-
min A or 25,000 to 50,000 IU (15 to 30 mg) of beta-carotene plus mixed
carotenoids.

Vitamin B Complex

Julie, a fifty-two-year-old artist, had a long history of episodes of manic
behavior once or twice a year interspersed with periods of low-grade
depression. She'd been taking homeopathic remedies and following a
healthful diet for a number of years, but by themselves these approaches
were not enough to alleviate her condition. After I started to see her,
among the most important supplements that I recommended was one
that contained optimal doses of various B-complex vitamins, associated
minerals, and cofactors specific to enhance brain cell metabolism. Their
influence on mind and mood soon began to help Julie. Along with some
amino acid supplements and some lifestyle adjustments, they've allowed
her to go for almost two years now without a manic episode. Her mental
and physical energy is considerably better and her depression is completely gone.

Marsha, a twenty-three-year-old student when she came to see me a
few years ago, had a similar experience. A conservatively dressed young
woman enrolled in business school, Marsha had started living with her
boyfriend, and taking birth control pills, about six months earlier. Normally outgoing and vivacious, within the past two months she had
begun to be troubled by a number of symptoms of depression, including
insomnia, unexplained episodes of anger and withdrawal, and problems
with eating well.

After talking with Marsha, I suspected that her mainly fast-food and
processed-food diet, in conjunction with the birth control pills, were
probably causing B vitamin deficiencies. Tests showed she was very deficient in B_6 and marginally low in B_{12} and another B vitamin, folic acid. I
believe that the daily B vitamin supplements, although they weren't the
only aspect of her treatment program (we talked a lot about establishing
better eating habits and switching to another method of birth control),
were an important reason why she felt much improved within three
weeks. Her depression lifted, her outbursts of anger subsided, and she
had increased physical energy. "My physical and emotional relationship
with my boyfriend has also improved," she told me.

In my experience, the B-complex vitamins have more dramatic mood-elevating effects than most other nutrients. Various B vitamins are crucial for proper nerve function and nerve cell metabolism, which produces optimal neurotransmitter levels. People who suffer from B-vitamin deficiencies often show symptoms of mild depression. Studies have found that, among patients who are admitted to the hospital for major depression, B vitamin status is often poor. Deficiencies or low blood levels in B-complex vitamins, particularly pyridoxine, B_{12}, and folate, as well as inositol, choline, and the up-and-coming NADH (which some nutritionists consider B vitamins), are common among psychiatric patients suffering from irritability, apathy, anxiety, fatigue, and other symptoms related to mood depression. Administering B vitamins to depressed patients often helps them improve faster than those who are not given such supplements. In some cases they recover completely from nothing more than supplementing their diet with the missing B vitamin nutrient.

The links between B-complex vitamins and depression should not be surprising, given the crucial functions these nutrients play in mind and body. Let's first consider the seven core B-complex vitamins.

Thiamine (B_1). Brain cells require thiamine to produce energy, and a deficiency of thiamine can impair mental function and even lead to psychosis. A recent study of 120 young adult females found that those given 50 mg thiamine daily reported being "more clearheaded, composed, and energetic." The influence was noted even in subjects with adequate thiamine status at the start of the study. Researchers have also noticed that psychiatric patients admitted to hospitals tend to have reduced thiamine levels in their blood.

Thiamine is found primarily in vegetables, whole grains, nuts, seeds, and legumes. It is also a popular nutrient for fortifying processed foods.

An optimal daily dose of thiamine for an adult is 25 to 50 mg.

Riboflavin (B_2). Riboflavin is necessary for essential fatty acid metabolism (see Chapter 7), improves energy production in certain brain cells, and promotes the antioxidant properties (the ability to neutralize free radicals) of the bodily compound glutathione.

Riboflavin occurs in significant amounts in whole grains, legumes, yogurt, soybeans, green leafy vegetables, beans, poultry, and fish.

An optimal daily dose of riboflavin for an adult is 25 to 50 mg.

Niacin (B₃). Niacin helps regulate blood sugar levels and energy production. It is a crucial component of another B-complex vitamin, NADH, with prominent antidepressant effects. It may have an indirect effect on serotonin levels, because the body uses tryptophan (see Chapter 5) to produce niacin, and on adrenal hormones. Psychosis and dementia are two of the common symptoms of a long-term deficiency in niacin. It is specifically deficient in some forms of schizophrenia.

Niacin is plentiful from such vegetarian sources as peanuts, sesame seeds, sunflower seeds, brown rice, whole grains, barley, and almonds.

An optimal daily dose of niacin for an adult is 25 to 50 mg.

Pantothenic acid (B₅). Along with niacin, pantothenic acid plays a role in forming coenzymes necessary for proper functioning of essential fatty acids, metabolism of carbohydrates, and the production of adrenal hormones. It is a vital nutrient for anyone subject to extreme stress.

Pantothenic acid is found in a wide range of foods (the Greek root of its name, *pan*, means all or every), including avocados, mushrooms, soybeans, bananas, collard greens, sunflower seeds, lentils, broccoli, brown rice, and eggs.

An optimal daily dose of pantothenic acid for an adult is 25 to 50 mg.

Pyridoxine. This B vitamin has one of the most dramatic mood-elevating effects of them all. Pyridoxine can help correct brain metabolism dysfunctions that can cause depression. It can heighten serotonin function through its ability to slow the destruction of tryptophan in the brain and to act as a cofactor for enzymes that convert tryptophan to serotonin as well as tyrosine to noradrenaline. A pyridoxine deficiency is common among depressed patients, many of whom find that taking supplemental pyridoxine provides an emotional boost. Because oral contraceptives can interfere with the tryptophan/serotonin cycle, women who take birth control pills are particularly likely to benefit from taking extra pyridoxine. People who need to increase serotonin activity should take pyridoxine with their tryptophan or 5-HTP supplements to promote these amino acids' conversion into serotonin in the brain.

Pyridoxine is concentrated in spinach, walnuts, eggs, fish, and poultry. *An optimal daily dose of pyridoxine for an adult is 25 to 50 mg.*

Cobalamin or cyanocobalamin (B_{12}). Vitamin B_{12} plays a number of key roles in the body, including aiding in the metabolism of essential fatty acids and another B vitamin with important effects on mood, folic acid. B_{12} also is necessary for the myelin sheath that insulates nerve fibers and allows for the free flow of neurotransmitters. A deficiency in B_{12} causes neurological problems and confusion, depression, and memory loss. A deficiency in the elderly has been linked to Alzheimer's disease. Taking vitamin B_{12} supplements helps treat fatigue (even with no evidence of a deficiency), depression, and infertility. Many of my clients get immediate relief from their depression with a B_{12} and folic acid injection.

Various studies done on older subjects have demonstrated links between B_{12} status and mood. For example, a 1984 study of female psychiatric patients aged sixty to ninety-three confirmed a high frequency of B_{12} deficiency. A retrospective study of sixty geriatric inpatients with severe mood disorders, including depression and manic depression, demonstrated numerous significant positive correlations between B_{12} and cognitive factors. Some recent evidence suggests that B_{12} helps the body secrete additional melatonin.

A number of factors may affect your ability to absorb B_{12}. Age is one factor; declining absorption with advancing age is not uncommon. In my clinical experience, stress appears to be a major factor in causing a B_{12} deficiency. I've also noticed that many of the depressed people I've treated need regular B_{12} supplementation for one to two years before they can cut back.

Although vitamin B_{12} is commonly thought of as an animal-source nutrient, it also occurs in high levels in plant sources such as

- tempeh
- various sea vegetables
- brewer's yeast
- green and blue-green algae such as spirulina, Klamath Lake algae, and chlorella
- bee pollen
- mushrooms

Vitamin B_{12} is nontoxic up to at least 1,000 mcg per day, much beyond what you need to take.

The optimal daily dose of vitamin B_{12} for an adult is 50 to 100 mcg.

Folic acid or folate. Vitamin B_{12} often works closely with folic acid to regulate functions relating to mood. Researchers say that folic acid and B_{12} help stimulate the formation of a compound necessary for the first step in synthesizing neurotransmitters, especially serotonin. A folic acid deficiency can lower brain levels of serotonin and S-adenosyl-methionine (SAM), the amino acid metabolite with mood-elevating properties (see Chapter 5).

Studies have found that people with major depression have a higher than normal rate of folic acid deficiency, which may aggravate psychiatric disturbances, particularly depression. Among nonpsychiatric patients, a folic acid deficiency can cause psychiatric symptoms. Researchers have also found that administering folic acid to patients who are deficient can help to alleviate symptoms of depression and other psychiatric conditions. In conjunction with B_6 and B_{12}, folic acid may help prevent Alzheimer's disease.

Folic acid occurs in both animal and plant foods, with dark green leafy vegetables such as spinach and kale being especially rich sources. Other sources include whole wheat and wheat bran, asparagus, brewer's yeast, and fruits such as bananas and cantaloupes. Whole, fresh foods typically have much higher levels than processed foods.

An optimal daily dose of folic acid for an adult is 400 to 800 mcg.

Prime candidates for vitamin B-complex use: You may gain special benefit from taking thiamine, riboflavin, niacin, and pyridoxine supplements if your depression is related to
  - an imbalance in blood sugar, and you are a slow oxidizer

You may gain special benefit from taking pantothenic acid or vitamin B_{12} if your depression is related to
  - an imbalance in blood sugar, and you are a fast oxidizer

You may gain special benefit from taking niacin and pyridoxine if your depression is related to
  - an imbalance or deficiency in essential fatty acids

Safety concerns: All of the B-complex vitamins are nontoxic at the doses mentioned here.

How to use it: B-complex vitamins are widely available as single nutrients, in B-complex formulas, and as components of multinutrient supplements. In general, it is best to take the B-complex vitamins as a group, to avoid an excess of one B vitamin leading to a deficiency of another. See specific B vitamins for suggested optimal doses.

Inositol

A number of studies have also shown beneficial effects from the B-complex nutrient inositol for treating depression, panic disorder, attention deficit disorder, and obsessive-compulsive disorders. A group of Israeli psychiatric researchers have been leading the way in exploring the link between inositol and mood disorders. For example, a double-blind study compared inositol and a placebo in twenty-eight depressed patients. After four weeks, eleven of thirteen patients given a high daily dose of inositol improved, while most of those taking the placebo stayed the same or worsened. Other studies have found that inositol was significantly more effective than a placebo at reducing subjects' average weekly number and intensity of panic attacks, and that large doses of inositol (up to 18 g for six weeks) were comparable to Prozac in treating obsessive-compulsive disorder.

Anecdotal evidence suggests that a 500 or 1,000 mg dose of inositol may reduce anxiety or promote sleep. This effect, however, has not yet been scientifically proven. I see inositol lift depression in about 5 percent of my clients. It also seems to be supportive for some of my clients with anxiety.

Inositol helps to protect cell membranes from damage, among other functions. Its mood-related effects may be due to its ability to act as a precursor for compounds that carry messages in the nervous system and the brain. The mineral lithium, a popular treatment for manic depression, is thought to work at least in part by inhibiting the formation of inositol in the brain.

Most adults consume an estimated gram or more of inositol from foods every day. Inositol is found in citrus fruits (an orange contains about 300 mg of inositol), cantaloupe, nuts, beans, whole grains, and brewer's yeast. Lecithin provides inositol, although lecithin is comparatively richer in choline. Inositol is also produced and stored in the body.

Prime candidates for inositol use: You may gain special benefit from taking inositol if your depression is related to an anxiety disorder.

Safety concerns: Inositol is safe and nontoxic at doses well beyond optimal ones.

How to use it: Inositol is sold as a powder and in capsules and tabs, most ranging from 500 to 1,000 mg.

An optimal daily dose of inositol for an adult is 250 to 500 mg.

Choline

Choline is a vitamin-like compound also found in phosphatidylcholine and lecithin and is intimately involved in the synthesis or release of certain neurotransmitters, particularly acetylcholine. When some types of neurons are deprived of adequate acetylcholine as a neurotransmitter, the result may be memory loss or mood disorders. Increases in acetylcholine in the brain seem to elevate mood and memory and improve alertness and mental energy, while low levels have been tied to depression and lack of concentration.

Choline has shown promise as a way to control mood swings. Many people who use choline as a smart drug notice an improvement in overall disposition. Studies have confirmed that choline boosts the mood of some Alzheimer's patients.

Approximately 500 to 1,000 mg per day of choline is consumed on average through the food we ingest. Dietary consumption may be falling, however, because people are cutting back on the foods that are rich in choline, such as eggs, to reduce cholesterol consumption. Leafy green vegetables, wheat germ, peanuts, and lecithin are also good sources of choline. A raw natural source is bee pollen, which is approximately 15 percent lecithin.

Prime candidates for choline use: You may gain special benefit from taking choline if your depression is related to underlying conditions associated with memory loss, cognitive problems, or reduced mental energy.

Safety concerns: Choline is generally safe and nontoxic even at much higher levels, although megadoses are usually reserved for treating manic depression and other serious psychiatric disorders. You should work closely with a qualified health practitioner if you have such conditions. Also, high doses of choline can be countereffective and may actually cause depression in some people. Avoid taking choline supplements if you have gastric ulcers, Parkinson's disease, or are taking prescription drugs meant to block the effects of acetylcholine, such as atropine and diphenhydramine.

How to use it: Choline is available in powders, tablets, capsules, and liquids. Lecithin typically comes in granule, oil-filled capsule, and liquid forms.

For an adult, an optimal daily dose is 1,000 to 2,000 mg of 90 percent pure phosphatidylcholine or 5 to 10 g of lecithin that is 20 percent phosphatidyl-choline.

NADH/Coenzyme 1

In some cases, nutrients also help to restore brain function. I remember one woman I treated, Evelyn, who was a seventy-one-year-old painter and grandmother. A few years earlier she had been involved in a car accident and had since experienced chronic mental confusion, sluggishness, and depression. Doctors had told her that her mental function would never fully return to normal. Within a few weeks after putting her on a fast-oxidizer vegetarian diet and a regimen of daily supplements, however, including the amino acid tyrosine and the little-known but potent vitamin NADH/coenzyme 1, she began to improve. She had more energy, her blood pressure went down, and she lost ten pounds in a month. Within three months her brain function had returned to normal and instead of often being depressed she reported a much greater sense of joyfulness in her everyday life. Evelyn is now very happily pursuing her creative and spiritual paths.

Medical practitioners are only beginning to recognize the memory-boosting and mood-elevating effects of NADH/coenzyme 1, a close relative of niacin. It is fast gaining prominence as a dietary supplement under its chemical name, nicotinamide adenine dinucleotide with hydrogen (NADH). First discovered in 1934 by American medical researcher Dr. Nathan Kaplan, NADH is a coenzyme form of niacin that occurs naturally in all living cells, from bacteria to animals, and is continuously synthesized in the human body. NADH is especially concentrated in bodily tissues that are intense users of energy, such as the brain and central nervous system. The heart, whose cells contain as much as 90 mcg of NADH per gram of muscle tissue, and other muscles are also major users of NADH.

In addition to being a potent antioxidant that may help slow the pace of aging, NADH plays an important role in how cells produce energy. Along with another coenzyme (Q10), NADH helps to synthesize adenosine triphosphate (ATP), the body's principal energy-carrying compound. Cells need NADH to produce ATP, and without sufficient stores of NADH, bodily function will eventually begin to suffer. NADH also affects the release of growth hormone and the repair of DNA.

Many of my patients who have tried NADH for a month or so report that they not only feel more energetic but that they experience better athletic performance and increased capacity to work. Although the findings are very preliminary, one recent study of seventeen athletes who took NADH for four weeks demonstrated improvements in reaction time, physical performance, and maximum oxygen uptake.

NADH also has important antidepressant effects through its action on the brain and central nervous system. Scientists know that NADH is a cofactor necessary for the brain to synthesize various neurotransmitters such as L-dopa, dopamine, and noradrenaline. The results of a brain cell culture study suggest that NADH can markedly increase the production of dopamine in particular by facilitating the breakdown of tyrosine into L-dopa, dopamine, and noradrenaline. And scientists have found higher levels of certain dopamine metabolites in the urine of individuals taking NADH. The upshot is that by providing cells with optimal levels of NADH, you can promote your body's ability to produce important mood-boosting brain chemicals.

The preeminent NADH researcher in the world over the past two decades, Jorg G. D. Birkmayer, M.D., Ph.D., of Vienna, Austria, has found that NADH activity decreases with advancing age. Birkmayer and various colleagues have studied the effects of NADH on patients with chronic fatigue as well as various age-related conditions, including Parkinson's and Alzheimer's. Their clinical trials have demonstrated improvements in symptoms related to motor skills as well as thinking, memory, and mood. Increased bioavailability of L-dopa is thought to be responsible for many of the positive effects. In studies done on patients with Parkinson's, the best outcomes have resulted from giving subjects 25 to 50 mg of NADH per day, often intravenously. A pilot study done on patients with Alzheimer's, however, found improvements in alertness and mental activity from taking only 10 mg of NADH every morning for eight to twelve weeks.

While doing studies on subjects with Parkinson's disease, Birkmayer also found that NADH helped reduce symptoms of depression. "This observation prompted us to study the clinical effect of NADH on patients suffering from psychic depression," he said. In a 1992 open label study (one conducted nonblind, in which subjects and experimenters know who's getting what) of 205 patients with depression who were treated with various doses of NADH for 5 to 310 days (the average was 19.5 days), Birkmayer says that 93 percent of the subjects experienced beneficial clinical effects.

Admittedly, research on NADH and especially its usefulness as an antidepressant is in its infancy. Large-scale, double-blind, and placebo-controlled studies have yet to be conducted, though it is likely these will be done in the near future. What we do know so far is that NADH is a naturally occurring and apparently very safe nutrient that plays a crucial role in brain chemistry. I think it is a very promising supplement to include in my *Depression-Free for Life* program. About 85 percent of my clients with depression seem to benefit from taking NADH. They usually need to take it for six months to a year before they can discontinue its use because their metabolism needs it, even though they may feel results from it within three weeks, sometimes sooner. I'm very pleased with its antidepressant effects.

NADH appears to be more concentrated in meat, poultry, and fish than in fresh vegetables. Brewer's yeast is another source. NADH levels in food are relatively low, however, and I think the best way to take it is in supplement form.

Prime candidates for NADH use: You may gain special benefit from taking NADH if your depression is related to
 - too little dopamine activity
 - underlying conditions that cause low energy levels or Parkinson-like neurological symptoms

Safety concerns: Like the other B vitamins, NADH appears to have very low potential for toxicity. Birkmayer says that he has not seen any adverse effects in the thousands of people treated with NADH so far. Also, toxicity tests suggest that the nutrient is safe in levels up to 500 mg per kg body weight, over 7,000 times the optimal level.

How to use it: Researchers recently produced a patented formulation of NADH that is said to remain stable for at least two years. (NADH is easily degraded by humidity, temperature, light, oxygen, or water.) This NADH is sold in tablet form (2.5 to 5.0 mg) as Enada, a registered trademark of Menuco Corporation of New York. Menuco officials say that they are in the eleventh year of seeking FDA approval of Enada as a new B vitamin. Menuco has licensed various natural product companies to sell Enada. Like coenzyme Q10, it is one of the most expensive supplements, with tablets retailing for approximately a dollar each.

An optimal daily dose of NADH for an adult is 5 to 10 mg.

Vitamin C

The brain has a much higher concentration of vitamin C than other parts of the body, and it needs vitamin C to synthesize the neurotransmitters noradrenaline and dopamine. Vitamin C is important for the metabolism of essential fatty acids. It also helps to strengthen the adrenals and other endocrine glands.

As I mentioned, depressed mood is an early symptom of scurvy. A number of studies in which emotionally disturbed subjects were administered vitamin C suggested that supplements can help elevate mood. For example, one random study of forty chronic psychiatric patients found that after three weeks, patients given vitamin C were less depressed than those given a placebo. Researchers have also found that in general, patients in mental hospitals tend to have low blood levels of vitamin C. At least 95 percent of my clients with depression require additional vitamin C.

Vitamin C is concentrated in a variety of foods, including citrus fruits but also green and red peppers, strawberries, broccoli, kiwi, papaya, Brussels sprouts, cauliflower, and mustard and turnip greens.

Prime candidates for vitamin C use: You may gain special benefit from taking vitamin C if your depression is related to
- too little noradrenaline or dopamine activity
- an imbalance or deficiency in essential fatty acids
- stress
- an underlying condition related to connective tissue problems

Safety concerns: Vitamin C rarely causes any side effects at levels up to 3,000 mg per day. Some people may develop diarrhea or loose stools at higher doses. Orthomolecular healers, who use large doses of nutrients to help treat ailments, often recommend at least 4,000 mg of vitamin C per day. Many people routinely take even higher amounts of vitamin C, without apparent ill effects.

How to use it: Supplement manufacturers offer vitamin C in tablet and capsule forms ranging from 250 mg to 1,500 mg. You can also find vitamin C in a wide variety of chewable or time-release tablets, buffered capsules (with added calcium, for example, to reduce C's natural acidity), powders, liquids, and even chewing gums. Depending on your constitution, you may need either the buffered form, which needs to be taken before meals, or the ascorbic form, which can be taken with meals.

An optimal daily dose of vitamin C for an adult is 1,000 to 3,000 mg.

Vitamin D

Reduced vitamin D levels among people who live in northern climates during the winter (and thus are not regularly exposed to sunlight, which reacts with cells in the skin to produce vitamin D) may be a factor in causing the mild depression, loss of appetite and interest in sex, and insomnia associated with seasonal affective disorder. A recent study published in the *New England Journal of Medicine* found that nearly 60 percent of some 300 patients hospitalized for various conditions had insufficient blood levels of D, and that almost one in four were severely deficient in the vitamin.

Your skin makes vitamin D naturally if you expose yourself to 20 to 30 minutes of sunlight every day or so. Vitamin D is found in egg yolk, sunflower seeds, and oily fish such as halibut, tuna, and cod. Food producers fortify various products with vitamin D, especially milk and other dairy products.

Prime candidates for vitamin D use: You may gain special benefit from taking vitamin D if your depression is related to a seasonal rhythm disturbance, or an indoor lifestyle in a northern climate.

Safety concerns: Like vitamin A, D is a fat-soluble vitamin capable of building to toxic levels in the body. Excess vitamin D may cause calcium deposits in certain tissues. The federal government has established a recommended upper limit of 1,000 IU per day from birth through twelve months, and 2,000 IU beyond age one. Levels up to approximately 5,000 IU per day don't adversely affect most people. Optimal levels are well under these upper limits.

How to use it: Because it is fat-soluble, vitamin D is better absorbed if it is taken with a small amount of oil or fat. The natural form of the vitamin, D-3, is preferable to synthetic D-2.

An optimal daily dose of vitamin D for an adult is 400 to 800 IU, or 600 to 1,000 IU if you're living in a northern climate during the winter, are a night-shift worker, or are over age seventy.

Vitamin E

A nutrient used by most of the tissues of the body, vitamin E is a powerful antioxidant that plays various crucial roles. By protecting the body against the harmful effects of free radicals, it has been shown to boost immunity, reduce heart disease, and possibly enhance athletic performance. Vitamin E can also protect neurons from free radical damage, which may be why researchers are finding that low blood levels of vitamin E can quickly begin to limit serotonin activity. Vitamin E is a major protector of brain cell membranes and even seems to help slow Alzheimer's disease.

Vitamin E occurs in high levels in vegetable oils, including safflower, wheat germ, and corn. The best food sources are dark green leafy vegetables, whole grains, wheat germ, nuts, seeds, and legumes. Meat and dairy products usually have low amounts.

Prime candidates for vitamin E use: You may gain special benefit from taking vitamin E if your depression is related to
- underlying conditions, especially heart disease and the onset of age-related mental impairment
- too little serotonin activity
- stress

Safety concerns: Some people may experience dizziness, elevated blood pressure, decreased blood coagulation, or other side effects at daily dosages of 1,200 to 1,600 IU. A recent well-designed clinical trial determined that four months of supplementation with 60 to 800 IU of vitamin E per day had no adverse effects. Average doses are clearly safe and nontoxic for long-term consumption.

How to use it: Vitamin E supplements most commonly are oil-filled capsules, softgels, or gelcaps. There are also dry capsules and tablets, sublingual forms, and liquids in 2- to 12-ounce containers. Potencies range from 100 to 1,500 IU, with 400 IU being the most common. The naturally occurring forms of vitamin E, designated "D-" (as in D-alpha tocopherol) are somewhat more absorbable than the synthetic "DL-" forms (DL-alpha tocopherol) of the vitamin.

An optimal daily dose of vitamin E for an adult is 400 to 600 IU.

Coenzyme Q10 (CoQ10)

CoQ10 is a vitamin-like compound also known as ubiquinone, so named because it is naturally ubiquitous throughout the body. Discovered in 1957, coQ10 plays a major role in overall metabolism, heart health, and immune function. It is a powerful antioxidant in the brain. Like many other vitamins, coQ10 acts as a coenzyme in the body to promote various chemical reactions. It is needed to help the body's cells use oxygen and generate energy. In particular it acts as a catalyst for the process by which the body produces ATP, necessary for energy at the cellular level. Deficiency symptoms include fatigue, mental lethargy, and depression. Some people take coQ10 to boost energy levels, strengthen muscles and improve physical performance and endurance, and lose weight.

Coenzyme Q10 is found primarily in cold-water fish such as sardines and tuna, whole grains, and a few other foods such as peanuts, polyunsaturated vegetable oils, and spinach. Plant foods generally have only trace levels. Take optimal levels of B-complex and vitamin C to help your body produce coQ10.

Prime candidates for coenzyme Q10 use: You may gain special benefit from taking coenzyme Q10 if your depression is related to

- an imbalance in blood sugar metabolism
- underlying conditions, especially heart disease and degenerative nerve ailments

Safety concerns: Adverse effects have been rare even at dosages up to 600 mg per day. If you have congestive heart failure and you're taking coenzyme Q10, don't suddenly stop taking it, as this might worsen your symptoms.

How to use it: CoQ10 comes in capsules, softgels, tablets, sublingual, liquid, and chewable forms. Potency ranges from 10 to 125 mg, with 30, 60, and 75 mg being popular strengths. Taking coenzyme Q10 at meal-time will improve absorption.

An optimal daily dose of coQ10 for an adult is 30 to 75 mg.

Calcium

Although best known for its role in the building of bones, this major mineral is also necessary in a proper balance for smooth functioning of the nervous system, sufficient serotonin activity, and prevention of irritability and depression. Taken before bed, calcium may have a slight sedating effect. Large doses of calcium in a person with too much noradrenaline activity, however, tend to aggravate rather than balance mood. Slow oxidizers don't do well with excess calcium.

Dairy foods are heavily promoted as a source of calcium, but dark green leafy vegetables such as kale and collard greens are very high in calcium and are more healthful than dairy foods in other respects. Pasteurization of dairy products reduces calcium absorption. Kelp, almonds and other nuts, sesame seeds and other seeds, and beans are relatively high in calcium. Foods that have a high ratio of phosphorous to calcium, such as meat and soft drinks, can reduce bodily levels of calcium. Foods such as fresh fruits and vegetables that are rich in the mineral boron help minimize loss of body calcium through the urine.

Prime candidates for calcium use: You may gain special benefit from taking calcium if your depression is related to
  - an imbalance in blood sugar, and you are a fast oxidizer (an excess of calcium may be aggravating for slow oxidizers)
  - an underlying condition, especially a disorder of the parathyroid glands

Safety concerns: The federal government recently recommended an upper limit of 2,500 mg calcium daily for all ages beyond one year (the infant upper limit was "not determinable").

How to use it: Although calcium is sometimes combined with magnesium in supplements, I've found that it is best not to take them at the same time. *An optimal daily dose of calcium for an adult is 800 to 1,500 mg.*

Magnesium

I estimate that four out of every five patients who come to see me are deficient in magnesium. Magnesium plays a role in blood sugar balance, the production of the omega-3 essential fatty acid DHA, and nervous system function. A deficiency in this essential major mineral has been known to lead to anxiety, irritability, fatigue, and depression. Studies that have compared the magnesium blood levels of patients in a psychiatric hospital to those of normal people have found that low magnesium levels have been associated with more symptoms of depression, sleep disturbances, and possibly even higher rates of suicide. In a 1991 study, researchers gave women twenty-four to thirty-nine years old with PMS either a placebo or 360 mg magnesium three times daily from day 15 of their cycles to onset of menstrual flow. The researchers found that magnesium treatment significantly affected the women's scores for "menstrual distress" and "negative effect." According to the researchers, "These data indicate that magnesium supplementation could represent an effective treatment of premenstrual symptoms related to mood changes." Many depressed persons find that magnesium will help improve their condition.

Dark-green leafy vegetables are a rich source of magnesium, as are whole grains, nuts, seeds, kelp and other sea vegetables, tofu, legumes, and fish. Other plant foods notably rich in magnesium include soybeans, almonds, black-eyed peas, avocados, oatmeal, apples, beets, dates, figs, peanuts, wheat germ, lentils, grapefruit, and kelp. Eggs and liver are other sources. Algae-based green food concentrates such as spirulina and chlorella are good sources of magnesium. Most vegetarians get plenty of magnesium in their diet, although low magnesium content in the soil can reduce a food's magnesium content. Processed foods such as refined grains, meats, and boiled vegetables also have lower magnesium contents.

Prime candidates for magnesium use: You may gain special benefit from taking magnesium if your depression is related to
- an imbalance in blood sugar, and you are a slow oxidizer
- an imbalance or deficiency in essential fatty acids

Safety concerns: The federal government has decreed that the upper limit (from supplements, exclusive of intake from food) ranges from 65 to 110 mg daily for ages one through eight, and 350 mg per day for all others. I think that 350 mg is an extremely conservative upper limit figure. Magnesium is among the safest minerals. High levels of magnesium may adversely affect some people with poor kidney function, but the vast majority of people would probably not experience symptoms of magnesium toxicity even if they took ten times the suggested upper limit. I believe that this upper limit figure is actually about average for an optimal supplement level.

How to use it: Most products are capsules, tablets, or liquids ranging in potency from 200 to 500 mg.

An optimal daily dose of magnesium for an adult is 250 to 450 mg.

Iron

I see a huge variation in my practice in how readily people absorb the mineral iron. Some people seem to get plenty from an average diet while others who are eating what should be a high-iron diet become deficient. Other foods and nutrients may be major factors. For example, I've noticed that dairy foods inhibit iron absorption, while vitamin C supplements enhance it.

Iron plays a key role in supplying cells with oxygen and producing energy. The form of anemia due to too little iron can lead to fatigue, lethargy, and other symptoms shared by depression. Some studies suggest that an iron deficiency can impair learning ability, attention span, and mental development. Iron also plays an indirect role in producing neurotransmitters. Along with NADH, iron is one of the cofactors in the process by which tyrosine is metabolized into L-dopa and dopamine.

Iron is found in both plants and animals, although the types of iron derived from these sources differ slightly. The point is often made that animal-derived iron is more readily absorbed, but the more relevant fact in my mind is that vegetarians have less anemia than meat-eaters. Among the best plant sources are kelp, brewer's yeast, wheat bran, pumpkin seeds, sesame seeds, wheat germ, sunflower seeds, almonds, cashews, and raisins. Most whole grains, legumes, and dark-green leafy vegetables provide reasonable amounts of iron. Iron is better absorbed with vitamin C, as from fresh fruits and vegetables.

Animal sources of iron include beef, egg yolks, chicken, clams, oysters, and salmon.

Women who are pregnant need additional iron for the developing fetus. Women who are menstruating may need additional iron because they're losing significant amounts with each period. Most other people, however, are probably getting enough iron if they're eating a reasonably healthy diet. Unless you're a pregnant or menstruating woman, I recommend you get tested for blood levels of iron before you start to take iron supplements, including multinutrient formulas containing additional iron.

Prime candidates for iron use: You may gain special benefit from taking iron if your depression is related to an underlying condition of iron deficiency anemia or one associated with a weakened immune system or low energy.

Safety concerns: The body readily stores iron, and too much iron can be toxic or contribute to cardiovascular disease. It can also be countereffective. For instance, high levels of iron may actually cause fatigue or compromise the immune system.

How to use it: Most nutritionists now recommend that iron supplementation be undertaken only if an iron deficiency has been clinically demonstrated. Because of concerns about its toxicity, many multinutrient formulas are now iron-free. The exception is multinutrients specially formulated for women. Check labels to make sure that, if you have not been diagnosed with an iron deficiency, your multinutrient does not contain iron. Most multinutrient products formulated especially for women contain 15 to 20 mg iron. Along with calcium, iron is the rare nutrient whose Recommended Dietary Allowance (RDA) is close to or even higher than what I think is an optimal level.

An optimal daily dose of iron for an adult is 15 to 20 mg.

Selenium

This essential trace mineral has become increasingly popular in recent years for its well-established antioxidant effects and its ability to protect against such age-related ailments as heart disease, cancer, and arthritis. A few recent studies have assessed the effects of selenium on mood. For example, a double-blind crossover trial of fifty British subjects given a placebo or 100 mcg selenium for five weeks found no mood effects from the placebo but substantial improvement after both 2.5 and 5 weeks taking selenium. According to the researchers, "Intake was associated with a general elevation of mood and in particular a decrease in anxiety." Other studies have linked low levels of selenium in the diet with increased symptoms of anxiety and depression. The mechanism for selenium's effect on mood may be related to its antioxidant activity and its ability to protect the integrity of cells' membranes, thus improving their overall function.

Selenium needs to be consumed in only minute amounts every day. Seafoods are probably the most reliable dietary source, because animal and plant foods can vary significantly in selenium content depending upon the selenium status of the foods animals are fed and the soil plants are grown in.

Prime candidates for selenium use: You may gain special benefit from taking selenium if your depression is related to an underlying condition, especially one associated with a viral infection or a weakened immune system.

Safety concerns: Selenium is safe to take on a daily basis at levels three to four times the adult RDA (50 to 75 mcg). Its potential toxicity does not appear to begin until dosages in excess of 800 to 1,000 mcg daily.

How to use it: Selenium is widely available in tablets and capsules ranging in size from 50 to 200 mcg.

An optimal daily dose of selenium for an adult is 100 to 200 mcg.

Chromium

Insulin is crucial for regulating the metabolism of proteins, carbohydrates, and fats, and scientists have known since the late 1950s that the mineral chromium is necessary for insulin to function properly. When the body is deprived of sufficient chromium, all sorts of health problems often follow, from blood sugar swings to obesity and diabetes. A recent study of chromium's influence on insulin metabolism found that chromium reduced the blood pressure–increasing effects of high sugar intake.

Taking optimal levels of chromium can also aid in controlling hunger, reducing body fat, and encouraging muscle development. Athletes and others have also been turning to chromium for help in lowering body fat levels, encouraging muscle development, and controlling hunger and weight. Chromium is part of an overall support approach, but I use it mainly when the person has a carbohydrate metabolism imbalance.

Chromium occurs only in low amounts in most foods. Among the best sources are brewer's yeast and whole grains, while potatoes and wheat germ may also provide reliable amounts. Processed foods usually lack chromium. Dietary surveys conducted by the U.S. Department of Agriculture and others indicate that 90 percent of Americans get insufficient chromium—an average of only 25 to 33 mcg—from their diet. Similar deficiencies have also been identified in European countries.

Strenuous physical activity increases your requirement for chromium; mental stress and eating large amounts of sugary foods deplete your body's chromium stores.

Prime candidates for chromium use: You may gain special benefit from taking chromium if your depression is related to
- an imbalance in blood sugar metabolism, and you are a slow oxidizer
- stress
- poor long-term dietary habits, especially overconsumption of refined sugar and flour products

Safety concerns: Chromium is very safe and does not cause side effects at dosages much greater than optimal. Diabetics taking insulin, however, should consult with their physician before taking chromium supplements.

How to use it: Chromium comes in tablets and capsules, from 100 to 500 mcg (200 mcg products are the most prevalent). It is a common ingredient in diet, weight-loss, and fat burner formulas. Chromium is sold in a number of forms and under a variety of brand names. Because the body cannot absorb elemental chromium, supplement manufacturers use a form called trivalent chromium, which is biologically more active. The type of chromium found naturally in brewer's yeast that researchers have determined has the most effect on insulin function is called Glucose Tolerance Factor (GTF) chromium. GTF is an organic chromium complex that contains niacin as well as cysteine and other nutrients. Chromium polynicotinate is also a niacin-bound form of chromium. Another well-absorbed form of chromium is chromium picolinate, a patented synthetic compound sold under various brand names. Some chromium supplements combine GTF chromium, chromium picolinate, and other nutrients—their effects are all similar.

An optimal daily dose of chromium for an adult is 200 to 400 mcg.

The Top 20 Depression-Relieving Nutrients

The following chart offers a snapshot of the twenty depression-relieving nutrients. I provide both the Daily Value (DV) and an optimal range. The Food and Drug Administration developed the DVs for use on food labels. Initially called U.S. Recommended Daily Allowances (USRDAs), the DV is similar to the Recommended Dietary Allowances (RDAs) established by the Food and Nutrition Board of the National Research Council. In essence, these figures are meant to be levels that are "adequate to meet the known nutrient needs of practically all healthy persons." DVs differ only slightly from the RDAs, chiefly in providing a single suggested nutrient level rather than a range based on the person's age and sex.

I believe that the DVs and RDAs, even in their latest incarnations, are inadequate. For one thing, doses should be individualized rather than applied as if any one individual is a "normal" or "healthy" person. Moreover, a huge gulf exists between the dosage level that is adequate to prevent a nutritional deficiency and the dosage level that truly optimizes a person's overall health. Finally, when a person is depressed, his or her nutritional requirements are often higher than what may be considered optimal for an average person. When your overall physiology is way out of balance, almost druglike doses of nutrients are required in order to restore optimal health.

NUTRIENT	DAILY VALUE	OPTIMAL INTAKE
Thiamine	1.5 mg	25–50 mg
Riboflavin	1.7 mg	25–50 mg
Niacin	20 mg	25–50 mg
Pantothenic Acid	10 mg	25–50 mg
Pyridoxine	2 mg	25–50 mg
Vitamin B_{12}	6 mcg	50–100 mcg
Folic acid	400 mcg	400–800 mcg
Inositol	n/a	250–500 mg

Choline	425–550 mg*	500–1,000 mg
NADH	n/a	2.5–5.0 mg
Vitamin A	5,000 IU	2,500–5,000 IU
Vitamin A activity from beta-carotene/ mixed carotenoids:	n/a	5,000–10,000 IU
Vitamin C	60 mg	1,000–2,000 mg
Vitamin D	400 IU	400–1,000 IU
Vitamin E	30 IU	400–800 IU
Coenzyme Q10	n/a	30–75 mg
Calcium	1,000 mg	800–1,500 mg
Magnesium	400 mg	250–450 mg
Selenium	70 mcg	100–200 mcg
Chromium	120 mcg	200–400 mcg
Iron	18 mg	15–20 mg

*Recommended daily intake, as no DV has yet been established

St. John's Wort: A Mood-Boosting Herb

I want to briefly mention the herb St. John's wort, which has been the subject of so much recent attention for its antidepressant effects. I have found that I really don't need to use St. John's wort very much, although I've had patients who have benefited from it. For example, I once treated a fifty-two-year-old woman who was taking not only Prozac but another antidepressant, the tricyclic desipramine, for depression. She told me that she did not feel fully functional—she felt as if she was just going through life in slow motion. Because she also had food allergies and sugar cravings, her treatment involved a number of nutrients, including GABA and NADH. She also seemed to do very well on St. John's wort when we tried it, and sure enough, within two months she was able to gradually discontinue both of the prescription antidepressants she was taking. Her depression lifted and mentally she became sharper and more alert. She also lost weight.

In this instance, the patient tested well for St. John's wort and it seemed to play a key role in her recovery from depression. Other patients of mine with significant depression who have tried the herb, however, haven't always noticed as much benefit. In most cases I've found that St. John's wort is not nearly as good as the amino acid neurotransmitter precursors. In my experience, St. John's wort seems to have somewhat milder effects on mood than SSRIs like Prozac, but it also has fewer adverse side effects. As such it can provide some short-term palliative benefits, but it's not an integral part of my five-step, drug-free program because it does not correct the cause of the imbalance. In essence it is a less invasive SSRI compared to Prozac, but not necessarily a substance capable of changing the brain metabolism. It also seems to present a viable short-term alternative to much more toxic conventional antidepressants such as the tricyclics.

St. John's wort studies have tended to confirm that the herb does have antidepressant properties. For example, a meta-analysis of twenty-three St. John's wort studies that was published in the *British Medical Journal* in 1996 determined that the herb was "significantly superior" to a placebo and "similarly effective as standard antidepressants" with a much lower rate of side effects. These studies involved outpatients with mainly mild or moderately severe depressive disorders. A recent study, however, found that a St. John's wort extract was as effective as the antidepressant imipramine for severely depressed patients.

Exactly which compounds in the plant account for St. John's wort's antidepressant properties is still a matter of dispute, as is the question of how it causes its effects in the body. The herb contains various compounds, including flavonoids, carotenoids, and an essential oil. Its depression-relieving effect may be due to the reddish pigment compound hypericin concentrated in the flowers' essential oil, or to a combination of hypericin and other compounds. Some evidence suggests that hypericin inhibits the activity in the body of monoamine oxidase (MAO), an enzyme found in nerve cells that can inactivate neurotransmitters and thus lower mood, much like the conventional MAO inhibitors. Thus it may raise the levels of such neurotransmitters as dopamine and noradrenaline in the brain. Recent studies have found evidence for other dopamine-related effects and for actions similar to the SSRIs. When these issues are resolved and more is known about how and why St. John's wort works, it may become easier to use as part of a program specific to your biochemistry.

Prime candidates for St. John's wort use: You may gain special benefit from taking St. John's wort if your depression is related to

- serotonin deficiency
- underlying conditions, especially sleep disorders and anxiety

Safety concerns: The most common side effects from taking St. John's wort include nausea, stomachache, lack of appetite, tiredness, restlessness, and dizziness. Very rarely St. John's wort may cause increased skin reactivity to light from the sun. Such photoreactivity has been noted in cows who have grazed the plant, but it is probably a concern only if you are fair-skinned, are out in the sun for long periods of time, and are taking high daily doses of St. John's wort. Women who are pregnant or breast-feeding should not take St. John's wort. Consult with your physician or medical practitioner if you want to substitute St. John's wort for a prescription antidepressant drug.

How to use it: The herb is usually sold dried and in concentrated drops, tinctures, and standardized extracts. A few companies combine St. John's wort with other herbs or with nutrients such as 5-HTP. St. John's wort may need to be taken for three to six weeks before its full mood-lifting action is evident.

An optimal daily dose of St. John's wort for an adult is 200 to 300 mg of a standardized extract containing 0.3 percent hypericin two to three times daily.

Ginkgo: The Herbal Smart Drug

Another herb worth mentioning for its potential to elevate mood and relieve depression is ginkgo. Often called a "living fossil" because it has survived some 200 million years, *Ginkgo biloba* is a tree with fan-shaped leaves that are used to make extracts with a broad range of therapeutic uses. It is now among the most widely used herbal medicines in Europe and the United States, where many people take it regularly as an energizer to improve mood and alertness, as a "smart drug" to stimulate brain function and boost memory, and as an antioxidant to slow the effects of aging and prevent degenerative diseases. Researchers who have tested ginkgo extracts on subjects with less-than-optimal brain circulation found that the herb can help reverse symptoms such as short-term memory loss, headache, lethargy, and depression. Researchers say that ginkgo stimulates circulation in the brain, ears, and other parts of the body and thus may help prevent hearing loss, stroke, Alzheimer's disease, and depression. Studies indicate it might help treat circulatory conditions, including impotence, that results from using some of the conventional antidepressant drugs.

Ginkgo is one of my favorite herbs, especially for people in their late forties and older. A number of my patients who have taken ginkgo have reported that they feel brighter and more alert and have an improved memory. Ginkgo helps create antidepressant support because it increases brain function and a sense of well-being. Ginkgo's ability to improve mind and mood may be due to increased blood flow to the brain, allowing for more oxygen and nutrients to reach crucial brain cells. Ginkgo also seems especially effective at protecting nerve cells from free radical damage. Many of ginkgo's positive effects are likely tied to its potency as an antioxidant and a regulator of blood platelet stickiness. Plant scientists believe that the most active constituents of ginkgo are certain flavonoid compounds known as "flavoglycosides" or "ginkgoheterosides," and certain complex terpene compounds, such as bilobalide and one or more of the ginkgolides.

Two recent well-designed studies, including a multicenter study published in the *Journal of the American Medical Association*, documented beneficial effects from using ginkgo extracts in the treatment of Alzheimer's disease. Another study found that ginkgo's ability to protect the nervous system from damage due to conditions such as hypoxia and seizure activity may be due to both the ginkgolides and the herb's free radical–scavenging flavonoids. Also, the mechanism for ginkgo's stress- and anxiety-reducing actions may be related to an inhibitory effect on MAO.

Prime candidates for ginkgo use: You may gain special benefit from taking ginkgo if your depression is related to underlying conditions, especially circulatory ailments, nerve-related diseases, and age-related or other mental impairments characterized by memory loss and loss of cognitive function.

Safety concerns: Ginkgo is safe and nontoxic even at doses well beyond average. It may cause mild digestive discomfort or headaches in some people, although these problems are rare.

How to use it: Among the most popular ginkgo products are encapsulated extracts standardized to 24 percent of flavoglycosides and 6 percent terpene lactones. Ginkgo also comes in softgels, tablets, liquids, and the powdered whole herb. Like St. John's wort, ginkgo may need to be taken for a number of months before its full effects are felt, though some people report benefits within two to three weeks. Research has found that ginkgo seems to have more obvious and lasting effects if it is taken for an extended duration. Ginkgo is usually a prominent component in brain and memory, and mind and mood, formulas. It is safe to take in conjunction with prescription antidepressants.

An optimal daily dose of a standardized ginkgo extract for an adult is 40 mg three times daily.

Thyroid Hormone Supplements

The prescription drugs that most doctors recommend to alleviate a thyroid hormone deficiency typically work by supplying additional hormone. For example, prescription drugs such as levothyroxine (Synthroid) and liothyronine are synthetic forms of thyroxine. These new products have been developed within the past few decades, mostly replacing the whole extract products such as desiccated thyroid. The whole extracts, derived from ground-up thyroid glands taken from pigs or cows, work in much the same way as the prescription drugs: they provide additional hormone. I'm like a few doctors, and most alternative practitioners, who still prefer to recommend these extracts because they provide a combination of hormones that more closely resembles the body's natural needs compared to the synthetic drugs. The drugs have the advantage of being more standardized in potency.

The nonprescription hormone supplements found in natural food stores work through a slightly different mechanism. They provide nutrients that the thyroid and other endocrine glands need to function optimally. These can often work as well as hormone replacement drugs—I've seen any number of patients who were able to reduce or even eliminate their thyroid hormone intake by boosting the overall health of their endocrine system, including the thyroid and pituitary. You should also keep in mind the importance of nourishing the thyroid gland and supporting its optimal function through diet and lifestyle choices.

If you're taking a thyroid hormone drug or supplement, have your doctor periodically monitor your TSH levels to determine the precise dosage that brings your TSH score into the normal range.

A number of researchers have determined that thyroid hormone can help to alleviate depression. Studies have tested it as an adjunct to tricyclic antidepressants, but a few studies show that it works on its own to elevate mood for many depressed people. How it works with SSRIs or other new antidepressants is still being determined.

Prime candidates for thyroid hormone supplement use: You may gain special benefit from taking thyroid hormone supplements if your depression is related to an underlying condition of hypothyroidism.

Safety concerns: FDA regulations prohibit over-the-counter (OTC) products from containing thyroxine, although in practice it is likely some products do contain small amounts. Potential toxicity and side effects should be minimal.

How to use it: The over-the-counter thyroid supplements sold in natural food stores are sometimes referred to as glandulars. Many are extracts derived from the endocrine organs of cows. Combination products often include hypothalamus, pituitary, thyroid, and adrenal gland extracts. Products differ widely in dosage range, so it is best to follow label instructions or work with an experienced health practitioner to determine how much to take. Symptoms and basal temperature (see Chapter 4) can be indicators of effectiveness.

Melatonin

Unlike with most remedies, the time of the day that you take melatonin is crucial. Melatonin seems to be most effective when taken in doses that mirror the body's natural melatonin secretion pattern. Most people secrete their lowest levels of melatonin between eight A.M. and four P.M. At the onset of darkness, secretion typically starts to rise and peaks (at a level ten times higher than daytime) around two or three A.M. Tiny amounts of melatonin taken orally are enough to support this natural cycle—recent studies have shown that doses of 0.1 to 0.3 mg of melatonin generated peak serum melatonin levels that were within the normal range of nighttime melatonin levels in untreated people.

Unless you work at night or otherwise want to dramatically shift your circadian rhythms (because you're flying across many time zones, for example), you should never take melatonin during the day. Doing so may cause unwanted effects, such as impaired memory, decreased alertness, and possibly even exaggerated symptoms of depression. You can avoid these side effects and enhance your body's natural biorhythms by taking melatonin in the evening before you go to bed. Generally, healthy people should take it at the same time every night within an hour of bedtime, to avoid causing a shift in their circadian rhythms. If you suffer from insomnia, try taking it two to three hours before bedtime.

Taken orally, melatonin is short-lived in the body. It is rapidly absorbed into the bloodstream, metabolized, and eliminated. After melatonin is taken orally, it reaches a maximum level in the blood after about an hour. You may notice its relaxant effects within twenty minutes, or not at all. Experiment to determine what works best for you.

It's possible to take too much supplemental melatonin. I used to see this more frequently a few years ago, when melatonin supplements first came onto the market. Many of the capsules provided 6 mg or more of melatonin per dose, which is now recognized to be more than most people need. I recommend that someone who wants to try melatonin start by taking no more than 0.5 to 0.75 mg—a level that has never caused side effects in any of my patients. If a person needs only a marginal boost in his or her melatonin levels, 6 to 12 mg can be a sledgehammer dose. I remember one patient I saw who, among other symptoms of depression, had low mood, extreme morning grogginess, and lethargy. It turned out he was taking 10 mg of melatonin every night because of a longstanding battle with insomnia. The melatonin did help him sleep, but the sleep-inducing effect turned out to be just as great at 3 mg, a dose that left him more alert and cheerful during the following day.

Prime candidates for melatonin use: You may gain special benefit from taking melatonin if your depression is related to
- seasonal depression
- underlying conditions that cause insomnia

Safety concerns: Melatonin has an enviable safety profile. No acute toxicity has been shown in human or animal studies, meaning that it is not possible to overdose on melatonin. Side effects are rare even at doses many times higher than what you need to take for depression or insomnia, for example. Some studies have administered as much as 1,000 and 6,000 mg for short periods (to test for melatonin's potential usefulness against cancer and other serious conditions) without showing toxic effects.

Minor side effects are possible, including next-day fatigue or grogginess, mild nausea, diarrhea, bad dreams, headaches, and reduced sex drive. Effects such as a worsening of mood and slower reaction time are possible if melatonin is taken at the wrong time, such as during the day.

Though relatively safe, melatonin is contraindicated for certain people nonetheless. It should not be taken by women who are pregnant or breast-feeding; by anyone suffering from kidney disease; or by people with autoimmune diseases or immune-system cancers such as lymphoma and leukemia (melatonin's ability to activate the immune system would be countereffective in such conditions). Because it may affect growth or sex hormone levels, melatonin should be avoided by anyone under the age of eighteen. People taking steroid drugs such as cortisone should also avoid melatonin.

How to use it: Melatonin comes in tablets, sublinguals, and capsules ranging in potency from 0.75 to 6 mg. I usually recommend that people start with a low dose, such as 0.5 to 0.75 mg, and see if that helps. Increase if necessary for greater effect. Older people may find they feel best from slightly higher doses, such as 1.5 to 3 mg.

An optimal daily dose of melatonin for an adult is 0.5 to 1 mg.

Siberian Ginseng/Eleuthero: The Stress-Busting Herb

I've found that this is one of the best herbs for supporting the adrenal glands and other organs especially affected by stress. Siberian ginseng is derived from the roots and sometimes the leaves of a relatively common thorny shrub (*Eleutherococcus senticosus,* hence its other common name, eleuthero) native to northeastern Asia. Siberian ginseng is not in the *Panax* (ginseng) genus, though it is in the same plant family as the Asian and American ginsengs and has somewhat similar effects and uses.

Siberian ginseng was a lesser-known strengthening or "tonic" herb of Russian and Chinese folk tradition until Russian scientists of the 1940s and 1950s focused on it as a more widely available (and considerably cheaper) substitute for Chinese ginseng. Like other ginsengs, it is an adaptogen, a substance that strengthens, normalizes, and regulates all of the body's systems. It supports the working of the adrenal glands and prevents the worst effects of nervous tension. It tends to increase energy, extend endurance, and fight off fatigue. Siberian ginseng boosts overall immune function and may play a role in the treatment of hypertension, blood sugar irregularities, and depressed mood and other psychological ailments.

Studies of Siberian ginseng have shown that it has considerable promise as an agent to increase longevity and improve overall health. Chemists have isolated more than three dozen compounds in Siberian ginseng that may affect the mind and body. Foremost among these is a series of a dozen glycosides known as eleutherosides, which occur in tiny amounts (less than 1 percent) in the plant's roots and are even less concentrated in the leaves. Studies have determined that the eleutherosides differ from the ginsenosides isolated from the *Panax* ginsengs, though some of their effects on the body are similar. Exactly how these compounds (or the whole herb—Siberian ginseng appears to be like other ginsengs in that the isolated components do not have the same tonic action as the whole plant) affect the body is still being determined.

Prime candidates for use of Siberian ginseng: You may gain special benefit from taking Siberian ginseng if your depression is related to stress.

Safety concerns: Adverse side effects from using Siberian ginseng are very rare. It is considered to be safe for daily consumption even in doses many times larger than average, though some people have been known to experience insomnia and other side effects from taking high amounts.

How to use it: Siberian ginseng is sold in capsules, tinctures, and extracts. Standardized Siberian ginseng products often specify the content of one or more of the eleutherosides.

An optimal daily dose of Siberian ginseng for an adult is 200 mg of an extract standardized for 1 percent eleutherosides.

Tips for Optimizing Your Supplement Use

- Take a high-quality multinutrient formula to meet most of your optimal requirements. This is much easier than trying to take each of the top twenty nutrients just listed as separate supplements. In order to get optimal levels, however, you'll have to take multiple doses—a "one-a-day" supplement just won't do. It can't be made big enough to contain optimal levels, especially of the macro minerals, and still be small enough to swallow. For example, a typical multinutrient supplement that calls for six capsules per day (take two with each meal) provides close to optimal levels for almost all of the depression-busting nutrients. The exceptions are likely to be the two coenzymes, NADH and coenzyme Q10. NADH is new and may start appearing in multinutrient formulas in the near future. Both NADH and coQ10, however, are costly and adding them to multinutrient formulas would make these products prohibitively expensive. So for the most part you need to take the coenzymes separately. Most multinutrients also will provide only 300 to 500 mg of vitamin C and calcium, so you may need to take separate supplements for these nutrients.

- Take your vitamin supplements with meals. Foods and supplements can work together to help the body absorb and metabolize nutrients. Taking supplements at meals also helps to spread your supplement intake over the day, allowing you to get blood levels of various nutrients up to an optimal level and keep them there.

- A few nutrients, such as the fat soluble vitamins A and D, and coQ10, are better absorbed when they're taken with a small amount of fat or oil.

- Store your supplements in a cool, dry, dark place, and out of the reach of young children. Light and moisture can cause vitamins to oxidize or become rancid. Try to buy nutritional supplements in quantities that you use up within a month or two.

- While it is likely you'll be able to reduce the dosage of antidepressant drugs after you've been on an optimal supplement program for a month or so, always consult with your doctor or health care practitioner about such changes.

Step Three: Make the Fatty Acids Essential

When I first saw Lisa, a forty-four-year-old artist with her own pottery studio, I was struck by her silver hair and dark blue eyes. She came to me complaining of mild depression as well as fatigue, overall weakness, minor skin problems, headaches, and nervousness. Lisa admitted that her depressed mood was interfering with her ability to function at work and at home.

I started Lisa on the five-step natural treatment program immediately. It was the essential fatty acid component, however, that seemed to offer her the most rapid and dramatic relief. At one point she told me, "When I take the fatty acids it feels like a coating goes over my nerves and I immediately feel happy and relaxed."

If you're like Lisa and suffer from depression that is accompanied by the symptoms she mentioned, plus others listed in Chapter 4 such as fingernails that break easily, constipation, lack of appetite, and low metabolic rate, it is possible that your problem is being caused—or worsened—by an imbalance in essential fatty acids. This is especially likely if you eat a diet all too typical nowadays:

- rich in simple sugars and saturated fat
- made up mostly of processed and refined foods, many containing hydrogenated fats, and "lite" and low-fat packaged foods

- uses lots of vegetable oils such as safflower and sunflower in cooking
- is mostly lacking in nuts, seeds, fish, and other sources of natural fats

All of these factors tend to concentrate one type of essential fatty acid in your blood at the expense of others. Furthermore, many people today have a greater-than-average need for certain essential fatty acids. That's because factors such as the following raise their requirement for these healthful fats:

- the type of modern diet just outlined
- age, because the body's ability to use essential fatty acids declines with advancing age
- body size, with a large man, for example, needing higher than average amounts than a small woman or a child
- body constitution, with a person who is thin, energetic, and has difficulty gaining weight needing higher levels of essential fatty acids compared to a person who is heavy-boned and gains weight easily
- stress, which can reduce the activity of enzymes necessary for the conversion of essential fatty acids to prostaglandins, which are fatty acids generated within the body that have hormonelike effects
- certain medical conditions, including diabetes, obesity, and viral infections
- nutritional deficiencies, especially insufficient blood levels of the vitamins pyridoxine, niacin, C, and E, and the minerals magnesium and selenium

Why are so many people getting an unbalanced or deficient supply of essential fatty acids nowadays?

First, the fear-of-fat mania has conspired to remove from many people's diets their principal sources of one particular family of essential fatty acids, the hard-to-get omega-3s. (Scientists classify essential fatty acids into "omega" families, chiefly the omega-3s and the omega-6s, based upon where in the fat molecule the first double-bond occurs.) Omega-3s are found in high concentrations in flaxseeds and hemp seeds as well as in certain cold-water fish and in some other animal and plant foods, although in general they are a somewhat elusive set of nutrients.

Second, people have begun to wildly overconsume the other main type of essential fatty acid, the omega-6s. These are more widely represented in foods, especially in processed foods containing hydrogenated fats. Refined vegetable oils such as safflower and sunflower oil also have high levels of omega-6s but virtually none of the omega-3s that are needed to keep the optimum ratio between omega-6s and omega-3s. Thus, people eating a low-fat diet of mostly refined foods may be consuming much higher levels of omega-6s than omega-3s.

And finally, researchers have determined that a diet rich in omega-6s actually reduces by as much as 50 percent the body's ability to convert certain fats into the omega-3s.

Recent evidence suggests that this imbalance between the two major families of essential fatty acids is worsening. People who are constantly dieting and children who eat large amounts of candy and refined junk food may be especially at risk. Strict vegetarians may also be overloading their diet with omega-6s compared to omega-3s. With the emphasis on a low-fat diet among some vegetarians, I have seen an increase in omega-3 deficiencies. A study determined that breast milk from American women has among the lowest levels of one of the omega-3s compared to the breast milk of women anywhere in the world. Estimates for the ratio of omega-6s consumed to omega-3s in the United States now range as high as 15:1 or 20:1.

How bad is that? Historic norms suggest it is threatening to veer off the chart. Researchers think that at an early point in human history the ratio was one part omega-6 to one part omega-3 or even 1:2. A few populations, such as traditional Inuits, still eat close to an even ratio of omega-6s to omega-3s. In modern industrialized countries such as the United States, however, the combination of an explosion in omega-6 consumption and a retreat from omega-3 foods has caused the pendulum to swing radically in favor of the omega-6s. What exactly constitutes an optimal dietary ratio of omega-6 to omega-3 fatty acids is still being debated, but the consensus among many nutritionists is that the current ratio needs to be rolled all the way back to a balance of approximately 4:1 of omega-6 to omega-3.

The good news is that plenty of options exist for doing just that. By making some simple adjustments in your diet and supplement programs, you can quickly begin to bring these ratios into a proper balance. As a result you are likely to experience significant improvements in daily mood while boosting your overall health.

The Healthful Fats

Before going further, we need to distinguish primary essential fatty acids from their derivatives. The latter are compounds that result from the breakdown of primary essential fatty acids after you ingest them. These derivatives can also be found in foods and consumed directly. For example, the body converts the primary omega-3 essential fatty acid (alpha linolenic acid) into eicosapentaenoic acid (EPA) and docosahexaenoic acid (DHA), as these compounds are required for various processes. Similarly, the primary omega-6 (linoleic acid) is used to produce gamma linolenic acid (GLA), another essential fatty acid derivative with prominent biochemical properties. Humans cannot convert alpha linolenic acid into linoleic acid, or vice versa.

Here is a simplified version of the distinction between primary and derivative essential fatty acids.

Omega-3s
Primary essential fatty acid: Alpha linolenic acid

Derivatives: eicosapentaenoic acid (EPA)
docosahexaenoic acid (DHA)

Omega-6s
Primary essential fatty acid: Linoleic acid

Derivatives: gamma linolenic acid (GLA)
dihomogamma linolenic acid (DGLA)
arachidonic acid (AA)

Later in this chapter we'll look more closely at the essential fatty acid content of foods, oils, and supplements, but first let's summarize how a deficiency or imbalance in the omega-3s and omega-6s can affect your health and in particular how they might trigger depression.

Mind, Mood, and Beyond

As do most nutrients, essential fatty acids play a variety of roles in the body. Cells in every part of the body need essential fatty acids to maintain fluid and healthy cellular membranes. These are the thin layers of fat surrounding cells that are crucial for processing nutrients, producing energy, and synthesizing hormones. You need to provide your eyes with the proper balance of essential fatty acids for sharp vision. The heart, the gastrointestinal tract, the sex glands, the stomach, the skin—every major organ system depends on essential fatty acids to perform its functions.

The omega-3s' role in maintaining cardiovascular health is probably among the best-known benefits of essential fatty acids. Numerous studies in recent years have found that consuming high amounts of fish and fish oils, which are rich in EPA, can reduce the risk of heart disease. Certain essential fatty acids are now known to make platelets less sticky, increase the "good" HDL cholesterol, and reduce total blood fats and "bad" LDL cholesterol. The EPA and DHA in fish oils have also been shown to reduce joint pain in patients with rheumatoid arthritis. Essential fatty acids can help prevent some skin conditions and treat others, such as atopic dermatitis. Although scientific studies have reached conflicting results, a number of them have determined that GLA, for example, helps to reduce the symptoms of PMS, including low mood.

Essential fatty acids' effects on mind and mood are due in part to the brain's very high concentration of essential fatty acids and other fats. In fact, lipids (fats) account for more than half of the weight of the brain. These fat compounds are necessary for proper nerve function, cognitive development, and mood regulation. Cells that are weakened by a deficiency of the right fats are unable to process serotonin and other neurotransmitters, which may result in adverse effects on mood and behavior.

Special Effects from DHA

Because a reduced level of DHA seems to be linked with depression, it may well be a factor in causing the common postpartum depression that many women suffer in the first week or two after birth. It is interesting to note that the incidence of postpartum depression increases with each birth and that the levels of DHA continue to fall with each successive pregnancy. Other researchers have noted that in many instances an onset or a worsening of obsessive-compulsive disorder seems to be linked to the post-pregnancy experience.

DHA is the most prominent fatty acid in the human brain, where it may function in a way that is distinct from EPA or other essential fatty acids. DHA is also concentrated in parts of the brain closely tied to consciousness and thinking abilities, such as the cerebral cortex. DHA may work as well through an influence on cells' production of adenosine triphosphate, the body's principal energy-carrying compound. As I mentioned in Chapter 4, adenosine triphosphate is also involved in the metabolic functions that determine whether you are a fast or slow oxidizer.

In the body, DHA's possibly unique properties are evident even before birth—the developing brain and central nervous system seem to have a special need for DHA. Infants and children suffer a number of serious consequences from poor early supply of DHA, such as impaired vision and delayed cognitive development. For example, an eighteen-year study of more than 1,000 New Zealand children found that those who were breast-fed as infants had higher intelligence and better academic achievement than children who were fed with infant formula. The authors noted that the effects were both "pervasive, being reflected in a range of measures" and "relatively long-lived, extending throughout childhood into young adulthood." While nondietary factors may be involved, the authors mentioned that DHA was likely the crucial nutrient found in breast milk and lacking in infant formula.

Another study that looked at nine-year-old children determined that those who had been fed with formula for the first three weeks of their lives had twice the rate of minor neurological dysfunction as children who had been breast-fed for the first three weeks. Again, essential fatty acids were cited as a likely factor. (Breast milk is full of DHA and other essential fatty acids, which is another reason why it is nutritionally preferable to infant formulas. Although commercial formulas for full-term infants with added DHA are now marketed in Europe and elsewhere, in the United States infant formulas are lacking these nutrients.)

Researchers have found a drop in the DHA levels of pregnant women, probably because these nutrients are being transported to the fetus for proper brain development. One study found that by the third trimester many pregnant women had developed significant essential fatty acid imbalances, with low levels of DHA and the omega-3s and high levels of the omega-6s. This imbalance has also been shown to persist at least six weeks after delivery, the time when postpartum depression can take hold.

Later in life as well, the brain and central nervous systems require a balanced supply of essential fatty acids in order to maintain wellness. Studies have found that elderly people with low levels of DHA are more likely to suffer from Alzheimer's and other forms of dementia. Researchers have also tied various other behavioral and neurological conditions to essential fatty acid imbalances, including depression and other mood disorders, reduced concentration, memory loss, and hostility. One recent study of children in Indiana found subjects with attention deficit hyperactivity disorder had significantly lower levels of DHA compared to control subjects.

How can DHA and other essential fatty acids have such important effects on mind and mood? Part of the answer relates to their role in creating prostaglandins. As you'll see, these intriguing and versatile hormone-like compounds are key factors in preventing or treating depression.

The Mystery of Aspirin Solved

Scientists discovered aspirin's surprising pain-relieving property in the mid-1800s, yet for more than a century exactly how this compound worked its magic remained one of the major mysteries of medicine. The Nobel Prize–winning efforts of researchers in the early 1980s uncovered the surprising answer: aspirin acts on certain series of prostaglandins. These complex compounds were identified in the mid-1930s, when scientists found them in the seminal fluid of animals. They named these substances prostaglandins, after the prostate gland. Scientists have since identified prostaglandins in other parts of the body, including the brain.

The prostaglandin-pain connection spurred an explosion of research into these little-understood biochemicals, with new findings coming almost weekly. Prostaglandins are now known to have numerous important functions in the body, including helping to regulate blood pressure, blood platelet stickiness, the contraction of the heart and other muscles, energy metabolism, and immune system health.

Prostaglandins are unlike the classic hormones testosterone and melatonin in that prostaglandins are very local. They're created by a process that allows hormonal messenger molecules from a gland to attach themselves to a cell and extract fatty acids from the cell's outer membrane. But rather than being sent out into the bloodstream to circulate throughout the body, once formed the prostaglandins stay more or less put. They work within the cell to fulfill the function that the original gland intended. Prostaglandins are short-lived. Cells need to constantly create more prostaglandins, and ultimately all those fatty acids being extracted from cellular membranes have to be replaced by consuming foods or supplements rich in essential fatty acids.

In recent years scientists have determined that prostaglandins have prominent effects on mind and mood. These complex biochemicals apparently play a key role in controlling the release of serotonin, which in turn affects further prostaglandin production. Prostaglandins also regulate aspects of sleep, appetite, sexual activity, energy levels, and stress. Of course, all of these are also major indicators of depression. Studies have also determined that certain prostaglandins are found in much higher levels in depressed subjects and that other prostaglandins can actually elevate mood.

Two additional, recently established facts suggest the necessity to address prostaglandin levels in any depression-treatment program. One, the body needs certain essential fatty acids in order to produce prostaglandins. And two, how the body handles fat, sugars, and proteins can influence prostaglandin levels. Clearly, prostaglandins and their dietary precursors, the essential fatty acids, are significant—and most important, *controllable*—factors in mood and depression.

The Good and Bad Prostaglandins

Scientists have grouped prostaglandins into loose families, based on chemical structure. Three of these families with prominent actions and effects are prostaglandin E series 1, 2, and 3. (Other prostaglandin series include the A series and F series.)

- Series E1 prostaglandins are derived from the omega-6 essential fatty acid DGLA, which in turn is derived from GLA.
- Series E2 prostaglandins, which are abundant in the body, are derived from an omega-6 essential fatty acid derivative.
- Series E3 prostaglandins are derived from the omega-3 essential fatty acid DHA, which in turn is derived from EPA.

Here is the metabolic pattern for both the omega-3s and the omega-6s with the prostaglandins added in:

Omega-3s

Primary essential fatty acid: Alpha linolenic acid

↓

Derivatives: eicosapentaenoic acid (EPA)

↓

docosahexaenoic acid (DHA)

→ Series 3 prostaglandins

Omega-6s

Primary essential fatty acid: Linoleic acid

↓

Derivatives: gamma linolenic acid (GLA)

dihomogamma linolenic acid (DGLA)

→ Series 1 prostaglandins

arachidonic acid (AA)

→ Series 2 prostaglandins

Knowing which prostaglandins come from which essential fatty acids is important because the three E prostaglandin series have different effects on the mind and body.

Like HDL cholesterol, series 1 and series 3 prostaglandins are becoming known as the "good" prostaglandins. Series 1 prostaglandins

- reduce pain and promote euphoria, possibly by promoting the activity of serotonin
- benefit cardiovascular health by relaxing blood vessels, lowering blood pressure, and preventing blood platelets from clumping together by making them less sticky
- decrease inflammation, promote immune response, contract the uterus, and improve insulin function

In my experience, I've noticed that some people, of mostly Irish, Scottish, or English descent, seem to have inherited a defect that reduces the conversion of essential fatty acids into series 1 prostaglandins, thus increasing their risk of depression. (These people often benefit from taking supplements rich in GLA, such as evening primrose oil.) Research in Scotland matched two groups of alcoholics whose essential fatty acid levels were 50 percent lower than normal. One group received essential fatty acid treatment and the other received a placebo. After one year, 83 percent of those who received the essential fatty acid replacement remained sober and depression-free, while only 28 percent of the placebo group remained sober and depression-free.

Series 2 prostaglandins are called the "bad" prostaglandins because many of their effects are opposite to those of series 1 prostaglandins.

Series 2 prostaglandins

- cause inflammation
- make platelets stickier (low-dose aspirin's positive blood-thinning effects are accomplished by helping to block series 2 prostaglandins)
- promote depression

A number of studies done over the past fifteen years have found that the bad series 2 prostaglandins are elevated in people suffering from depression as well as sleep disorders. This may be due to interactions with tryptophan (decreased availability of tryptophan may be related to the inflammatory system response); low levels of melatonin (the hormone may help limit series 2 prostaglandins); or blood sugar (low insulin levels promote the release of series 2 prostaglandins).

Series 3 prostaglandins are also "good," since one of their main functions is to keep levels of the bad series 2 prostaglandins under control. The series 3 prostaglandins do this by preventing the metabolism of DGLA into AA. DGLA is also the source for the other good prostaglandins, the series 1. If too much DGLA breaks down into AA, you have lots of bad series 2 prostaglandins and a dearth of good series 1 prostaglandins.

Ideally, your body gets just the right amounts of the various essential fatty acids and is able to balance the actions of the prostaglandins. For example, overly sticky blood platelets may clog up heart vessels, but if platelets didn't clump at all, you might bleed to death from a minor cut. Effects on mood work similarly. If the prostaglandins are balanced, you feel alive and joyful. If the bad series 2 prostaglandins dominate, as can happen as a result of too much omega-6 action, depression may ensue.

The Effects of Essential Fatty Acids and Prostaglandins on Mind and Mood

The consequences of omega-6s overwhelming omega-3s in the diet are becoming clearer every day. A number of studies have pointed to dramatic effects of this imbalance on mind and mood, including an increase in rates of hostility, suicide, and depression. Population studies in various countries and in the United States suggest that reduced omega-3 fatty acid consumption is linked to increasing rates of depression. One prominent researcher in the field has postulated that consuming adequate amounts of essential fatty acids, and DHA in particular, may reduce the development of depression just as omega-3s have consistently been shown to reduce heart disease. Studies have also determined that higher blood levels of EPA and DHA correlate with higher levels of the mood-boosting neurotransmitter serotonin.

Researchers have noted that societies such as Japan with relatively high rates of consumption of cold-water fish also have correspondingly low rates of major depression. Low fish consumption may be an important factor in why some countries have as much as sixty times the rate of major depression compared to other countries. A study done on the effects of administering DHA determined that the supplements could reduce aggression and hostility in Japanese students. On the other side of the same coin, a study determined that violent, impulsive prisoners were deficient in DHA. Higher blood levels of EPA have been linked to a reduced likelihood of suicide.

A particularly dramatic study was recently done on some fifty patients suffering from manic depression. Half the subjects were given 10 g per day of omega-3s and the other half received an olive oil–based placebo. Although the researchers intended to study the effects for nine months, after only four months the results were so favorable for the omega-3 group (which was approximately twice as likely to go into remission as the placebo group) that the researchers stopped the study early. Other researchers have had success using essential fatty acid supplements in the treatment of schizophrenia.

A recent study also suggests that an imbalanced essential fatty acid intake can adversely affect thinking and memory. Physician Sandra Kalmijn examined the diets of elderly Dutch men and determined that those who ate lots of omega-3-rich fish and lesser amounts of linoleic acid, the source of omega-6s, from corn and sunflower oil were mentally sharper, based on standard psychological tests. According to Kalmijn, "The most important food groups that predicted absolute intake of linoleic acid in this population were margarine, butter, baking fats, sauces, and cheeses."

The Surprising Cholesterol Connection

Although cholesterol is not a fatty acid, it too may be a factor in how recent dietary trends are promoting mood disorders. Cholesterol is a fat in the sterol family. The link between high blood levels of LDL cholesterol, the bad cholesterol, and cardiovascular disease has caused many people to try to avoid it at all costs. Like the essential fatty acids, however, cholesterol performs a number of valuable functions in the body. It helps in the synthesis of various hormones, including a number that may play a crucial role in mood regulation. Cholesterol also promotes the absorption of essential fatty acids.

A growing number of recent studies have in fact linked very low blood cholesterol rates to an increased risk of depression and even suicide. For example, one recent study suggests that lower blood levels of HDL, the "good" cholesterol, are a marker for major depression and suicidal behavior in depressed men. Of course, cause and effect need to be considered: researchers speculated that the low HDL levels might have been induced by a bodily response to depression. While not every study confirms a link between low cholesterol (such as total cholesterol below 160 mg/dl) and depressive disorders, a number of recent studies have. For example:

- A study of blood fat concentrations in 100 subjects with major depression and 100 matched healthy controls found that total blood cholesterol among the depressed subjects was significantly lower than that of the controls. The authors concluded, "These results suggest an association between low serum total cholesterol and depression in both sexes and at all age groups."
- An Italian study of sixty depressed men and women over the age of sixty-five and eighty controls determined that those with cholesterol scores below 160 mg/dl experienced a rate of depression three times greater than subjects with higher cholesterol.
- A study of 300 healthy women aged thirty-one to sixty-five living in the area of Stockholm, Sweden, determined that those in the lowest tenth of the cholesterol distribution reported significantly more depressive symptoms. "Low cholesterol was found to be strongly associated with lack of social support," the authors noted.

This doesn't mean that I think you should start to eat a slab of bacon and a half-dozen eggs every day. A diet that is dominated by saturated animal fats and cholesterol is deadly. But so is a diet that is dominated by refined oils and popular cooking oils such as sunflower and safflower, which as we'll see in the next chapter are lacking in a balance of essential fatty acids. Fats are not the enemy. The trick is eating the right fats in the optimal levels. Fortunately, various foods, seed oils, and supplements can provide essential fatty acids in a form that most benefits your body. I'll offer guidelines for how to use all three forms. But first, a few words on the important issue of daily intake.

How Much Is Enough?

Essential fatty acids are macronutrients, like protein. That is, your optimal daily dose is measured in grams, rather than in milligrams like the B vitamins or in micrograms like selenium and other trace elements. The World Health Organization suggests that total caloric intake from essential fatty acids should be 3 percent for adults and 6 percent for children and pregnant and lactating women. Nutritionists have estimated that in order to avoid conditions associated with deficiencies of the essential fatty acids, you need to consume approximately 1 to 2 percent of your total calories in the form of linoleic acid for the omega-6s and .4 to .7 percent in the form of alpha linolenic for the omega-3s.

Optimal daily amounts are on the order of three times as high, such as 4 to 6 percent of calories for the omega-6s and 1 to 2 percent of calories for the omega-3s. These optimal levels are consistent with a number of studies that have administered essential fatty acid dosages of 5 g or more for therapeutic effects. Notice that these levels are also consistent with an approximate 4:1 ratio of omega-6s to omega-3s, which I identified earlier as much more healthful than the widespread imbalance in favor of omega-6s common today. The following chart translates these figures into grams per day.

MINIMAL AND OPTIMAL ESSENTIAL FATTY ACID NEEDS	LINOLEIC (OMEGA-6s)	ALPHA LINOLENIC (OMEGA-3s)
If you eat approximately 2,000 calories per day		
Minimum daily requirement	2.4 to 4.8 g	.8 to 1.6 g
Optimal daily requirement	8.8 to 13.6 g	2.4 to 4 g
If you eat approximately 2,500 calories per day		
Minimum daily requirement	3 to 6 g	1 to 2 g
Optimal daily requirement	11 to 17 g	3 to 5 g
If you eat approximately 3,500 calories per day		
Minimum daily requirement	4 to 8 g	2 to 3 g
Optimal daily requirement	15 to 24 g	4 to 7 g

The relatively large amounts of essential fatty acids necessary for preventing depression and maintaining optimal health emphasize the need to become more aware of the essential fatty acid balance of your diet. Unless your symptoms indicate an existing essential fatty acid imbalance, you should try to consume more of the omega-3s and fewer of the omega-6s. In my experience, many depressed people benefit when they either add more omega-3-rich foods to their diet (the ideal choice) or take an omega-3 essential fatty acid oil or supplement.

The Best Choice: Eating More Foods That Are Rich in the Omega-3 Essential Fatty Acids

As I've mentioned, it is much easier to fall into eating a diet that loads your body with omega-6 essential fatty acids than with omega-3s. The omega-6s are found in lots of processed foods, so one way to improve your ratio of omega-6 to omega-3 intake is to cut back on these unhealthful omega-6 foods. At the same time, you should try to incorporate into your diet healthful sources of the omega-3 essential fatty acids. These are relatively limited but are available.

The most common food that is rich in the desirable omega-3s is various fish usually found in the wild in deep, cold water, such as tuna, salmon, sardines, mackerel, bluefish, halibut, herring, striped bass, and cod. The natural oils found in these fish have a high content of the omega-3 derivatives EPA and (to a lesser extent) DHA.

Red meat and animal fat contain essential fatty acids or derivatives, particularly DHA. These do not, however, rival the cold-water fish as a concentrated source. The richest animal-based sources of essential fatty acids include eggs, organ meats, cream, and butter. These foods are not healthful for regular daily consumption, however, because they tend to be high in the omega-6 derivative arachidonic acid, which in excess is inflammatory, and of course they are also high in saturated fat and cholesterol.

If you do like to eat fish or meat, I encourage you to seek out high-quality sources for products that are free of toxins, hormonal residues, and environmental pollutants. Take some time to educate yourself by talking to the people who sell these foods in your local markets, or by contacting organic food organizations that can vouch for growers, providers, or retailers.

Many of my clients are vegetarians, and they have no trouble getting sufficient omega-3s from plant sources. A number of fresh vegetables have appreciable levels of essential fatty acids, though primarily the omega-6s rather than the omega-3s. The plants with the most significant omega-6 content include three (evening primrose, borage, and black currant) that are rarely eaten but whose seeds have become the sources for oils that have become popular GLA supplements. I'll talk more about them in the later section on omega-6 essential fatty acid supplements.

Sea vegetables such as nori, hijiki, and kombu contain a balance of essential fatty acids, as do a number of nuts, seeds, and beans. Among those with the highest levels of the desirable omega-3s are

- walnuts
- pumpkin seeds
- soybeans
- kidney beans
- flaxseeds

Many people are unfamiliar with flaxseeds, but flaxseeds have a history of food use that goes back many thousands of years. They can be eaten whole but are more commonly ground. Unlike many other plant foods, flaxseeds are one of the richest known sources of a special fiber called lignin that is converted in the colon to lignans. These natural compounds help to fortify the immune system and have specific anticancer, antifungal, and antiviral properties. High levels of lignans are associated with reduced rates of colon, prostate, and breast cancer. Lignans may have antioxidant and heart-protective properties. Flaxseeds also contain protein, potassium, calcium, magnesium, B-complex vitamins, and other nutrients.

Flaxseeds are not the easiest food to eat but I think it is well worth the additional effort, as they are the most concentrated animal or plant source of omega-3s—much more concentrated than cold-water fish. Making ground flaxseeds a regular element of your diet is probably the single best way to take advantage of the healthful properties of essential fatty acids, and it is safer and more effective than taking seed oils or any of the essential fatty acid supplements.

Whole flaxseeds are becoming more widely available in natural food stores and through mail-order supplement companies. All that you need to get started is some premium flaxseeds (South Dakota and other states grow it) and a high-quality electric grinder. A coffee-bean grinder works fine, though you won't want to switch back and forth from grinding flax and coffee beans in the same unit.

Start by taking one to two teaspoons per day of ground flaxseeds. This represents approximately 750 to 1,500 mg of essential fatty acids. Ground flaxseeds can be sprinkled on cereals, yogurt, applesauce, or salads to add a mildly nutty flavor. You can also put the ground seeds in a blender and mix them with fruits and ice into smoothies, or mix with some honey and nuts for a dessertlike treat. Some people add ground flaxseeds to bread dough, although the heat of baking will deactivate some of the essential fatty acid content. Sprinkling flaxseeds onto hot cereal or soup as they're being served only minimally affects their healthful qualities.

The quickest and easiest way to take ground flaxseeds is to mix them into a few ounces of water or juice, stir, and drink. The flax doesn't readily dissolve (instead it absorbs liquids) so it's not the most appealing drink in terms of appearance and texture, but you'll be surprised at how easily it goes down.

Although unground flaxseeds have a long shelf life, it is best to store them in a tightly closed container in a cool, dry place. Grind only as much as you intend to take immediately, because once grinding has removed the seeds' protective shells, flaxseeds are similar to the oil and will begin to oxidize and lose their healthful qualities.

Your Second-Best Choice: Taking the Omega-Balanced Seed Oils

Flaxseed and hemp seed oils, both of which provide a balanced mix of omega-3s and omega-6s, straddle the line between foods and supplements. These oils are available as liquids in 4- to 32-ounce bottles but are relatively hard to find in capsules. Most of the flaxseed and hemp seed oil that is sold today is taken like a supplement—people gulp a teaspoon or more a day for the benefits of the balanced essential fatty acids. Less frequently these oils are used in salad dressings or other foods.

The seed oil from flax is rich in both omega-3s (57 to 58 percent) as well as containing approximately 15 percent omega-6s. The oil does not, however, contain the healthful lignin found in flaxseed shells. Compared to fish oils, flaxseed oil tends to have a lighter taste and smell. The flax plant (*Linum usitatissimum*) is also used to make linen fiber, which is why another name for flaxseed oil is linseed oil. (Most products for human consumption are called flaxseed oil; industrial grades of linseed oil, such as those used to thin paints, should not be ingested.)

Hemp is, of course, the plant (*Cannabis sativa*) that is the source of the mind-altering drug marijuana. The seed oil, however, is pressed from sterilized seeds and is perfectly legal (and without any potential psychoactivity). Hemp seed oil has approximately three times as much omega-6 content (58 percent, including about 2 percent GLA) as omega-3 (20 percent).

Seed oils are easier to take than eating ground flaxseeds but have the disadvantage of being much less stable. Highly unsaturated oils like flaxseed and hemp can readily turn rancid when exposed to heat or light. To ensure that these oils are fresh and potent, look for products that

- have been extracted by processes that do not involve chemical solvents or high temperatures (look for terms such as "expeller pressed" and "modified atmospheric packing" on labels; "cold pressed" is insufficient as a guide to oil quality, since in the United States it means that the product may nevertheless have been exposed to high temperatures)
- have been refrigerated
- have a "pressing" and "better before" date on the bottle
- are sold in opaque containers

Prime candidates for omega-balanced seed oil supplements: You may gain special benefit from taking omega-balanced seed oil supplements if your depression is related to an imbalance or deficiency in essential fatty acids.

Safety concerns: The omega-balanced seed oils (as well as ground flaxseeds) are safer to use than most essential fatty acid supplements, such as fish oils. That is because ground flaxseeds and the seed oils provide the primary essential fatty acid substances—alpha linolenic and linoleic acids—rather than the derivatives such as EPA, DHA, and GLA. The alpha linolenic acid is a basic building block in the human body for many bodily functions, only one of which is to make EPA and other derivatives. By supplying EPA directly, fish oils limit the body's options to make what it needs from alpha linolenic acid. An analogy is to compare flaxseed oil, for example, to the plant-based vitamin A precursor beta-carotene, which is essentially nontoxic even in huge doses since the body converts to vitamin A only what it needs. EPA and DHA in this analogy are like preformed, animal-derived vitamin A, which can more easily reach toxic levels in the body if overconsumed.

One safety concern that should be kept in mind is the danger from oils going rancid or oxidizing. Oxidation forms highly reactive free radicals that compromise oils' healthful properties or can actually be toxic.

How to use it: Barlean's Organic Oils and Omega Nutrition (see Supplement Resources) offer high-quality flaxseed oil products. One teaspoon of the oil per day is a good starting point for most people; this is approximately equal to consuming 3 teaspoons of the ground seeds. You can also use the oil to make salad dressings, salsas, and condiments (preferably uncooked to preserve the essential fatty acid activity). Once you've opened the container, consume the contents within four to six weeks. Unopened, the oil retains its potency for approximately four months, longer if you freeze it. Many people would rather consume oil in a softgel than drink it, so I think in the near future these oils will become more widely available in softgel capsules.

Rating the Omega-3 Essential Fatty Acid Supplements

Two primary sources exist for omega-3 derivative supplements. The best known is fish oils. Producers express and concentrate the fatty liquids from salmon, tuna, and other cold-water, deep-sea fish to make fish oil supplements, usually rich in both EPA and DHA.

Essential fatty acids are essential for fish, too. That is, fish don't produce sufficient quantities in their bodies and thus need to consume it in their diet. So where do they get it from originally? They get it by consuming microalgae, which is now being exploited as a source for omega-3 DHA supplements.

Fish oil supplements are still the most popular and have been more widely used than any other type of essential fatty acid supplement in scientific studies. On the other hand, fish living in polluted waters can concentrate toxins in their oils. There are also ethical concerns about killing animals, including fish. The microalgae supplements provide only DHA, but DHA has been more reliably tied to beneficial effects on mind and mood than EPA. I think these are all valid reasons to prefer the new microalgae supplements to fish oil supplements for people who need or want to take omega-3 derivatives.

Prime candidates for omega-3 supplement use: You may gain special benefit from taking omega-3 supplements if your depression is related to
- a history of postpartum depression in yourself or your mother
- an extremely low-fat diet

Safety concerns: In general, essential fatty acid supplements are safe and nontoxic. Most people will not experience any side effects from taking the types of doses recommended here. Talk to your doctor before taking essential fatty acids, however, if you have a medical condition that causes you to bleed excessively. That's because the blood-thinning effects of essential fatty acids could theoretically present a hazard, although problems associated with increased bleeding time or blood loss have not been demonstrated in any clinical trials of essential fatty acids. The same advice applies if you're taking anticoagulant drugs such as warfarin (Coumadin) for a heart condition. Combining essential fatty acids with aspirin should also be approached with caution. Some evidence suggests that diabetics and people suffering from immune dysfunctions should also limit essential fatty acid consumption. Because of the potential for bleeding, pregnant women and infants should not take fish oils—flaxseeds or one of the omega-balanced oils are preferable.

Signs that you may be consuming too much of the omega-3s include

- oily skin
- diarrhea
- intestinal gas
- fatigue or lack of energy

Cod liver oil, which has been traditionally taken as a supplement, presents unique safety concerns. Unless vitamins A and D have been removed during processing, cod liver oil is an extremely concentrated source of these nutrients. Because they are fat-soluble, vitamins A and D can readily accumulate in the body to toxic levels and may affect liver function. Because of this safety concern and the fact that cod liver oil has lower levels of essential fatty acids (approximately 7 percent EPA and 7 percent DHA) than most fish oil capsules, I don't recommend using cod liver oil.

How to use it: A popular new microalgae-source DHA product is Neuromins DHA. It is the best vegetarian source of DHA. It comes in two potencies, providing either 100 or 200 mg of DHA per capsule. I usually suggest the 100 mg size if it is the woman's first pregnancy, for example, and 200 mg for subsequent pregnancies. A number of leading natural product companies, including Nature's Way, Solgar, Solaray, Natrol, and Source Naturals, have been licensed by developer Martek Biosciences Corporation (see Supplement Resources) of Columbia, Maryland, to sell Neuromins DHA.

If you prefer fish oils, most omega-3 supplements are liquid-filled softgels that contain 1,000 to 1,250 mg of fish oil concentrate, representing an EPA range of 180 to 360 mg and a DHA range of 120 to 240 mg. One capsule per day is a good starting point to help alleviate depression.

Rating the Omega-6 Essential Fatty Acid Supplements

The fatty liquids extracted from the seeds of three plants—evening primrose, borage, and black currant—are the source of the most popular omega-6 GLA supplements. Evening primrose is a yellow-flowering willow family plant that is a popular healing herb in Europe but mainly an essential fatty acid supplement in the United States. Its oil has approximately 10 percent GLA content. Borage is a blue-flowering plant that has also traditionally been used as an herb in Europe, primarily to make a sore throat remedy. The oil derived from borage seeds is approximately 20 to 25 percent GLA, making it among the most concentrated natural sources of this essential fatty acid. The oil from black currant usually contains approximately 5 to 15 percent GLA content.

I don't see much difference among the omega-6 source supplements. Evening primrose is the most popular, although borage has a slightly higher percentage of GLA content. If I am treating someone who has an obvious omega-6 deficiency, I usually recommend evening primrose capsules, but if you prefer another type of supplement that's fine.

Prime candidates for omega-6 supplement use: You may gain special benefit from taking omega-6 supplements if your depression is related to
- an omega-6 essential fatty acid deficiency
- habitual use of alcohol

Safety concerns: (The same general safety concerns apply as for the omega-3 supplements.)
Signs that you may be taking too much of the omega-6s include:
- constipation
- fatigue
- anxiety
- irritation

How to use it: Evening primrose oil is widely available in 500 to 1,000 mg softgels, with GLA content approximately 50 to 100 mg. Capsules providing 1,000 to 1,300 mg of borage oil usually have 240 to 300 mg of GLA. An average 1,000 mg capsule of black currant oil provides 100 mg of GLA.

FDA-in-Wonderland

I think it is important to mention that a number of the seed oil essential fatty acid supplements were the focus of a heated regulatory battle in the late 1980s and early 1990s. In 1988 the Food and Drug Administration banned the importation of evening primrose oil supplements, on the illogical grounds that encapsulating the nutrient somehow turned it into an "unapproved food additive." Legally, that meant that the oil was considered unsafe until producers petitioned the FDA with proof that it was safe (which can be a lengthy and expensive process). The FDA seized some evening primrose shipments and instituted an automatic detention policy on flaxseed oil. The agency also began a court action against an importer/manufacturer of black currant oil. Companies sued the FDA in district and circuit courts, claiming that the FDA was misusing its authority in attempting to ban a whole category of nutritional supplements. Judges agreed with essential fatty acid supplement companies all along the way, with one characterizing the FDA's reasoning as "an Alice-in-Wonderland approach."

In the final analysis, the FDA's draconian actions against the essential fatty acid supplements backfired. The FDA's legal harassment of essential fatty acid producers and importers served as one of the most dramatic examples of the agency's refusal to institute a rational regulatory approach to nutritional supplements. This prompted Congress in 1994 to pass and President Clinton to sign the Dietary Supplement Health and Education Act (DSHEA), which, among other provisions, forbids the FDA from regulating dietary supplements as food additives. It wasn't until more than a year after the passage of the DSHEA that the FDA formally gave up and rescinded its import alert on evening primrose oil and a number of other herbs and supplements. While this unnecessary and unwarranted regulatory battle may have slightly retarded public acceptance of essential fatty acid supplements over the past decade, some measure of regulatory sanity has been restored and essential fatty acid supplements are now widely available and recognized as safe and effective nutrients.

Keep It Simple

Correcting an essential fatty acid imbalance or deficiency is not a panacea for relieving depression, but it can have dramatic effects in some cases. Often, it needs to be recognized for what it is: one step among the five in the natural program for beating depression. On the other hand, I've had patients who've responded particularly well to eating flaxseeds or taking essential fatty acid supplements. One woman, a somewhat shy and retiring accountant in her mid-forties, had been depressed for years when she first came to see me. I helped her make many adjustments to her diet, lifestyle, and nutrient program, but she seemed to really improve with the addition of flaxseed oil. After six months, I found we could cut back on some of the amino acid supplements that were modifying her neurotransmitter levels. When we tried to reduce the essential fatty acid source, however, she began to feel tired and remote, signs that her depression was returning. Her overall mood benefited greatly from staying with the essential fatty acid program.

It's clear there is no easy answer to the question "What essential fatty acids should I take and at what levels?" For the foreseeable future, the process will involve some trial and error and self-observation for improvements in mood or avoidance of adverse side effects. Following a few simple guidelines, however, can improve your chances of benefiting from the depression-busting effects of essential fatty acids.

- Eat primarily foods that are low in saturated fats, hydrogenated fats, or trans fatty acids, such as fresh vegetables, fruits, and grains. Try to avoid margarine, processed snack foods, and highly refined polyunsaturated cooking oils, which competitively inhibit the absorption of healthful essential fatty acids.
- If you cook with oils, use olive or sesame oil and try to use small amounts and quick-cooking techniques.
- Meet most of your daily essential fatty acid requirements with unprocessed, uncooked whole foods, such as flax or other seeds, nuts, and soybeans, or by eating salmon or other essential fatty acid–rich fish two to three times per week if you are not vegetarian.
- Your body needs optimal levels of various vitamins and minerals to convert linoleic acid to GLA, to synthesize cholesterol from dietary nutrients, and to act as antioxidants to protect these nutrients and your body from the harmful effects of free radicals. Among the most

important of these nutrients are vitamin A and mixed carotenoids, niacin, pyridoxine, vitamin C, and magnesium. (See Chapter 6 for optimal levels for these and other nutrients.)

- More so than powdered and encapsulated supplements, fish and seed oils tend to be very perishable. Even though many essential fatty acid supplements have vitamin E oil added to prevent rancidity, you need to store them in the refrigerator or some other cool, dry, and dark place. Keep the container tightly closed to limit exposure to light and air and thus reduce oxidation. Once opened, most oil products are best consumed within four to six weeks.

8

Step Four:
Diet for Mental Health

Few of my patients would be surprised if I were to tell them that there was no one pill that could treat every person's depression. Each person has a unique mind and body, a different set of life experiences, and a personal biochemical balance. Yet patients are surprised when I tell them that there is no "best diet" for depression, either. Just as with drugs and supplements, what works for one person may not work for another, even when those two people seem to have the same symptoms. One of the most crucial factors in determining a person's optimal diet, I've found, is whether the person is best described as a fast oxidizer or slow oxidizer.

Let me give you an example. Michael and Brad both came to see me within a month or so of each other about two years ago. On the surface, the cases seemed similar. They were both thirty-something professionals without histories of depression but with recent episodes of variable mood, insomnia, inability to concentrate at work, and anxiety. Some amino acids and nutritional supplements proved to be beneficial for both, but in each case the most notable improvement came after we made certain dietary adjustments.

The questionnaire "Your Personal Biochemistry: Are You a Fast or Slow Oxidizer?" in Chapter 4 established that Michael's system was quick and efficient at metabolizing sugar. He was your typical fast oxidizer who needed more than average amounts of protein, while Brad was just the opposite and needed somewhat less protein. Michael had been trying to follow a high-carbohydrate diet (mostly refined carbohydrates, in his case, unfortunately) and just hadn't been getting enough protein. When he started to eat fewer carbohydrates and more whole foods and high-quality protein such as from soy foods and spirulina, his mood swings leveled off, he slept better, and his mental energy returned. Brad, on the other hand, was eating a high-protein "Zone-based" diet. But it was the wrong diet for his system and was contributing to his anxiety and fatigue. When I put him on a high-complex-carbohydrate, lower-protein, slow oxidation diet, the effects were noticeable almost immediately: his pulse rate came down, he felt less anxious, and his sense of purposefulness in life returned.

This is an example of an important principle I've seen demonstrated again and again: both overall diet (ratio of proteins, carbohydrates, and fats) and specific foods can have a tremendous effect on mind and mood. Specific foods can affect mood in various ways:

- amino acids transported to the brain can affect neurotransmitter levels (for example, most protein-rich foods boost dopamine and noradrenaline and reduce serotonin, thus increasing arousal)
- nutrients can raise or lower blood sugar (for example, complex carbohydrates can raise serotonin levels and promote relaxation)
- overall fat content can alter metabolic pathways (for example, certain types of fat are inefficiently processed by the body, clogging circulation and thus potentially adversely affecting mind and mood)
- essential fatty acid content can affect prostaglandin levels (for example, consuming flaxseeds or cold-water fish can increase bodily levels of the mood-boosting prostaglandins)
- hormones and circadian rhythms can interact with diet (for example, many people feel better by adjusting the percentages of protein, fat, and carbohydrates they eat from morning to evening)

The key principle to keep in mind is that there is no such thing as an optimal diet for everyone. Each person is biologically unique and has a different need for protein, fat, and carbohydrates. Advocates for various diets, whether it be macrobiotics, the Zone, or the Pritikin diet, claim their diet is the best. How can this be? All these diets do seem to work— for about one-third to one-half of those who try them. The people who succeed on the diet are those who provide the glowing testimonials used in the promotional literature. The people who fail on the diet don't garner as much attention.

As the Roman philosopher Lucretius said, "One man's meat is another man's poison." When you determine the optimal amounts and ratios of protein, fat, and carbohydrates for your body, you can reach an optimal state characterized by three key signs that must hold over time:

- you feel balanced emotionally and mentally immediately after eating
- you feel physically energized in a way that lasts for at least several hours
- you feel satisfied after the meal

You need to observe which overall diet and foods provide you with optimal energy, emotional balance, and no cravings. A few simple tools can help you to learn how to better balance your ratio of carbohydrates, proteins, and fats, both in any one meal and in your overall diet. For example, I've found that the glycemic index, which indicates how quickly a food is metabolized into glucose, is an excellent scale for judging a carbohydrate food's potential for mood-related effects, although you do need to keep in mind other factors (like whether you're a fast or slow oxidizer) when you use it. So let's look at how you can balance each of the three major food groups to achieve a lasting positive mood.

Carbohydrates: How the Glycemic Index Affects Fast and Slow Oxidizers

I've noticed that people tend to have love/hate relationships with carbohydrates. Clients have told me that eating carbohydrates puts them to sleep, or that carbohydrates make them go crazy, or that they can't wake up in the morning until they've had their carbohydrates. For most people, carbohydrates mean energy—that's what they eat to fuel mind and body.

Carbohydrates can do this because they are digested easily, breaking down in the body into simple sugars such as glucose and fructose. Various bodily cells—but especially brain cells—need glucose to function. Without glucose, you'd have no fuel to support your ability to think, or even remember or decide to eat, for that matter. Glucose is also important because it can be converted to glycogen, which can be stored and then converted back to glucose when the body needs more heat or energy.

Carbohydrates are the fuel that keep you going, but some carbohydrates are higher-octane than others. The most basic classification is simple and complex carbohydrates. Simple carbohydrates are mainly sugars, such as glucose, galactose, and fructose, discussed above. Complex carbohydrates contain other compounds in addition to sugars, such as starch and cellulose.

How quickly the body responds to the fuel supplied by carbohydrates is a crucial issue. Some carbohydrates travel like a rocket to the brain and provide an almost immediate burst of energy. Others take a more leisurely "turtle" route and provide a more steady supply of energy. The problem with the rocket foods is that eating them tends to cause wild swings in blood sugar, a high followed by a low. And the low, hypoglycemic state is one that has been closely associated with low mood, a feeling of tense arousal or tense tiredness, and a reduced ability to experience pleasure.

Which foods are rockets and which are turtles? The glycemic index answers just that question. It provides a measure of how quickly a food's sugars are absorbed and metabolized in the body. Those high on the glycemic index are most quickly converted. They tend to be refined carbohydrates. Those low on the index tend to be more complex carbohydrates, although other factors also come into play (especially fat content).

Research into various foods' glycemic ratings continues, and in some cases researchers disagree and various glycemic indices differ. I've looked at many charts and have incorporated their findings with my own and my patients' experiences to develop the following index. My chart is also unique in that while most others offer only low, moderate, and high ratings, I find it useful to distinguish foods that are "super high." These foods are so quickly converted to glucose that they're unhealthy for virtually everybody except in small and infrequent amounts.

Glycemic Index

SUPER HIGH
- white bread and other white flour products
- mashed or instant potatoes
- refined and sweetened cereals
- candy bars

- processed fruit juice (added sugar)
- white and instant rice
- corn chips
- donuts
- cookies
- puffed rice and rice cakes

HIGH
- cornflakes
- raisins and other dried fruits
- boiled and baked potatoes and French fries
- bananas, mango, apricots, pineapple, watermelon
- cooked carrots
- refined pastas and spaghetti
- honey

MODERATE
- whole wheat bread
- brown rice
- whole grain cereals without sugar
- orange and grapefruit juice
- whole/mixed grain pasta
- corn
- sweet potatoes
- green peas
- grapes, oranges, peaches, blueberries
- lentil and split pea soup
- instant noodles
- popcorn

LOW
- leafy green vegetables
- yogurt (low-fat, unsweetened)
- dried beans: kidney, black, brown
- dried/split peas
- lentils
- chickpeas
- apples, pears, plums, cherries, grapefruit
- soybeans

- tomatoes
- mushrooms
- peanuts

In my experience, depending upon their constitution, some people do better eating foods in the low to moderate categories while others do better eating foods in the moderate to high categories. One exception is leafy green vegetables, which are healthful for virtually everyone and should be eaten daily. On the other hand, foods in the super high category are not healthful for everyday intake by anybody. They are acceptable as an occasional indulgence, although fast oxidizers feel much better over the long term by avoiding them completely.

If you are a slow oxidizer: Slow oxidizers should obtain approximately 55 percent of their calories from complex carbohydrates, especially those in the moderate glycemic range. They can do all right with some high glycemic foods as well.

If you are a fast oxidizer: Foods moderate to low on the glycemic index are the healthiest for fast oxidizers, who should obtain approximately 35 percent of their diet from complex carbohydrates. These foods are the ones that result in optimal energy production for the fast oxidizer. Although essential for fast oxidizers, low to moderate glycemic foods may also form the basis for a vegetarian slow oxidizer diet.

If you are a balanced oxidizer: Consume approximately 45 percent of your diet from complex carbohydrates, especially those in the low to moderate glycemic range.

Switching to the right diet can often be the most important step for defeating depression. I've treated many persons like David, a forty-four-year-old lawyer who was very active in his spare time playing tennis and basketball. Over the previous year or so he had begun to travel more and had not only become less active but had started to eat a diet much higher in refined and high glycemic foods. He was a classic fast oxidizer, and not surprisingly began to feel depressed and chronically fatigued. I recommended that David take some nutritional supplements, but the main thing was that over the next two months he started to pay more attention to his diet, minimizing high-glycemic and refined foods. As a result, he quickly regained his physical and mental energy. In fact, he told me,

"I feel mentally sharper than I have in years and I also feel ten years younger out on the court. Everybody who knows me recognizes that I've lost body fat and added muscle and that my overall mood and disposition are much better."

The Serotonin Effect

Low-fat foods that are rich in carbohydrates tend to boost the activity of serotonin. This can not only improve mood but help to control appetite and reduce bingeing. But wait a minute, you might say. Serotonin is derived from tryptophan, and tryptophan is found in protein foods. So why should eating carbohydrates instead of protein boost serotonin?

The answer has to do with how tryptophan is handled by the body. Foods rich in protein actually send very little tryptophan to the brain. That's because tryptophan competes with other amino acids, like phenylalanine, that are also found in protein foods—and often in larger numbers than tryptophan. The brain uses phenylalanine to make not serotonin but the more stimulating or arousing neurotransmitters dopamine and noradrenaline. So protein foods tend to rev you up rather than calm you down.

Complex carbohydrates stimulate serotonin synthesis through an interaction with insulin, the hormone secreted by the pancreas. The body secretes insulin into the bloodstream in response to the glucose, one of the sugars derived from the digestion of complex carbs. It so happens that insulin causes amino acids in the bloodstream to enter muscle cells. The amino acid tryptophan, however, is exempted from this insulin effect. That leaves a relative abundance of tryptophan in the bloodstream, where it can travel to the brain and where nerve cells can process it into serotonin.

Various studies by researchers at M.I.T. and elsewhere over the past twenty years have confirmed that carbohydrates have this serotonin-boosting effect. Researchers have also found that eating carbohydrate-rich meals can elevate mood, relax mind and body, and help to dispel anger and anxiety.

Protein and Mood

If you're a balanced oxidizer, your optimum diet is going to be approximately 45 percent from high-protein foods, while slow oxidizers need approximately 35 percent from high-protein foods and fast oxidizers approximately 50 percent from high-protein foods.

The specific amino acids that are most concentrated in the protein foods you eat can have noticeable effects on your mood. One method, as we've just seen, for controlling amino acid uptake in the brain is to eat more complex carbohydrates, which promotes tryptophan uptake and thus serotonin action. You can combine this method with an increased consumption of foods relatively rich in tryptophan for even greater serotonin activity.

PROTEIN FOODS WITH A HIGH CONCENTRATION OF TRYPTOPHAN
RELATIVE TO OTHER AMINO ACIDS:
- pumpkin seeds
- sunflower seeds
- milk
- bananas
- peanuts
- lentils

PROTEIN FOODS WITH A LOW CONCENTRATION OF TRYPTOPHAN
RELATIVE TO OTHER AMINO ACIDS:
- meat
- poultry
- seafood
- beans
- tofu
- corn
- cereal grains
- legumes

Prime candidates for foods high in tryptophan: You may gain special benefit from emphasizing tryptophan in your diet if your depression is related to
- too little serotonin activity in the brain
- seasonal rhythms

Prime candidates for foods low in tryptophan: You may gain special benefit from avoiding tryptophan if your depression is related to
- too little noradrenaline activity in the brain

- too little dopamine activity in the brain
- too little endorphin activity in the brain

Fast oxidizers also benefit from eating whole food high-protein supplements (such as chlorella, spirulina, and other microalgae, brewer's yeast, and bee pollen, which are concentrated sources of amino acids, vitamins, minerals, and other nutrients) and sea vegetables such as nori, hijiki, and kombu.

Sea vegetables are also the richest source of iodine among foods. Iodine plays a key role in thyroid function, and a deficiency can cause hypothyroidism. Sea vegetables have actually been used for hundreds of years as a treatment for goiter. Consuming soy protein can also boost the body's ability to secrete thyroid hormone. Other foods rich in iodine include watercress, squash, asparagus, citrus fruits, watermelon, and pineapple. (Note that iodine content in foods is affected by the iodine content of the soil in which the foods are grown. Soils in coastal areas tend to have higher iodine content than inland soils.) Most people get the bulk of their iodine, and in some cases too much, from highly processed, iodine-fortified salt. My preference is to use more natural types of salt, like sea salt or Celtic salt (a sun-dried sea salt that is very high in minerals), and obtain iodine from foods such as sea vegetables. An organic tamari (soy sauce) can also substitute for salt.

The Fat Factor

The amount of your daily diet made up of fats should vary slightly depending on whether you are a balanced, fast, or slow oxidizer. Slow oxidizers do better consuming less fat (approximately 10 to 15 percent of the total diet). Various types of fat, however, can have different effects on mind and mood. Many people with chronic low mood benefit from reducing their intake of foods rich in the omega-6s and increasing their consumption of foods rich in the omega-3s. Here is a quick review of those foods:

FOODS RELATIVELY HIGH IN THE HARD-TO-GET OMEGA-3s:
- various cold-water fish such as salmon, mackerel, cod, and tuna
- sea vegetables such as nori, hijiki, and kombu
- walnuts and other nuts
- pumpkin seeds and other seeds
- soybeans

- kidney beans
- flaxseeds
- flaxseed oil
- hemp seed oil

FOODS RELATIVELY HIGH IN THE OFTEN OVERCONSUMED OMEGA-6s:
- vegetable oils like safflower, sunflower, corn, and peanut

You'll notice that the second category of foods, those high in the often overconsumed omega-6s, is not very large. Another factor, however, considerably alters the picture. That is, foods that are high in other types of fats tend to concentrate the omega-6s in your blood at the expense of the omega-3s. These other, mostly unhealthful types of fat include hydrogenated fats and the related trans fatty acids, and saturated fats.

Food manufacturers add hydrogen to fats to make processed foods that are more stable and will stay fresh on the shelf longer. This process is known as hydrogenation. When you hydrogenate a polyunsaturated oil, such as safflower or sunflower, you can turn a mostly liquid fat into a semisolid one, like margarine. In the process, however, you change the chemical composition of fats from their natural "cis" configuration into an abnormal "trans" form, one with different chemical and physical properties. These trans fatty acids are biologically inactive forms of fat that are poorly processed by the body. They concentrate in the cell membranes, which become less fluid. This weakens the cells' function and particularly their resistance to viral invasion. Trans fatty acids also act much like saturated fats to raise blood fat and total cholesterol levels. They clog metabolic pathways, disrupt cellular processes, deplete other nutrients, and possibly even impair production of prostaglandins. The trans fatty acids also block DHA production and metabolism and inhibit the body's ability to convert linoleic acid/omega-6s into GLA.

PROCESSED FOODS HIGH IN THE UNDESIRABLE TRANS FATTY ACIDS:
- margarine
- cookies
- white bread
- candies
- cakes
- doughnuts
- chips

Take the time to check labels for hydrogenated fats. Higher-quality cookies, chips, and so forth are made without resort to these harmful fats.

Most people are already familiar with the adverse properties of foods high in saturated fats, from an increased risk of heart disease to obesity and diabetes. High-fat foods also have subtle effects on mood and alertness, according to researchers. Studies have found that high-fat meals, for example, cause a decline in alertness and concentration compared to low-fat meals. Subjects have also been shown to feel less vigorous and imaginative and more feeble and fatigued from eating high-fat meals.

FOODS HIGH IN THE UNDESIRABLE SATURATED FATS:
- beef
- pork
- lamb
- luncheon meats
- sausage
- hot dogs
- butter
- mayonnaise
- ice cream
- cream cheese
- egg yolks
- cheese
- whole milk and dairy products
- coconut

Although nuts, seeds, and avocados have fat contents proportionately as high as or higher than meat and dairy foods, for example, I think that these plant foods are much more healthful because they do not introduce harmful trans fatty acids into the body. This is especially the case if the nuts and seeds are eaten raw rather than cooked. An even better way to derive their benefits is to soak them overnight before cooking, which makes them easier to digest. Nuts, seeds, and avocados have the comparative advantage over animal fats in not containing cholesterol and in not storing in their fats ingested estrogen and other potentially toxic chemicals.

A final factor in fat consumption that is just beginning to gain the attention it deserves is that fat activates the brain chemical galanin, which competes with serotonin. Too much galanin activity can make you feel fatigued and "out of it." Its effects can linger until the source of the fats has been fully digested, which may mean hours rather than the shorter period necessary for the body to digest carbohydrates, for example.

The Problem with Most Cooking Oils

Ideally the body attains a balance of approximately four parts omega-6s for one part omega-3 in the diet. Unfortunately, the somewhat narrow range of dietary choices, as well as shifting cultural dietary patterns, can make it tough to achieve that balance. People tend to get much of their essential fatty acids from less-than-ideal sources, like cooking oils.

A number of cooking oils derived from nuts, seeds, and grains have relatively high concentrations of omega-6s and no omega-3s. This includes vegetable oils derived from safflower, sunflower, corn, and peanuts. Oils derived from rapeseed (canola oil), soybeans, and sesame have somewhat lower levels of omega-6s accompanied by minor amounts of omega-3s. Another popular cooking oil, olive, has relatively low levels of both omega-6s and omega-3s. The following chart summarizes the approximate fatty acid content of these popular cooking oils as well as two animal fats. Keep in mind that saturated fats (the term saturation refers to the relative number of hydrogen molecules attached to carbon molecules) are generally more stable at room temperature than unsaturated fats but contribute heavily to heart disease and other health problems. Monounsaturated fats have a more neutral effect on blood fat levels.

Fatty Acid Content of Common Cooking Oils and Animal Fats

■ ■ ■ ■

OILS	SATURATED	MONOUNSATURATED	POLYUNSATURATED	
			OMEGA-6s	OMEGA-3s
		(figures represent percent of total fat content)		
Safflower	9	13	78	0
Sunflower	11	20	69	0
Corn	14	25	60	0
Peanut	18	48	34	0
Canola	7	61	21	11
Soybean	15	24	54	7
Sesame	14	40	45	1
Olive	14	77	8	1
Animal fats				
Butter fat	66	30	2	2
Lard	41	47	11	1

Source: USDA Agricultural Handbook No. 8-4, product literature. Note that these values should be considered averages—oils may differ in fatty acid content depending upon factors such as source, processing, and growing climate.

As you can see from this chart, one problem with cooking oils is that they're overabundant in the omega-6s. An equally worrisome health consideration relates to what happens when these oils are heated and used for cooking. I must emphasize, however, that this problem affects all cooking oils. That's because heat (as well as light) breaks down oils and creates free radicals that can be harmful if consumed in large amounts.

Because olive oil is highly monounsaturated, it has a slight advantage over the polyunsaturated oils in this regard. Therefore, I recommend a high-quality olive oil for use in cooking. Even with olive oil, you should try to use small amounts of oil and heat the oil as briefly as possible. Traditional Asian wok cooking, for example, exposes food to small amounts of heated oil relatively briefly.

If you don't like olive oil, I think that sesame oil is the next best choice. I've found that a number of companies offer high-quality sesame seed oil products, while soybean and canola oil products tend to be overrefined and I don't recommend them for that reason. (Canadian researchers developed canola in the 1970s by breeding a new variety of the rape plant with seeds that have an improved fatty acid profile. The new oil was dubbed "Canada oil" or canola for short. It has become increasingly popular as a cooking oil in recent years.)

The animal fats in butter and lard are no better, by the way, and have additional drawbacks. Plants don't store ingested estrogen and other chemicals in their oil as animals do. The plant-based oils also have the advantage of being lower in saturated fat compared to animal sources of essential fatty acids. The saturated animal fats that have come to dominate modern diets are nonessential. Your body not only doesn't need these unhealthful fats, it works better without them. This is especially true when these other nonessential fats are consumed in high quantities.

Balancing Protein, Carbohydrates, and Fat

Let me summarize my dietary recommendations for various types of oxidizers. Remember that these are just starting points. Even though you may be in a certain category, there is a continuum within each category. As you learn more about what works best for you, the dietary guidelines can be more finely tuned. The basic idea is that you should have the same ratio of protein, carbohydrates, and fat at each meal or snack that specifically optimizes your cellular metabolism. Rather than recommending calorie levels, I've found it is more helpful to talk in terms of types of foods, such as high-protein foods (nuts, seeds, fish) and high-complex-carbohydrate foods (whole grains). The key is not how much you eat or how many total calories you consume, but rather the approximate ratio of high-protein, high-complex-carbohydrate, and fatty foods on your plate. I've taken this approach because, in my experience, most people find it much easier and more practical to work with this ratio in mind than to worry or obsess about total calories. The ratios I recommend for these foods, depending upon what type of oxidizer the individual is, are meant to be starting points. Over time people will fine-tune these ratios for optimal effects. For example, if you're a fast oxidizer, approximately 50 percent of your intake at an average meal should be in the form of high-protein foods. Your total protein intake, depending upon how much food you eat per meal, should be within the norm for active Americans—such as 30 to 70 grams per day. The point I want to emphasize is that a fast oxidizer diet should not provide excessive amounts of protein, which is unhealthy for you, but rather a healthy balance of protein, carbohydrates, and fats.

- If you are balanced midway between being a fast and slow oxidizer, your optimum diet is going to be approximately 45 percent from high-protein foods, 40 percent from high-complex-carbohydrate foods, and 15 to 20 percent from fatty foods.
- The general diet for slow oxidizers is approximately 30 percent from high-protein foods, 55 percent from high-complex-carbohydrate foods, and 10 to 15 percent from fatty foods.
- The general diet for fast oxidizers is approximately 50 percent from high-protein foods, 30 percent from high-complex-carbohydrate foods, and 20 to 25 percent from fatty foods.

Keeping these general guidelines in mind, it is time to switch the emphasis slightly, from theoretical guidelines to practical tips. That is, given your body and metabolism, which foods and dishes should you be looking to emphasize, and which should you minimize? Notice that I'm not saying that you need to totally eliminate any food from your diet. Rather, try to reach a balance within meals and throughout the day, so that your overall diet elevates your mood and supports your long-term health.

Foods for Fast Oxidizers

PROTEINS

Nuts and seeds	Soy protein
Whole food supplements, such as microalgae (chlorella, spirulina), bee pollen, and brewer's yeast	Lentils
	Beans

CARBOHYDRATES

All grains, except wheat	Carrots
Cauliflower	Celery
Asparagus	Avocados
Artichokes	Olives
Spinach	

FRUITS (MINIMAL, AND LOW ON THE GLYCEMIC INDEX)

Apples (especially Granny Smith)	Pears
Peaches	Oranges

JUICES

Carrot (diluted 50/50
  with water)
Beet (diluted 50/50
  with water)

All vegetable
Minimal fruit

FATS

Nuts and seeds
Olive oil
Flaxseed oil
Sesame oil

Hemp seed oil
Borage oil
Walnut oil
Sunflower oil

OTHER FOODS

Mushrooms
Peanuts
Peas

Herbs and spices
Herbal teas
Sea salt

FOODS FOR FAST OXIDIZERS TO AVOID OR MINIMIZE

Sugar, candy
Coffee, tea, soft drinks, alcohol
Table salt
Wheat
Potatoes

White rice
White flour
Dried fruits
Sweet fruits, such as bananas,
  grapes, and dates

Foods for Slow Oxidizers

CARBOHYDRATES

All grains
Beets
Broccoli
Brussels sprouts
Cabbage
Chard
Collard greens
Cucumbers
Eggplant
Hot peppers
Kale

Leeks
Lettuce
Mustard greens
Okra
Onions
Potatoes
Scallions
Sweet peppers
Squash
Yams

FRUITS (ALL RIPE FRUITS)

Apples	Nectarines
Apricots	Oranges
Berries	Pears
Cherries	Plums
Grapefruit	Pineapple
Grapes	Tangerines
Lemons	Melons

JUICES

All fruit juices	All vegetable juices

PROTEINS (MODERATE TO MINIMAL)

Nuts and seeds	Whole food supplements, such as microalgae (chlorella, spirulina), bee pollen, and brewer's yeast

FATS

Nuts and seeds	High-quality vegetable oils, such as flaxseed and sesame

OTHER FOODS

All herbs and spices	Mustard
Herbal teas	Ketchup
Rice milk	Horseradish (no salt)
Soy milk	Vinegar
Honey	Pepper
Maple syrup	Sea salt

FOODS FOR SLOW OXIDIZERS TO AVOID OR MINIMIZE

Sugar, candy	White flour
Coffee, tea, soft drinks, alcohol	White rice
Table salt	

Typical Daily Meals

We'll look at meals and even specific recipes in a minute, but first let me briefly summarize what I think are healthful daily meals for fast and slow oxidizers. Let these daily meal plans serve as general guidelines. If you'd like a more specific plan of menus, refer to the *Depression-Free for Life* menus on page 181 and their recipes.

For Fast Oxidizers

BREAKFAST
Unsweetened yogurt
Orange
2 tablespoons Brewers yeast or other high-quality vegetarian protein

LUNCH
Sautéed vegetables, sea vegetables, and beans with avocado, nuts, or seeds

MIDAFTERNOON SNACK
Nuts or seeds

DINNER
Salad
Sweet potatoes
Lentil or bean soup
1 tablespoon spirulina, tofu, or tempeh

For Slow Oxidizers

BREAKFAST
Whole grain cereal
Banana, pineapple, orange, or apple
Fresh fruit juice

LUNCH
Mixed-grain pasta with steamed vegetables and salad

MIDAFTERNOON SNACK
Fruit

DINNER
Salad
Carrots
Vegetarian entrée

Concentrated Vegetarian High-Quality Protein Sources

Spirulina: gram for gram, spirulina may be the most nutritious, well-rounded food on the planet. It is about 60 percent assimilable protein, containing all the essential amino acids in correct proportions. It also contains the omega-3 and omega-6 essential fatty acids, has 14 times the daily recommended dose of vitamin B_{12} in 100 grams, has seventeen different carotenoids, over 2000 enzymes, and a full spectrum of assimilable minerals. Spirulina also enhances the immune system. It contains about six grams of protein per tablespoon.

Chlorella contains about 65 percent assimilable protein and is more protein-dense than spirulina. It has about 9 grams of protein per tablespoon. It is also high in carotenoids, magnesium, and iron. It is exceptionally good at pulling heavy metals such as mercury, lead, cadmium, uranium, and arsenic out of the body. It also boosts the immune system.

Brewers yeast contains approximately 60 percent protein by weight. One tablespoon yields 8 grams of protein. Yeast is high in the B vitamins, especially B_{12}, magnesium, zinc, copper, chromium, potassium, manganese, selenium, RNA and DNA, and inositol. Because it is high in phosphorous, it is best to get a yeast to which calcium has been added or take a calcium supplement with the yeast.

Bee pollen is a general life enhancer, a potent anti-radiation food, and an immune system enhancer. It contains all the essential amino acids, over 5000 enzymes, vitamins A, B, C, and E, 15 percent lecithin, selenium, calcium, magnesium, vitamin B_{12}, and RNA and DNA. It is about 20 percent protein. It boosts vitality and the immune system. Three heaping teaspoons can supply the minimal daily protein need.

Bee pollen, brewers yeast, spirulina, and chlorella can be taken directly, stirred into a drink, or sprinkled over food. These particular proteins are all easy to absorb.

Those readers who are not prepared to give up all animal protein may substitute 3 ounces of fish or chicken wherever these high-quality vegetarian protein sources are specified in the recipes and meal plans.

Depression-Free for Life Menus

The two following seven-day menus, co-created with the chefs at the Tree of Life Rejuvenation Center, follow the pattern of being somewhat higher in protein for fast oxidizers and higher in carbohydrates for slow oxidizers. Taken together, these two menu plans represent an exciting and healthful cuisine and a sophisticated approach to personalizing your own diet. Each meal reflects a balance of nutrients, and the diet as a whole presents a full spectrum of international tastes, including American, Mexican, Italian, Middle Eastern, Greek, Nepalese, Turkish, French, Japanese, Chinese, and Italian. The dishes in boldface denote the recipes that follow, while all of the others are popular dishes with recipes readily found in many natural food cookbooks. In a few cases I recommend a specific dressing or sauce with an entrée or salads, but most are listed merely "with dressing." Choose from any of the half-dozen recipes provided in the dressings and sauces section. This menu is vegetarian, but you can substitute high-protein foods such as fish for the protein portion of the meal. Fast oxidizers can take somewhat larger portions of such protein foods, especially at lunch and dinner, compared to slow oxidizers.

The Depression-Free for Life Seven-Day Menu for Fast Oxidizers

■ ■ ■ ■

BREAKFAST	LUNCH	DINNER
DAY 1		
Buckwheat Granola with blanched soaked almonds	**Yam Burger with dressing** **Mixed Greens and Sprout Salad with dressing**	Pea Soup **"Spanakopita"** Salad with dressing and ¼ cup nuts or seeds
DAY 2		
Date Oatmeal Porridge with ½–1 cup soaked sunflower seeds	Veggie Burger Salad with dressing Nuts and Seeds	**Minestrone Soup** Pizza **Mixed Greens and Sprout Salad with dressing**

DAY 3

Tree of Life Seven-Fruit Haroset
1 tablespoon bee pollen

Almond "Falafel" sandwich
Mixed Greens and Sprout Salad with dressing

Spinach-Avocado Salad with ¼ cup walnuts
"Tabouli"
Spicy Corn Soup
Daikon Ginger Salad with dressing with ⅓ cup almonds

DAY 4

Lassi
Bagel with Nut Butter
Bowl of Fruit
1 tablespoon of bee pollen

Nori Rolls
Spinach Avocado Salad with dressing
1 tablespoon of spirulina

Raita
Salad with Tahini Apple dressing

DAY 5

Buckwheat Granola
1 piece of fruit
1 tablespoon brewers yeast

Yam Burgers
Daikon Ginger Salad with tahini dressing

Sun Squash Soup
Festive Wild Rice with ⅓ cup soaked sunflower seeds
Salad with dressing

DAY 6

Curry Apple Sunflax Drink

Kimchee Delight
Mixed Greens and Sprout Salad with dressing
1 tablesoon chlorella

Minestrone Soup
Spaghetti
Salad with dressing and ¼ cup soaked sunflower and pumpkin seeds

DAY 7

Granola
1 tablespoon brewers yeast

Almond Hummus Sandwich on Whole-Grain Bread
Steamed Vegetables

Spicy Corn Soup
Tempeh "Steak"
Mixed Greens and Sprout Salad with sweet dill dressing

The Depression-Free for Life Seven-Day
Menu for Slow Oxidizers

■ ■ ■ ■

BREAKFAST	LUNCH	DINNER
DAY 1		
Oatmeal	Pasta with Pesto	**Heavenly Garden**
Bagel	**Mixed Greens and**	**Soup**
Bowl of Fruit	**Sprout Salad with**	Salad with dressing
	dressing	
DAY 2		
Bowl of Fruit	**Nori Rolls**	**Raita**
	Mixed Greens and	**Carrot Hijiki**
	Sprout Salad with	**Salad**
	dressing	
DAY 3		
Whole Grain Pancakes	**"Tabouli"**	Whole Wheat Pasta
Bowl of Fruit	**Salad with Apple**	Greek Salad with
	Cinnamon Nut	dressing
	Sauce	
DAY 4		
Whole-Grain Bread	Vegetable Quiche	**Minestrone Soup**
with Honey or Jam	Pasta Salad	Salad with Red Top
Bowl of Fruit	**Spanish Salsa**	Salad Dressing
	Dressing	Festive Wild Rice
DAY 5		
Wheat Treat Cereal	Lasagne	**Sun Squash Soup**
Bowl of Fruit	**Salad with Red Top**	Whole-Grain Burger
	Salad Dressing	**Daikon Ginger Salad**
		with Italian dressing
DAY 6		
Date Oatmeal Porridge	**"Spanakopita"**	Broccoli Soup
Bowl of Fruit	**Salad with Tahini**	**Mixed Greens and**
	Apple Dressing	**Sprout Salad with**
		Creamy Miso
		Dressing
		Corn on the Cob

DAY 7

Buckwheat Granola   **Yam Burger**   **Heavenly Garden**
Bowl of Fruit   Sweet Potato Chips   **Soup**
                               Mixed Greens and   **Daikon Ginger**
                                 Sprout Salad with   **Salad with sweet**
                                 dressing   **dill dressing**

To find the best combination of foods and recipes for your particular body and lifestyle, you need to be willing to experiment with these menu guidelines. In my experience, most people do much better on a basically vegetarian diet than they do when they derive most of their protein and fat from animal foods. I realize that this is a difficult step from most people. As a meat-eating football player from the Midwest, I grew up without meeting a single vegetarian until I was in my late twenties. Even after I began to accept the physical and mental advantages of vegetarianism, I took a number of years to make a full transition to vegetarianism. It's usually easier with the support of friends and family, and taking incremental steps such as first giving up red meat. Making idealistic yet drastic changes often creates imbalances.

Depression-Free for Life Recipes

What follows are thirty of my favorite recipes, all of which are flexible enough to serve various individuals' needs. You can use the lists of foods for fast and slow oxidizers (pages 176–179), as well as your own taste preferences, to substitute ingredients and adjust these recipes to your personal situation.

First, a few general comments. I recommend always using organic produce—the fresher the better. Garden fresh, which is what we have at the Tree of Life Rejuvenation Center, is ideal. High-quality organic produce, however, is available through whole food stores, farmers' markets, co-ops, mail order, and in some grocery stores. Although organic produce is generally more expensive than commercially grown produce, it is significantly higher in its content of vitamins, minerals, trace elements, enzymes, and other nutrients. In addition to avoiding the detrimental effects of pesticides, irradiation, and produce waxes, you actually get a lot more nutrition for your money.

In order to reap the benefits of all the enzymes in your food, I recommend using fresh juices, ideally within one hour of juicing.

Soaking and Sprouting Guidelines

At the Tree of Life Rejuvenation Center, all of the nuts, seeds, and grains used are sprouted and/or soaked. The recipes included here also use these techniques. If you are just beginning your transition to a primarily vegetarian diet, this may seem like a lot of trouble. Yet soaking and sprouting are wonderful ways to optimize the vitality and nutrient content of grains, nuts, and seeds. During the soaking and sprouting process, nutrients break down into simpler compounds, making digestion and assimilation much more efficient.

We are including basic instructions for soaking and sprouting here, but if you are not yet prepared to make the extra effort, you can still derive enormous benefit from following the general guidelines in this chapter. Simply follow the typical daily meal plans given on pages 181–184, using your own recipes or recipes from any good vegetarian cookbook.

Soaking Instructions

1. Fill a glass or ceramic container half full with nuts, seeds, or grains.
2. Fill the container with water and soak a minimum of 6 hours or overnight.
3. Rinse with fresh water several times (using a small strainer or colander if necessary) and use in the recipe. You can store the soaked food in the refrigerator for up to 2 days.

Unless otherwise noted, all nuts, seeds, and grains should be drained after soaking before being used in recipes.

Sprouting Instructions

Soak first before sprouting for the time specified, following the general guidelines above.

Wheatberries. Soak 1 cup wheatberries in warm water 6 hours or overnight before sprouting. The grains will sprout in 2 to 3 days and are ready for eating when the shoot is ¼ to ½ inch long.

Quinoa. Soak ⅓ cup quinoa in warm water 2 to 4 hours before sprouting. The grains will sprout in 1 to 4 days and are ready for eating when the shoot is ¼ to 1 inch long.

Alfalfa. Soak 2 tablespoons seeds in cool water 3 to 6 hours before sprouting. Sprouts will appear in 7 days and are ready for eating when 1½ to 2 inches long.

Clover. Soak 2 tablespoons seeds in cool water for 3 to 6 hours before sprouting. Sprouts will appear in 6 days and are ready to eat when 1½ to 2 inches long.

To sprout:

1. Place soaked, drained grains or seeds in a glass jar with a fine-mesh screen secured over the top with a rubber band.
2. Place the jar in a dark place for 24 hours, then expose to indirect sunlight.
3. Rinse the sprouts 2 to 3 times a day by filling the jar with water and lightly swishing and draining with the screen in place. For proper drainage, store the jar upside down at an angle of 50 to 70 degrees (an angled dish rack works well).
4. When sprouts reach their specified length (see above), store in the refrigerator to slow growth and preserve freshness.

The following recipes are for breakfast dishes, entrées, salads, soups, and dressings and sauces, enough for two to four persons.

Breakfast Dishes

Tree of Life Seven-Fruit Haroset

1 cup shredded coconut
1 cup walnuts and almonds, soaked, drained, and chopped (see page 185)
1 cup raisins, soaked for ½ hour in warm water and drained
1 cup chopped apples
½ cup chopped pears
¼ cup prunes, soaked for ½ hour in warm water, drained, and chopped
2 tablespoons raw honey
1 tablespoon cinnamon
Zest of ½ lemon, grated
Fresh grape juice

In a bowl, combine all ingredients except for the grape juice and mix well with a spoon. Add the grape juice and stir until the mixture reaches the desired consistency.

Curry Apple Sunflax Drink

1 cup fresh apple juice
½ cup sunflower seeds, soaked (see page 185)
1 tablespoon flaxseeds, soaked (see page 185)
½ teaspoon curry powder

Combine all ingredients in a blender or food processor. Blend until smooth. (Adding 1 garlic clove or ½ teaspoon sun-dried garlic "heats up" this drink for the winter months.)

Wheat Treat Cereal

1 apple, shredded
1 cup wheatberries, sprouted (see page 185)
¼ cup raisins, soaked for ½ hour in warm water and drained
2 teaspoons raw maple syrup
½ teaspoon cinnamon
½ teaspoon grated nutmeg

In a bowl, combine the ingredients and mix with a spoon. Serve.

Lassi

½ cup low-fat yogurt of your choice
1 ripe banana, mango, or slice of papaya
¼ cup fresh mint or 1 tablespoon dried mint leaves
2 dates, soaked for ½ hour in warm water, drained, and pitted
Ginger to taste
1½ cups water

Combine all the ingredients in a blender or a food processor. Blend until smooth and enjoy.

Buckwheat Granola

½ cup seeds and nuts of your choice, soaked (see page 185)
1 cup wheatberries, sprouted (see page 185)
¼ cup raisins, soaked for ½ hour in warm water and drained
1 apple, chopped
5 dates, soaked for ½ hour in warm water, pitted, and chopped
½ tablespoon cinnamon

Preheat the oven to 250°F. Place the seeds and nuts in a food processor and grind into chunks. Add the wheatberries and remaining ingredients and mix with a spoon. Serve plain or with low-fat milk.

Date Oatmeal Porridge

1½ cups oat groats, soaked (see page 185)
½ cup dates, soaked for ½ hour in warm water
¾ cup date soak water
½ teaspoon cinnamon
½ teaspoon grated nutmeg

Combine all ingredients in a blender or food processor. Blend and serve warm if desired.

Entrées

Yam Burgers

4 cups grated yams
4 cups sunflower seeds, soaked (see page 185)
2 cups chopped celery
1 tablespoon oregano
1 tablespoon Celtic salt

Preheat the oven to 350°F. In a food processor using an S blade, blend all ingredients to make a paste. Scoop out individual portions, shape into patties, and place on a baking tray. Bake for 30 minutes, then grill. Cook 5 minutes per side over medium heat and serve with your favorite spread or sauce.

Almond "Falafel"

3 cups almonds, soaked (see page 185)
⅓ cup tahini
¼ cup ground sesame seeds
¼ cup lemon juice
¼ cup chopped cilantro
¼ cup chopped parsley
2 tablespoons cumin seed, soaked (see page 185)
Celtic salt to taste
Pita for serving

Preheat the oven to 275°F. Blanch the soaked almonds by placing in boiled water for 15 to 20 seconds. Rinse in cool water and remove the skins. Use a high-quality juicer to homogenize all the ingredients. Shape into round disks, patties, or balls and place on baking trays. Bake for 35 minutes. Turn and bake for an additional 10 minutes. Serve as appetizers or as a sandwich with chopped tomatoes and onions in whole wheat pita.

Kimchee Delight

Juice of 5 carrots
1 tablespoon cumin seed, soaked
½ teaspoon cayenne
1 teaspoon ground dried red pepper
1 teaspoon light miso
Juice of 1 head green or red cabbage
1 head green or red cabbage, chopped
5 carrots, chopped
¼ cup grated fresh ginger
2 garlic cloves, finely chopped

In a blender or food processor, blend the carrot juice, cumin seed, cayenne, red pepper, and miso. Add the remaining ingredients and mix with a spoon. Pour the mixture into a jar. Be sure that the vegetables are well covered by the juice. Cover the jar by placing several cabbage leaves on top. Place a weight on top of the cabbage leaves and leave to ferment for 3 to 4 days in the refrigerator.

"Spanakopita"

1 ripe avocado
4 cups chopped spinach
2 tablespoons lemon juice
2 tablespoons tamari sauce or 1 teaspoon Celtic salt
1 teaspoon dried dill weed or ¼ cup fresh dill
¼ teaspoon grated nutmeg
Additional spinach leaves for wrapping

Preheat the oven to 300°F. Scoop out the flesh of the avocado and combine with all the remaining ingredients (except spinach for wrapping) in a food processor bowl and process until smooth. Spoon 2 tablespoons of the mixture into each spinach leaf. Roll up the leaves and place on a baking sheet. Bake for 35 minutes, or until the spinach wrap is flaky. Serve warm.

"Tabouli"

1 tablespoon light miso
1 tablespoon virgin olive oil
1 cup quinoa, sprouted (see page 185)
1 small bunch kale, chopped
3 ripe tomatoes, chopped
4 fresh basil stalks
1 garlic clove
Juice of 1 lemon

In a bowl, mix together the miso and olive oil. Add the remaining ingredients and mix well.

Festive Wild Rice

1 cup raw black long-grain wild rice
¼ cup diced red pepper
¼ cup fresh corn kernels
1 teaspoon virgin olive oil
1 teaspoon paprika
1 teaspoon chili powder

Cook the wild rice according to the package directions. Then mix with the remaining ingredients and serve.

Nori Rolls

4 cups sunflower seeds, soaked (see page 185)
2 tablespoons lemon juice
4 raw nori sheets
3 carrots, shredded
2 zucchini, shredded
1 beet, shredded
½ head cabbage, thinly sliced
2 tablespoons light miso
2 tablespoons umeboshi (Japanese pickled plum) paste
Pickled ginger cut into thin strips
Wasabi (Japanese horseradish; optional)
Tamari (optional)

Place the sunflower seeds and lemon juice in a food processor bowl and process until you've created a very thick paste, stopping the processor periodically to scrape the sides of the bowl. Spread approximately ½ cup of sunflower paste onto the rough side of each nori sheet, covering half of each sheet. Place the shredded vegetables over the sunflower paste. Smear a small amount of miso and umeboshi paste on the unfilled portion of the nori. Roll up tightly and seal by rubbing miso along the edge and/or by applying a little water with your fingertips along the edge of the nori sheet. Cut into ½-inch cylinders. Serve with wasabi and tamari as condiments, if desired.

Almond Hummus

2½ *cups almonds, soaked (see page 185)*
3 *tablespoons tahini or* ½ *cup sesame oil*
2 *garlic cloves*
Juice of 1 lemon
Cayenne to taste
Celtic salt to taste
Pita or crackers for serving

Blanch the soaked almonds by placing in boiled water for 15 to 20 seconds. Rinse in cool water and remove the skins. Place all the ingredients in a food processor and process until smooth. (For maximum thickness, run the almonds and garlic through a juicer before processing, then proceed as above.) Serve as a sandwich spread on whole wheat pita or as a dip with vegetables or whole-grain crackers.

Salads

Mixed Greens and Sprout Salad

4 *romaine lettuce leaves*
4 *butter lettuce leaves*
4 *red leaf lettuce leaves*
4 *arugula leaves*
1 *tomato, chopped*
1 *cup mixed alfalfa and clover sprouts*
½ *cup chopped parsley*
⅓ *cup dressing of your choice*
1 *avocado, sliced*

Tear the lettuces and arugula into bite-size pieces and place in a bowl. Add the tomato, sprouts, and parsley and toss with the dressing. Garnish with the sliced avocado and a sprig of parsley and serve. Alfalfa and clover sprouts can be purchased at health food and organic food markets, or you can grow your own according to the instructions on page 186.

Carrot Hijiki Salad

½ *avocado, sliced*
¼ *teaspoon cayenne*
Juice of 1 lemon plus water to equal ½ *cup liquid*
1 handful of alfalfa sprouts (follow the instructions on page 186 to grow
    your own, or purchase at a health food or organic food market)
1 red bell pepper, cut into strips
3 carrots, grated
¼ *cup hijiki (a dark brown sea vegetable), soaked*
½ *cup pine nuts, soaked (see page 185)*

In a blender or food processor, blend the avocado, cayenne, and diluted lemon juice to create a dressing. Line your salad bowl with the sprouts and place the bell pepper, carrots, hijiki, and pine nuts on top. Pour on the dressing and serve.

Daikon Ginger Salad

¼ *cup finely grated ginger*
¼ *teaspoon cayenne*
⅓ *cup lemon juice*
1 daikon (Japanese radish), grated

In a bowl, combine the grated ginger, cayenne, and lemon juice and marinate at room temperature for several hours. Pour the marinade over the daikon and serve.

Spinach Avocado Salad

1 bunch spinach
1 tomato, diced
1 handful of alfalfa sprouts (follow the instructions on page 186 to grow
   your own, or purchase at a health food or organic food market)
¼ cup dulse (a reddish-purple sea vegetable), soaked ½ hour in warm
   water and drained
⅓ cup dressing of your choice
1 avocado, sliced

In a bowl, combine all the ingredients, except the avocado, and toss with
the dressing. Garnish with the sliced avocado and serve.

Soups

Minestrone Soup

1 cup chopped carrot
1 cup chopped celery
½ cup chopped zucchini
2 cups chopped tomatoes
1 cup each of the following vegetables, chopped: carrot, zucchini, broccoli,
   green beans, corn, spinach
¾ cup chopped celery
¼ cup minced parsley
⅛ cup virgin olive oil
1 teaspoon dried basil
½ teaspoon dried oregano
¼ teaspoon dried rosemary
1 bay leaf
½ garlic clove, minced
Celtic salt and pepper to taste

Soak the carrot, celery, and zucchini in 4 cups of water overnight. Blend
in a blender or food processor and strain. Set aside. Combine the remaining ingredients with the broth in a blender or food processor. Process for
15 to 30 seconds, being sure to maintain a chunky quality. Heat if desired
before serving, but don't boil. This soup is also good chilled.

Three Carrot Soup

3 carrots, diced
1 avocado, sliced into chunks
1 cup fresh carrot juice
1 teaspoon cumin

Combine all ingredients in a blender or food processor, blend, and serve chilled.

Spicy Corn Soup

2 cups water
Kernels from 3 fresh corncobs
1 hot red pepper
2 tablespoons dulse (see page 194), soaked
½ teaspoon fresh ginger juice

Heat the water to warm but below a simmer. Blend in the other ingredients and serve warm or hot.

Sun Squash Soup

1 medium yellow crookneck or other summer squash, cut into cubes
1 cup alfalfa sprouts (follow the instructions on page 186 to grow your own, or purchase at a health food or organic food market)
¼ cup sunflower seeds, soaked (see page 185)
2 tablespoons apple cider vinegar
1 tablespoon flaxseeds, soaked(see page 185)
1 teaspoon dried basil
1 garlic clove or ½ teaspoon sun-dried garlic
1 cup water

Combine all the ingredients in a blender or food processor. Blend until smooth, adding more water if necessary, until reaching the desired consistency. Serve hot or at room temperature.

Heavenly Garden Soup

2 quarts water
1 sweet potato, chopped
1 yam, chopped
1 purple potato, chopped
1 Yellow Finn potato, chopped
2 carrots, chopped
1 stalk celery, chopped
¼ purple cabbage, chopped
¼ green cabbage, chopped
¼ head cauliflower, chopped
⅛ bunch spinach, chopped
Handful of shiitake mushrooms, chopped
½ clove garlic, chopped
¼ tablespoon dill
¼ teaspoon basil
⅛ teaspoon grated ginger
⅛ bunch cilantro, chopped
3 tablespoons light miso

Heat the water. Add all the ingredients except for the cilantro and miso. Simmer for 3 to 4 hours, adding the cilantro during the last 30 minutes. When the soup is ready, remove ½ cup of broth, add the miso, stir, and mix back into the soup. Then remove 1 cup of soup mixture (with vegetables). Blend in a food processor or blender and stir back into the soup. Serve hot.

Raita

1 cup plain yogurt
¼ cup chopped mint
¼ cup chopped cilantro
1 teaspoon cumin
1 teaspoon coriander
1 teaspoon mustard seed, soaked (see page 185)
Juice of 1 lemon
Grated ginger, Celtic salt, and cayenne to taste
2 cups water
2 cups each of cauliflower, broccoli, cucumber, and zucchini, chopped
1 large tomato, chopped

In a blender or food processor, blend all the ingredients except the chopped vegetables until smooth. Add the vegetables, stir, and serve chilled or at room temperature.

Dressings and Sauces

Apple Cinnamon Nut Sauce

2 cups almonds, soaked (see page 185)
2 cups diced apples
2 cups raisin soak water (soak 1 cup raisins in 2 cups warm water for
  ½ hour and reserve raisins for another use)
1 tablespoon cinnamon
Additional water as needed

Blanch the soaked almonds by placing in boiled water for 15 to 20 seconds. Rinse in cool water and remove the skins. Combine the ingredients in a food processor or blender. Blend, adding more water if needed to achieve the desired consistency.

Zucchini Sun Dressing

1 cup chopped zucchini
1 cup fresh apple juice
½ cup sunflower seeds, soaked (see page 185)
1 tablespoon flaxseeds, soaked (see page 185)
1½ teaspoons dried dill

Combine the ingredients in a food processor or blender. Blend and serve.

Red Top Salad Dressing

1 cup carrot juice
½ red bell pepper, chopped
2 tablespoons flaxseeds, soaked (see page 185)
¼ teaspoon cayenne

Combine the ingredients in a food processor or blender. Blend until smooth and serve.

Creamy Miso Dressing

¼ cup flaxseed oil
2 tablespoons lemon juice
1 tablespoon light miso
¼ cup water

Combine the ingredients in a food processor or blender. Blend until smooth and creamy and serve.

Tahini Apple Dressing

⅓ cup fresh apple juice
2 tablespoons apple cider vinegar
1 tablespoon tahini
½ teaspoon black pepper
½ teaspoon curry powder

Combine the ingredients in a food processor or blender. Blend and serve.

Spanish Salsa Dressing

½ cup pumpkin or sunflower seeds, soaked (see page 185)
½ cup apple cider vinegar
½ cup chopped cilantro
3 medium tomatoes, chopped
1 clove garlic
¼ teaspoon cayenne or to taste

Combine all ingredients except for the cilantro in a food processor or blender. Process until smooth. Add the cilantro, mix well, and serve. This flavorful dressing is good in the fall but can be used in any season. In the summer, increase the cilantro and decrease the cayenne.

Making the Transition

You need both common sense and a flexible approach to create an individualized diet. In his efforts to develop an appropriate diet for himself, Gandhi made one shift every four months. Often a change in diet or lifestyle may feel good the first week, but may not be so good for you after several months. For example, I have treated many people with hypoglycemia who told me that in the past they had felt much better in the first few weeks from eating a high-protein diet. But they also reported that after a number of months, they began to feel worse. That's because it takes a couple of months to experience the toxic load of a diet that is high in animal protein. (Concentrated animal proteins have a high nitrogen content that prevents them from being "cleanly burned" in the body. The nitrogen is metabolized into uric acid, which has a toxic effect when an excess builds up in bodily tissues.) A better long-term solution for hypoglycemia is to eat a healthful, primarily vegetarian diet that is rich in complex carbohydrates for slow oxidizers or high in vegetable protein for fast oxidizers.

9

Step Five: Eight Lifestyle Choices You Can Make to Help Beat Depression

Depression is a multidimensional condition. It affects various aspects of your health, and in turn the choices you make on a daily basis about how you live your life can affect your depression. For most people, merely taking an amino acid supplement every day is helpful, but not as powerful as various lifestyle changes that can dramatically alter your depression. Your everyday actions and your interactions with those around you deeply affect body and mind and ultimately determine whether you can attain a state in which you feel love for yourself, others, and the world. Exercise, relationships, family, relaxation, and other prominent mood-elevating lifestyle choices are crucial factors in the success of your depression-busting efforts. Let me show you what I mean by introducing you to Joe.

Joe is thirty-one and lives alone. He commutes to work on congested freeways, typically taking almost an hour to travel about twenty miles. During his time in the car he listens to an all-news station that presents the usual morbid headlines from around the world. He works at a desk job, hunched over a computer console. The job doesn't challenge him and he is overqualified for it, considering his education and prior work experience. He needs to drink coffee throughout the day to stay alert and motivated. Joe stays at his job because "the money is decent." When he gets home he's often too tired to prepare a healthful meal. Instead he throws a prepared dinner in the microwave. After having a few drinks with dinner, he's too tired to make it to the gym or even to take a walk around the block. So he lounges in front of the television for hours at a time, watching sit-coms and sporting events. He needs another drink or two before bed to offset his all-day caffeine jag and help him to fall asleep.

On the weekends Joe may go to a movie but he has few outside interests and no creative hobbies that engage him. Joe's main connection to nature is mowing his lawn, which he has regularly treated with pesticides to keep it artificially green. His family is distant; he keeps in touch intermittently by phone. His main activity with the few friends he's made at work is to go out drinking with them occasionally. His sex life is mostly solo. The last massage he had was of the adult variety and lasted twelve minutes. He'll tell you he believes in God if you ask him but he neither attends church nor practices any form of spiritual endeavor.

Joe isn't a real person—or at least he's no one I know. Rather, he's a caricature I've created to demonstrate someone whose lifestyle violates virtually every commonsense rule for maintaining emotional wellness. Joe fails to

1. exercise or stay physically active
2. stay connected to close friends and family
3. have a creative outlet
4. cultivate a sense of humor
5. breathe right
6. sleep well
7. relax in a mindful manner
8. touch and be touched in a nurturing way

If Joe were a real patient of mine, no matter how many nutritional supplements or dietary adjustments I prescribed, I doubt Joe would ever begin to realize his full emotional health until he had also addressed at least a few of these eight crucial lifestyle factors that were in all likelihood contributing to an undiagnosed depression.

Joe's example should also serve as a warning to health care practitioners that a truly holistic program must avoid falling into the one-dimensional view of depression typical of some drug-only therapies. Substituting amino acids and vitamins for Prozac is only a partial answer.

Move That Body

More than 100 studies conducted in the past decade have proven a close connection between regular physical exertion, increased bodily levels of biochemicals such as serotonin and endorphins, and antidepressant and antianxiety effects. The mood-enhancing effects of exercise seem to be even more pronounced for people suffering from various forms of depression than for average persons. Some studies suggest that exercise alone is enough to alleviate many cases of depression:

- A 1996 review of two decades of studies concluded that "these studies suggest that both clinical and nonclinical subjects may benefit acutely from even a single bout of exercise."
- Even people who exercise relatively infrequently benefit. A 1993 study done on women who took aerobic classes found that both high- and low-frequency exercisers experienced significant mood enhancement after taking a class.
- A 1993 study on the effects of aerobic exercise on the mood of adult women found that it provided significant beneficial effects whether performed in the morning or the evening, that it boosted all dimensions of mood, and that benefits persisted (mood scores had not fully regressed to pre-exercise levels 24 hours later).
- According to a 1996 study, exercise can cancel some of the adverse effects on mood caused by beta blockers, drugs widely used to help treat heart disorders. The researchers determined that the tension, depression, and "total mood disturbance" caused by two beta blockers were all reduced by exercise.
- Regular runners have increased positive mood and decreased negative mood after a three-mile run, according to a 1994 study. Women experienced greater improvements in mood than men.
- Jogging can help prevent the increase in depression and the overall deterioration of mental well-being common during the winter months, especially among women, according to a 1991 study.

While almost all of the studies have focused on the effects of exercise, I like to emphasize to my patients that exercise need not be intense and aerobic to benefit mood. In fact, any type of physical exertion or activity can be beneficial. For example, a 1988 study that compared single sessions of high- and low-intensity exercise found that high-intensity aerobic sessions led to increases in tension/anxiety and fatigue. On the other hand, the low-intensity exercise led to positive mood changes and an increase in vigor and exhilaration. And two studies published in early 1999 in the same issue of the *Journal of the American Medical Association* have confirmed that staying physically active in your everyday life can be just as beneficial to body, mind, and mood as regular workouts at the health club.

These two studies deserve attention because they were both long-term and well-controlled. One compared two exercise approaches among forty obese, middle-aged women for sixty-eight weeks. The first group was assigned to a vigorous sixteen-week aerobic exercise program, with forty-five-minute sessions using stepping-platform exercises and similar routines. The second group attended a four-month class in how to become more active in their everyday lives, by looking, for example, for more opportunities to walk, climb stairs, and do household chores. Both groups followed a similar low-calorie diet. Guess what? At the end of the four months, both groups had lost the same amount of weight, about seventeen pounds. Not only that, but after a year the "lifestyle exercisers" had done better than the aerobics group in keeping the lost weight off.

The other study had similar results. It looked at the effects of two strategies among 235 previously sedentary men and women. One group took classes on how to stay active for at least thirty minutes per day. The other group got six months of intensive gym workouts on treadmills, stair climbers, and the like. After two years the researchers found similar benefits among both groups in terms of improvements in mood, blood pressure, cardiovascular fitness, body fat, and other measurements of health status.

I think that it is unfortunate that the distinction between exercise and physical activity has grown in recent years. Many people give little thought to how they might increase their fitness in ways that don't involve aerobics classes, exercise machines, or spending money. Until fairly recently, "exercising" was built into life. Nowadays it is something that occurs only at the health club, or in the daily jog around the local track. Meanwhile, as many as 60 percent of Americans are almost totally sedentary, and perhaps as few as 10 percent actually make it to the gym two to three times per week. And most Americans no longer even have to get up from the couch to change the television channel—which is especially disheartening because the average American watches television four to five hours every day of the week!

The result of the lack of physical activity is seen not only in a high rate of heart disease and other physical ailments but in high rates of depression as well. Physical activity or exercise can enhance the metabolism of fats, help suppress appetite, and lead to increased resting metabolic rate for some time afterward, thus promoting optimal body weight. Staying active also promotes relief from stress.

Many of my patients offer similar reasons for why they've become what one of them referred to as a "slouch potato." These reasons are often along the lines of "exercise is boring," "I'm so fat, so old, I'll never be able to do enough exercise to make a difference," and "I don't have time." Here's what I say to these objections.

If you find exercise boring, don't exercise. But wait—don't expect me to recommend those machines that promise washboard abs by convulsing your stomach muscles with tiny currents of electricity. You don't have to exercise, but if you don't exercise, you do have to play some sport, dance, or stay physically active in your everyday life.

If you think you can never get enough physical activity to make a difference, I disagree. Various studies have found that some activity promotes better health than no activity. There's no threshold—even people who take an occasional brisk walk live longer and happier lives than those who are sedentary. Any movement is better than no movement.

If time is your major concern, keep in mind that it's possible to expend much more energy going about your everyday activities than from exercising for an isolated period of time during the day. Plenty of ways exist to help stay fit by integrating physical activity into your daily life. For example, if you're a homeowner, I don't have to tell you that you have plenty of opportunities to stay active year-round without ever setting foot in the health club. You can get a tremendous whole-body workout by raking, shoveling, sweeping, and the like. Even in the kitchen, limit your use of physical-activity-preventing (also known as "labor-saving") devices. Do you really need to use a food processor to chop vegetables or knead bread?

You can also try to walk more frequently, whether it is to shops, work, or the local library. Even a short walk can invigorate mind and body. Leave a little earlier in the morning for your commute to work. Get off the train or subway a stop or two before your exit and walk the rest of the way. If you drive, park some blocks away and walk. Vertical walking, otherwise known as climbing stairs, is also a great workout. Unless the building is a skyscraper, avoid the elevator or escalator in favor of the stairwell. My conclusion from reading many of the studies done on walking and exercising is that walking briskly four times per week for thirty to forty minutes will give you 90 percent of the benefits of an Olympic workout schedule. I especially like walking in parks because it invigorates mind and body as well as exposing you to the healing effects of being in nature—you breathe fresh air, and you can get the thirty minutes or so of beneficial natural sunlight you need every day. Walking doesn't cost anything and it comes naturally—it's what the body is designed to do.

Of course, for many people a third option is much more attractive than either exercise or increasing your daily physical activity: playing a sport regularly. Find one that's appropriate for your body and temperament, or take up one like tennis that virtually anyone can learn with some practice.

If you really want to be sure 'of keeping the blues at bay, you'll do a little of each of these three things. Exercise, if only by walking, at least twice a week; stay a little more physically active in your everyday life; and play a sport at least twice a week.

Stay Connected

Numerous studies have tied close personal relationships and a viable social network to overall health. A long-term study of American adults even found that it was easier to predict how long a person would live by looking at the strength of his or her social networks than by looking at the state of the person's health. Loneliness and social isolation suppress the immune system, lead to chronic stress, and increase your risk of depression as well as heart attack, chronic pain, and debilitating diseases.

As a psychiatrist, it was not at all a surprise to me when I read recently that two in five married adults describe themselves as very happy, compared to only one in four of those who never married and one in eight of those who are divorced. Partners and family are a close corollary to the issue of social networks. In fact, your family is your most intimate and your most important social network. Yet families today face tremendous challenges as the opportunities for mobility and relocation rise. Both parents are now often working and thus out of the home much of the day. Young adults leave home to go to college and never return. Grandparents retire to warmer climates. Large extended families of three or four generations, including cousins and in-laws and all the rest, living in close proximity to each other are now rare, and with one in two marriages ending in divorce, even immediate families are nowadays often scattered across the country and even around the world.

Depressed people are at a double disadvantage. Their condition can often be dramatically helped if they have the support of other people. Yet their symptoms of hopelessness, anger, and sadness can be off-putting to others. Friends start to avoid them, the person is further depressed by the exclusion, and a vicious cycle of withdrawal and isolation begins.

Researchers have developed scales for measuring social networks and social support, and dozens of recent studies have begun to confirm the link between social support, social networks, and mood disorders. Studies have been conducted on African-American men and women aged sixty years or older, Korean immigrants in the United States, Norwegian men and women with symptomatic heart failure, noninstitutionalized older adults in France, and many other groups. Contact with and support from family members and close friends typically leads to fewer symptoms of depression and other mood disorders.

Other studies have tied marital status and close personal relations to depression. For example, a 1994 study of 115 patients during the first twelve weeks of cognitive-behavioral therapy for depression found that depressed married people were more likely to improve with treatment. This study also suggested chronic, low-level depression was more likely than major depression to be strongly associated with interpersonal problems.

Do you have the types of strong social and family connections you need to maintain an optimal mood? Consider how many of the following questions you answer "yes" to.

- Do you have a special person who is available when you feel in need?
- Do you get the emotional help and support you need from family and friends?
- Can you count on your friends when things go wrong?
- Can you talk about your problems with family and friends?
- Do you have special friends with whom you can share your joys and sorrows?

If you answer "yes" to only one or two of these questions, it is quite likely that your social isolation is contributing to your lingering depression. Intimate personal relations and a strong social network don't happen by accident. You need to constantly be considering how you can cultivate both close friends and casual acquaintances.

- Don't forget how to listen. Friends can easily be scared away by depressed persons who always want to talk about their depression. Many people cannot help but absorb some of this sorrow, which is often consoling to the depressed person but can be draining for the friend. Only the truly compassionate (or clinically intrigued) will keep coming back for more. Friendships are a two-way street.

- Keep up the activities and interests you've shared with friends. Even if this involves just going out to lunch once a week, the connection can often provide long-term benefits.

- Find a special partner with whom you can openly and freely share your thoughts, feelings, and desires. Even a difficult close relationship, unless one of the partners is abusive, can benefit mood over the long term.

- If you work at home, you have to take special steps to make sure you stay involved and avoid social isolation. Look for opportunities to extend your network of friends and coworkers through involvement in sports teams, professional or trade associations, your church or synagogue, and other outlets. Volunteering for community organizations, political parties, and the like can help you make friends and can also boost your self-esteem and mood.

- Buy a friend. An animal friend, that is. Owning a pet can relieve isolation and reduce anxiety and depression.

Developing a greater sense of family and deepening your relationship with a spouse or partner are lifelong activities. Many seemingly minor activities—staying in contact with family members through letters, phone calls, or e-mail; taking weekend-long joint vacations; setting aside face-to-face time to equitably work out conflicts—can go a long way toward renewing bonds and restoring closeness.

Find a Creative Outlet

An unfortunate archetype exists of the genius or the artist tortured by his or her creativity and falling into a self-destructive cycle of depression and suicide. Some elements of this archetype do seem to have a basis in reality. From Van Gogh to Hemingway, examples abound of creativity coexisting with depression.

I think it is fair to ask, however, whether this is the norm. A number of studies have attempted to examine the connection and have found that indeed visual artists and creative writers do seem to be more likely than other people to suffer from pathological personalities and high rates of depression and alcoholism. One researcher attributed this to "differences in the nature and intensity of their emotional imagination." This does not mean, however, that creativity itself has some adverse effects on mood. In my opinion, and in the opinion of many psychological counselors who have successfully used painting and other creative arts as a part of the treatment of depression, quite the opposite is true. That is, the passion, intensity of purpose, and self-confidence that accompany creativity are powerful antidotes to depression.

The act of creation, whether it be at the highest level of artistic endeavor or expressed at more mundane everyday levels, can bolster your self-esteem and connect you to your highest self. Creative therapies for the treatment of depression may "reactivate the nondominant sphere of the brain," according to one researcher, thus serving "to open up to the patient new perspectives for the solution of the problems that drive him into depression." Another study concluded that persons who are both schizophrenic and depressed can most benefit "from therapy that involves them socially in creative and physical activities."

"A false belief exists that depressed patients are not creative," noted an Israeli researcher. "On the contrary, they have an urge to create...They express their repressed feelings and ideas...and in some cases, the spontaneous paintings have prophetic meaning."

Plenty of routes exist to creative fulfillment.

- Recognize the creative spirit you carry within you. You may not be fully aware of how creative you are in the work you do, for example.
- Be willing to take a risk on a new idea. The creative process involves trial and error, hits and misses. Many of the best ideas never get off the ground because the creative impulse is overwhelmed by doubts and inner criticisms. Learn to trust your intuition once again and brave the sometimes icy waters of translating your creative ideas into action.
- Become a creator rather than a consumer of entertainment. The entertainment industry today is such a juggernaut that it can overwhelm individual initiative. People end up as passive consumers of movies, television, books, and music. Yet there is no reason why people cannot become active creators of their own entertainment, whether by playing music, making videos, or writing poetry. Granted, you won't compose like Mozart or direct like Fellini, but the creative process itself benefits moods and emotions, regardless of the commercial appeal or artistic merit of the final product.
- Have a hobby. This can be painting watercolors, collecting movie

posters, woodworking, rock climbing, knitting—the choices are limited only by your imagination and initiative.

- See it live. Going to a play, a live musical performance, or a literary reading puts you in closer contact with other people's creative endeavors and is often more fulfilling than seeing a movie or watching television.
- Gardening is especially mood enhancing, with its ability to connect you to the earth and its rhythms of birth, life, death, and rebirth.

The bottom line is that you should follow the creative urges of your heart. Believe in yourself and express that belief through your creativity. What is being reborn is a new you.

Learn to Love to Laugh

Maintaining (or acquiring) a sense of humor can have a tremendously therapeutic effect on depression. The physical act of laughing has prominent effects on biochemicals, including neurotransmitters and endorphins, that can elevate mood, alleviate depression, and relieve pain. Studies have found that laughter can enhance circulation, boost the immune system, stimulate digestion, and oxygenate the blood. Researchers have also found that exposure to humor reduces stress and anxiety. Hospitals, nursing homes, and other institutions now take advantage of humor's therapeutic potential to promote recovery from disease.

Because depressed persons laugh and smile more infrequently than others, researchers have even lately begun to recognize humor-recognition as a behavioral marker that can help to diagnose depression. (Other such markers include a blank stare, social inactivity, and withdrawal.) A 1990 study confirmed the hypothesis that humor may be used to relieve the symptoms of depression. A group of female undergraduates who were shown depressive slides (this is a way researchers can induce a type of temporary depression) and then heard a humorous audiotape were much less depressed than control groups who heard a nonhumorous tape or no tape.

Gerontologist J. Richman of the Albert Einstein College of Medicine in Bronx, New York, has posited five principles of therapeutic humor:

1. A positive doctor-patient relationship includes the freedom to be humorous. Both partners in the healing relationship bear a responsibility to make this possible.

2. The humor is life-affirming.
3. The humor increases social cohesion. This principle and the previous one point to the need for humor that does not denigrate or debase other individuals or groups. Vicious humor can be momentarily funny, but if it goes against your core values it leaves a sour aftertaste that deadens its positive effects.
4. The humor is interactive. In other words, get involved; don't just respond passively to other people's humor.
5. The humor reduces stress. If it's creating rather than reducing stress, it's likely because humor is not appropriate for the situation.

Increasing your daily ration of laughs and chuckles can be as important as taking your daily nutritional supplements in keeping your mind and body functioning optimally. Many opportunities exist for incorporating humor into your daily life and making laughter a frequent companion.

- Recognize the humor in your daily surroundings. Going to comedy clubs or seeing funny movies is fine but you can't do such things every day. Rather, try to keep an active eye and an open mind for the outrageous, the absurd, and the silly in your everyday life.
- Learn to relish the unique sound of your own laughter. We all sound different when we laugh. Whether yours is a high whinny or a deep bellow, recognize it as a joyous yawp that can inspire merriment in others.
- Hang out with kids. Children are much quicker and more willing to laugh than adults, as well as more likely to be wild and crazy in a humorous way. Take advantage of their constant sense of mirth.
- Discover what makes you laugh and follow your heart. Humor is like sex in its polymorphous perversity—find out what turns you on and seek friends or partners who can share your point of view. I enjoy the subtlety of puns and try my hand at them frequently, with varying degrees of success at entertaining others but always with much self-enjoyment.
- Take advantage of the widespread availability of funny videos and audiotapes. Instead of listening to the litany of disasters related on news radio shows while you're commuting to work, lighten your mood and boost your health by finding laugh-inspiring comedy routines and readings of popular humor books.

- Share what you find humorous with others, whether it is cartoons clipped from the daily paper, a joke you've been e-mailed, the funny part of a book you're reading, or something absurd that happened at work. When humor is shared, even when it is the second time around, it can provoke renewed laughter and appreciation.

Breathe Deeply

What's there to know about breathing, you may ask—you take in air and blow it out. Yes, breathing is simple, like walking. But try walking all hunched over, taking only short steps, with your feet splayed out to the side. You'll tire more easily and unnecessarily strain your body. Similarly, it is possible to breathe more fully and efficiently. If you're tense, have poor posture, and take rapid, shallow breaths through the mouth, you limit your breathing capacity and promote fatigue and anxiety. Improper breathing in some people can contribute to panic attacks, hyperventilation, and chest pains, leading some to think they're having a heart attack. The result is less potential energy for the body and the release of fewer endorphins and other natural mood-boosting biochemicals in the brain.

Every breath you take delivers oxygen to the lungs and every exhalation releases cellular waste in the form of carbon dioxide. Your body can store some forms of energy, like fat, but oxygen needs to be constantly replenished in the lungs for you to live. The health and spiritual practices of yoga, Buddhism, and Taoism have long made use of specialized breathing techniques to activate "spirit" or "life force." For example, the traditional yogis of India believe that by controlling your breath you can control the flow of *prana,* or vital energy, throughout your body. Deep, diaphragmatic breathing promotes calmness, a centered feeling, and elevated spirits. Learning to breathe deeply in your everyday life can help you gain greater control of your mind and reduce tendencies toward depression. When the breath is steady, the mind becomes steady and calm.

One of the first things you need to do is come to recognize the signs of poor breathing. People who suck in their stomachs to inhale are not taking full advantage of their lungs' size and capacity. Most people fill only the upper portions of lungs with air and take in only about 15 percent of the lungs' fully expanded capacity for air. They need seven or eight breaths to turn over all the air in their lungs. Shallow exhalations leave behind residual carbon dioxide. Deep breathing is also preferable to shallow breathing even when you are breathing polluted air because it increases filtration.

Take a moment every once in a while to become conscious of your breath during one of your daily activities. Whether you are sitting, standing, or exercising, are you breathing deeply through the nose, expanding the diaphragm on the inhalation and contracting it on exhalation? Breathing deeply is a much more efficient way to increase your lungs' ability to deliver oxygen to the blood than taking shallow, rapid breaths. When it has become your normal way of breathing, you'll be inhaling and exhaling more fully and will be providing increased levels of oxygen to your body's cells.

I suggest that my patients practice a simple deep-breathing technique for a few minutes every day. One of the easiest ones to do is called pursed lip breathing. This full, deep, abdominal breathing method is often taught to women taking natural birthing classes and to people with lung conditions like asthma. To do it, inhale deeply through your nose. On the inhalation, your diaphragm (the partition of muscles between the chest cavity and the abdominal cavity) should move down while your ribs move outward. The effect is to expand your stomach. Exhale slowly while puckering your lips as if to blow out a candle. On the exhalation pull the diaphragm in and up and relax the chest muscles. Try to achieve a slow, even, rhythmic rate. Pursed lip breathing can help open your lungs' airways and strengthen the respiratory system.

You can also do a similar type of full or "yogic" breathing by keeping the lips closed and inhaling and exhaling through the nose. Visualize filling and emptying both the lower and upper parts of your lungs. Doing this type of deep breathing while walking can be a powerful way to double the endorphin-elevating effects of exercise.

Here are some other simple ideas for improving your breathing capacity:

- Aerobic exercise, endurance training, or some form of sustained physical exertion can increase your oxygen uptake, force more carbon dioxide out of your lungs, and strengthen your respiratory system.
- Take up singing or playing a wind instrument. These are excellent activities for strengthening your abdominal muscles and developing better control of your diaphragm and your breath.
- Become more conscious of the connection between proper posture and correct breathing. For example, in a proper sitting position you should have the weight of your upper body poised over the two arches of the pelvic bone, your thighs parallel to the ground, your

shoulders back, and your head and neck balanced over the spine. This position allows your rib cage and diaphragm a full range of movement. Try to take a deep, abdominal breath when you're leaning over with your shoulders hunched forward. This position prevents your lungs from fully expanding and can quickly make you become short of breath.

Sleep Well

Lack of restful sleep can have obvious effects on mood. Anybody who has stayed up all night to study for an exam or for whatever reason has been able to sleep only a few hours knows what it feels like the next day. You're likely to be irritable and withdrawn. Even a relatively minor sleep deficit, if it is allowed to accumulate over weeks and months, can take its toll on mood.

Poor sleep is a common symptom of depression. Depressed persons suffer from insomnia, often awaken too early anxious and tired from not sleeping, or they oversleep and find it difficult to get out of bed. Others may sleep restlessly most of the night, only to fall into a deep sleep in the morning when they should be arising alert and rested. Such sleeping problems have terrible consequences on all aspects of life and health. Lack of proper sleep disrupts hormonal balance and taxes the heart and lungs. Poor sleep depresses the immune system while proper sleep enhances it—the first few hours of sleep from ten P.M. to two A.M. are particularly helpful in boosting immune function. Chronic sleeping problems have also been tied to an increased risk of depression and reduced creativity. Sleep deprivation probably played a role in recent environmental disasters such as the Exxon Valdez oil spill and the nuclear power accident at Chernobyl.

A number of studies, including a 1998 study of seventy-eight people with major depression who were not being treated with antidepressant drugs, have attempted to determine whether sleep problems in depressed individuals are inherent to the condition. The consensus seems to be that sleep problems associated with depression may in some cases be persistent but in other respects can be addressed and reversed.

Sleeping allows your brain to slow down and muscles to relax. Dreaming sets your mind free to work on unresolved anxieties and fears. If you're like most people, you could probably benefit from longer sleep time. With sufficient sleep you'll awaken refreshed and energized, ready to enjoy the day. Many people need a full eight hours, but nowadays few adults get even seven. Sleep is seen as an indulgence or a luxury instead of as a requirement for better health. You should take steps to increase your nighttime sleep if you find yourself nodding off during the day or napping frequently, signs of sleep deficiency.

Everybody suffers from sleep problems once in a while. If your sleep-lessness is habitual, you should consult a health practitioner for advice. For many people, though, the following suggestions are all that are needed to help them get a good night's sleep.

- Cut back on your daytime stimulant use. Caffeine is the most common stimulant but others include the methylxanthines in chocolate, nicotine in tobacco, and drugs in various medications.
- If you do need occasional help falling asleep, turn to a natural remedy (1 to 3 mg of melatonin taken before bed works fine for most people, while a cup of chamomile tea is an option for children) rather than alcohol or over-the-counter sedatives or antihistamines, or prescription sleeping pills. Alcohol can make you drowsy but it interferes with your body's sleep cycles and prevents sound sleep. Sleeping pills can cause addiction and harmful side effects, alter normal sleeping cycles, and suppress dreaming. A 1998 study found that slow-release melatonin improved the sleep of individuals with major depressive disorder taking Prozac, and that there were no adverse effects from combining the two substances. I often prescribe trypto-phan because it is so effective for depression and anxiety as well as sleep. It can be obtained from compounding pharmacies (see Supplement Resources).
- Develop a nighttime ritual that readies your body for sleep. This can be as simple as meditating for a few minutes, doing a series of light stretches, or reading some inspiring literature. (Aerobic exercise is stimulating for most people, though if it is done early in the evening it can help tire the body and ultimately promote restful sleep.) Don't actually get into bed until your ritual has promoted some initial sleepiness. You want to associate lying in bed primarily with sleeping, not other activities.
- Don't eat after dinner. Your body will benefit greatly from a twelve- to fourteen-hour daily fast, from dinner to breakfast. If you must eat, choose a complex carbohydrate rather than protein food. Carbohydrates promote absorption of calming tryptophan while proteins

promote the more arousing neurotransmitters that may interfere with sleep.

- Try the relaxing yoga pose known as "the corpse" while lying on your back in bed. Put your arms at your side, palms up. Stretch your legs out and allow your feet to fall open. Maintain a deep and even breathing pattern, inhaling and exhaling through the nose. Consciously tell each part of the body to relax, starting at the top of the head and proceeding to the scalp, eyes, face, neck, and so on down the body. After you've relaxed all of the major muscle groups, concentrate on full, abdominal breathing and clear your mind of distractions. Identify any muscle tension that creeps back into your body and gently release it.
- Take a warm bath to which you've added four to five drops of a calming essential oil such as lavender or chamomile.

Adequate sleep is one of the most important lifestyle patterns for healing from depression. Sleep plays a more important role in your health than you may realize. Insomnia is often a sign of nervous system breakdown, and for some people lack of sleep seems to actually induce depression. I know that everyday demands often cause us to consider sleep "wasted" time—in fact, getting proper sleep is one of the hardest health habits for me to maintain—but sleep recharges the body and mind and can actually increase your ability to get the most from your waking hours.

Relax in a Mindful Manner

Conscious relaxation techniques provoke what doctors call the "relaxation response." This physical change in the body is characterized by an immediate relaxing of muscles, slowing of breath and heartbeat, lowering of blood pressure, and decreasing of metabolism. These effects are the exact opposite of what happens to the body when it is experiencing stress. Consciously relaxing is both easier on the body and more difficult to really do well. It can help you attain a state of apparent opposites: aware yet passive, calm yet alert, relaxed yet focused, resting yet awake.

Many methods for conscious relaxation exist, including various forms of meditation such as transcendental meditation, Vipassana or "insight meditation," cabalistic meditation, Christian contemplative meditation, and Zen Buddhist meditation. Other methods for conscious relaxation include deep breathing, prayer, progressive muscular relaxation, yoga, visualizations, and t'ai chi. Find a technique that appeals to you and try to do it a short time, even if it is only five to ten minutes, every day. You may find that the benefits you feel will make you want to do it for longer periods as you become more experienced at it.

A 1992 study compared students taking classes in Hatha yoga (a system of postures and slow stretches) and swimming with controls in a lecture class. The yoga students and the swimmers scored better on mood tests not only for depression but also for less anger, confusion, and tension. Yoga seemed to be especially beneficial for men, who showed significantly less tension, fatigue, and anger than those who took the class in swimming.

Spiritual centers, adult education courses, and individuals teach meditation in all parts of the country, including my Tree of Life Rejuvenation Center in Patagonia, Arizona, where all these health habits are taught. "Body/mind centers" around the country feature flotation tanks as well as other high-tech meditation tools, such as biofeedback machines and light-and-sound goggles.

In its most basic form meditation generally needs to be done in a quiet place where you won't be interrupted. If you are sitting, sit comfortably with your back straight. Close your eyes and keep still. If you want you can use a sound or "mantra" repeated over and over, such as "om" (drawn out in meditation to sound like "aaah-oh-ooom") or a favorite inspirational phrase. Here are some other practices:

- Contemplate a familiar object, such as a burning candle, a "mandala" (an intricate painting of circles and other shapes or symbols that to the Hindus represents the order of the universe), or in the cabalistic tradition letters that spell the name of God. Calmly gaze at the object or symbol.
- Practice the deep, abdominal, pursed lip breathing exercise described in the section on breath. Focus your thoughts on your in-breath and out-breath. If it helps to keep you focused on the moment, count each exhale. Stop your count at five and start over. If you lose count or count higher than five, your focus is wandering and you need to gently bring it back to your breath and your count.
- Combine meditation with exercise or movement. While aerobic exercise done to booming music probably won't provoke the relaxation response, certain types of movement can be combined with medita-

tion to provide some of the body/mind benefits of both of these activities. Such meditation is now being called "mindful exercise." For example, you can walk or ride a stationary bicycle while listening to a relaxation tape or repeating a mantra. You could also combine the Oriental discipline of t'ai chi (a series of slow, fluid movements) with visualization. Yoga is another ancient movement discipline that naturally combines exercise and meditation. These can be useful ways to introduce meditative techniques to men who tend to be more movement oriented.

- At the Tree of Life, we find the combination of dance-movement, breathing exercises, walking in nature, and meditation creates an optimal activation of endorphins, neurotransmitters, and heightened self-esteem. The reconnection with nature is one of our most powerful tools. The result is an increased sense of love for ourselves, those around us, and all of nature. It is difficult to feel depressed when you feel this global love.

Touch and Be Touched

Forms of touching exist across a broad spectrum, from handshakes to hugging to massage to sexual intimacy. In its entirety, close physical contact between individuals is an important element of mental health. To touch is to reach out and connect with another person, to show concern, empathy, and warmth. To be touched is to feel acknowledged, valued, perhaps loved. Inappropriate touching, on the other hand, is recognized as a violation of the self and can cause severely adverse effects on mind and mood. Common sense and sensitivity to a person's cultural background is helpful in this regard.

We know this intuitively from our experiences with family and friends, as well as from the results of various studies that have examined the effects of touching and physical intimacy. Studies show that premature babies thrive and gain weight much more quickly than babies who are left alone in incubators. Children who aren't touched and held as they are growing up are more likely to feel alone and isolated. They are also somewhat more likely to become physically aggressive toward each other and engage in violence. Studies have also looked more specifically at the effects of massage, for example, as a treatment for depression. A 1996 study of thirty-two depressed adolescent mothers found that those who received ten thirty-minute sessions of massage or relaxation therapy over a five-week period reported reduced anxiety. Only the massage group, however, also showed changes in stress hormones (a decrease in urine cortisol levels) and a slower pulse. Another study found that a thirty-minute neck and back massage reduced depression and left people more alert, less restless, and better able to sleep. The effects were noticeable in a variety of subjects, including some who were not touch-starved but whose depression arose from trauma.

I have observed that in the one-week rejuvenation program we offer at Tree of Life, when a person with depression receives a daily massage (administered by two people at a time), his or her depression seems to melt away. I view all forms of appropriate touching as healing to mind and body. The physical intimacy of spouses or long-term partners is the most potent balm for the spirit, and perhaps may be a major reason why surveys consistently find that married people report higher levels of happiness than unmarried and divorced individuals, and that married men live longer than single men. A full and rich sex life can profoundly benefit mind, body, and spirit by expressing the love and commitment you share with another. Emotional closeness and intimacy deepens the connections between two people while also reinforcing each individual's sense of wholeness and self-worth.

Whether you have a close personal partner or not, you can still experience many of the benefits of touching. One of the best forms of nonsexual touching is massage, which is now widely available in a dazzling variety. Swedish massage, foot massage, the ten-minute shoulder rub, Japanese shiatsu—what these have in common is using the fingers, hands, and other body parts to touch and rub either one's own or another person's body. Kneading muscles and gliding over skin helps to stimulate circulation, slow the rate of heartbeat and breathing, relax muscles, reduce anxiety, and calm the nerves.

You don't need to be a professional masseuse to provide these benefits, although if you can afford a regular session with a bodyworker, his or her additional experience can make the massage supremely pleasurable. Or you can incorporate massage into your everyday life by, for example, giving a partner or close coworker an occasional shoulder and neck massage. The upper back is easy to work on while the person is sitting at a desk. It is also an area of the body that frequently becomes tense from hours of deskwork. Work while standing behind the seated person, who remains fully clothed. Without even encouraging the recipient, you'll find that he or she may reciprocate.

I also encourage you to be open to the opportunities to touch and be touched in your everyday life. If you have a spouse or partner, touch in as many ways as possible. Trade massages, hugs, kisses, caresses, and cuddles. The boost in your spirits will likely be matched by an increase in the joy of those around you.

A Place for Spirit

Finally, I want to mention an element in everyone's lifestyle that can have a subtle but notable effect on mind, mood, and behavior. A sensitivity to the sacred in life, whether we call this spirituality or religion, seems to have a positive effect on mood. Surveys conducted in more than a dozen societies have confirmed an association between spirituality and depression. Overall, people with an appreciation for the spiritual side of life are twice as likely as those with no spiritual connection to consider themselves very happy.

I encourage my patients to promote their own happiness and life satisfaction by tuning in to the sacred in their lives. I don't necessarily mean that you should start to go to church or synagogue. Rather, determine for yourself what it is that connects you to your deepest sense of self and enhances your feelings of belonging to the greater whole. You need to find a way to live and do things that connects you with the sacred design of your life. When you access this on a regular basis, it is a natural antidepressant. I also call this following the deepest avenues of your heart. Some of the most unhappy people I've met are those who have ignored the inner messages of their hearts. Their lives become filled with a painful angst because they know they are not realizing their life purpose or living in a way that encourages the time and space for the sacred moments in their lives.

I feel great compassion for these people. For some the answer may be hiking in the wilderness, attending yoga classes, or reading poetry. For others it may be prayer, meditation, ceremonial activities, living in gratitude, or serving others. A variety of ways exist—your task is to explore and embrace this aspect of your life, recognizing it as an essential element in your mental and emotional health.

A New Approach to Alcoholism: Breaking Addictions and Cravings

When Tom, a businessman in his early sixties, first came to me, his cravings for—and consumption of—sugar were enormous. He had been alcoholic for some thirty years, a fact that was evident in the broken blood vessels on his face and in his sunken, almost lifeless eyes. Other aspects of his physical health also showed sign of degeneration, including the functioning of his nervous and circulatory systems. He suffered from high blood pressure, low energy, notable anxiety and irritability, and insomnia. Tom was unable to walk without experiencing extreme pain in his legs.

As is the case with many long-term alcoholics, Tom's drug addiction had alienated many of the people in his circle. He was able to maintain only a marginal relationship with his girlfriend and was becoming increasingly isolated from friends and family. His alcoholism had caused him to lose a number of jobs and had probably limited his career advancement.

The treatment program that we worked out for Tom included daily high doses of B-complex vitamins and other nutrients; supplements containing the milk thistle compound silymarin to support the functioning of the liver; tryptophan to promote better sleep; omega-3 and omega-6 essential fatty acid supplements; DL-phenylalanine for pain and to build up endorphin and dopamine activity; and glutamine to support brain neurotransmitter function and to decrease sugar cravings. Group therapy and lifestyle counseling helped him begin to confront the personal demons he'd long been too numbed to face. Within two weeks Tom was walking without pain and sleeping soundly. A feeling of inner calm began to replace his normal irritability. The alcoholism, sugar cravings, and depression that had plagued him for three decades were gone, a state of affairs that has continued over the two years since that time.

Tom's experience offers a prime example of the interplay of depression, alcoholism, and biochemical balance. It also illustrates the fact that, by activating the brain's pleasure centers, the remarkable mood-elevating and health-benefiting effects of the five-step *Depression-Free for Life* program go beyond treating depression. As we've seen, serotonin, endorphins, melatonin, blood sugar, and a number of the other biochemicals so crucial to emotional well-being are also intimately involved in aspects of appetite and weight control, normal sleeping patterns, and levels of sexual desire. Perhaps most significantly, if less obviously, these natural biological builders and the program to balance them also touch directly upon another major health issue: the role of addictions and cravings, especially with regard to alcohol and other drugs. In my experience, a major overlap exists in the physiology of depression and addiction.

Beyond the Twelve Steps

Drug addiction represents a health problem that is at least as widespread as depression and is in many ways just as difficult to address. Addictive behaviors are common in modern society, with as many as two of every five persons afflicted to some degree. Significantly more men than women suffer from addictions. Some studies suggest that men are five times more likely than women to be alcoholic and two to three times more likely to abuse other drugs.

America is undergoing what has been described as an unprecedented epidemic of psychoactive drug use. Use of potent, mind-altering conventional drugs is widespread—Americans consume 5 billion tranquilizers per year. Among legal drugs an estimated 11 million Americans abuse alcohol and 61 million are addicted to nicotine. One third of all United States high school students binge drink every two weeks, and 100,000 children ages ten to eleven get drunk weekly. A recent survey on illicit drug use found that during the previous month an estimated

- 200,000 Americans had used heroin
- 800,000 had taken amphetamines

- 1.5 million had used cocaine or crack
- 10 million had smoked marijuana

Despite the ongoing efforts of public health agencies and medical therapists, this epidemic of drug and alcohol abuse in modern society shows no signs of abating. Its adverse consequences on individuals, families, and society are incalculable. Nearly half the violent deaths from accidents, homicide, and traffic fatalities are alcohol related. Much of the rampant physical and sexual abuse of women is due to men who have been drinking. Among young alcoholics the rates of suicide and cirrhosis of the liver are ten times normal. Alcoholics die approximately twenty years sooner than the average population.

Much as prescription antidepressants are not the magic bullets that can cure depression, so the conventional twelve-step and the secularized "rational recovery" approaches to alcoholism provide some benefit but stop short of full success. Anyone who has attended a typical Alcoholics Anonymous meeting is likely to come away inspired by the courage and dedication so obvious among the participants, men and women who are struggling with their addiction to alcohol. Many observers have also noted, however, that AA meetings are not always free from other addictions, cravings, and unhealthful behaviors. The haze of cigarette smoke often fouls the air, and the amount of caffeine from coffee and sugar from donuts consumed is sometimes enough to fuel a small city's police department for a month.

Which is fine, on one level—alcoholism is a terribly debilitating disease that is not easy to cure in the best of circumstances. Focusing exclusively on the psychospiritual aspects of chronic drinking has helped many people to break free from this drug. But I believe it is necessary to take a more holistic viewpoint, one that includes the role of biochemical imbalances and nutritional deficiencies in alcoholism. In my experience these are so closely associated with alcoholism that they must be a principal part of any program that hopes to deliver long-term mental and physical health.

Most of my work is with alcoholics who have already stopped using alcohol for months or years and want to go to the next level of mind and body repair. (I do some work with alcoholics who have just stopped abusing alcohol, but my center is not equipped to serve as an acute alcohol detox center.) I am not the only practitioner emphasizing a biochemical approach to alcoholism and addiction. Many naturopaths and even some large treatment centers now recognize the value of combining diet, supplements, counseling, and other aspects of addiction treatment into a holistic approach.

Preliminary studies on the results of this new approach suggest that it can be even more effective than one-dimensional psychospiritual treatments. Estimates vary, but most alcohol researchers would agree that on average only one in four graduates of the conventional twelve-step programs are able to maintain abstinence or control their drinking over as short a period as a single year. After five years the relevant figure may be as low as one in ten. In one study of more than 900 alcoholics attending conventional psychospiritual programs, the abstinence rate after four years was 7 percent.

That's not a terribly high hurdle for the holistic programs to surpass, and a recent pilot study shows that such programs are indeed clearing the bar. This study, conducted by researchers at Bowling Green University in Ohio, was designed to assess the effects of nutrition therapy added to a conventional rehabilitation program based on the twelve-step program of Alcoholics Anonymous. One study group received conventional twelve-step therapy while another received the same plus nutrition therapy consisting of modified menus and individualized nutrition counseling. The researchers concluded, "Patients who received nutrition therapy reported significantly fewer hypoglycemic symptoms, lower sugar intake, and less alcohol craving as well as significantly greater nutrient intakes; a greater number abstained from alcohol. These findings indicate that nutrition therapy can aid in the recovery from alcoholism."

Other signs suggest that the conventional twelve-step programs, while admittedly providing tremendous social support for sober alcoholics, don't go far enough. For example, the suicide rate among sober alcoholics and active alcoholics is about the same. Moreover, the mortality rate among treated and untreated alcoholics is about three times higher than the general population. I believe these statistics reflect the fact that recovering alcoholics continue to suffer from the causes that initially brought them to alcohol in the first place. These include depression, anxiety, insomnia, irritability, and a lack of joy. Their sobriety, of course, protects them from the bodily ravages of chronic alcoholism, but not from the physical and emotional consequences of these other issues.

Researchers have also begun to investigate the biochemical underpinnings of alcoholism and addiction, with some interesting results. For example, recent studies suggest that as many as three out of five alcoholics have a brain imbalance that makes it harder for them to experience pleasure. For these people, the use of alcohol may be primarily an attempt to stimulate poorly functioning pleasure centers.

We also know that symptoms of depression are likely to develop during alcoholism, and that depression can be both a cause and an effect from alcoholism and addiction to other drugs. Various studies have found that alcoholics and drug addicts are more susceptible to mood disorders. For example, a recent study found that compared to nonalcoholics over a lifetime, alcoholics are twenty times more likely to suffer from antisocial personality disorder, four to six times as likely to suffer from mania or schizophrenia, and almost twice as likely to be depressed. In many ways, depression and addiction are blood brothers that resist being separated.

Not surprisingly from my perspective, the same natural, five-step program to alleviate depression can also be a crucial element of any drug treatment program. I believe that in order to more fully understand the issues of addiction we must go beyond the conventional psychological and spiritual approach to addiction. This conventional view is admittedly an improvement upon outmoded views linking alcoholism and addiction to a weak personality, low morals, and lack of willpower. The new concept of alcoholism as a progressive and only marginally controllable disease has spawned many theories but few really effective long-term treatment or prevention programs in the past forty years. On the other hand, in the last few years some exciting breakthroughs in the biochemical underpinnings of drug use and addiction have opened new perspectives. This aspect of the problem continues to be overshadowed by psycho-social-spiritual programs, despite evidence indicating that the two could easily be combined into an effective holistic approach.

In summary, my holistic approach has four parts:

1. As is recommended by the conventional twelve-step programs, the individual must make a commitment to stop abusing alcohol. I also ask the person to avoid as well other addictive substances such as mind-altering drugs (licit and illicit), sugar, nicotine, and caffeine.
2. The individual needs to correct endorphin and neurotransmitter deficiencies that are genetically present or that are environmentally caused from long-term intake of alcohol, drugs, and industrial toxins and allergens.
3. All nutritional deficiencies and any other disorders that are directly related to the alcohol intake, such as hypoglycemia and allergies, must be treated.

4. The final component is the psychospiritual support and healing every addicted person seems to need.

The following discussion focuses on alcohol, partly because it is the most studied drug but also because it can serve as a model for how to understand most drug addictions, including those to nicotine, caffeine, and even gambling and sex.

The Genetic Component of Alcoholism

A great deal of research in recent years has focused on a genetic component of alcoholism, and I believe a hereditary link is now fairly well established. For example:

- In one study, researchers found that in identical twins, if one twin was alcoholic the chance that the other one was also alcoholic was four times greater than if one fraternal twin is alcoholic. This directly suggests a strong genetic component, since identical twins have the same genetic makeup, while fraternal twins do not.
- A study of 3,000 adoptees in Sweden showed that the rate for alcoholics in those with one biological parent who was alcoholic was three times greater than those adoptees who did not have a biological parent who was alcoholic. In a reverse study, it was found that children whose biological parents were not alcoholic but who were adopted by alcoholic parents did not have a higher rate of alcoholism than the normal population.
- Another study involved 133 boys who were raised by nonalcoholic parents but whose fathers were alcoholics. These boys were compared to a similar group of boys whose biological parents were not alcoholic. The sons of alcoholics had an alcoholism rate three times greater than the biological sons of nonalcoholic parents.
- In a genetic study at UCLA, researchers found that the sons of recovering alcoholics had neurocognitive defects similar to those of their fathers. They also found that these sons of alcoholic fathers had a serious risk at an early age of developing cravings for addictive drugs such as nicotine, marijuana, and alcohol. Their data suggested that sons of alcoholics had psychomotor, neuroelectric, and hormonal imbalances compared to control groups of sons of nonalcoholics.

In the past decade, researchers have continued to do comparative studies, but they have also begun to identify genes that might help to control alcoholic behaviors. One of the best candidates is the so-called D2 dopamine receptor gene and its alternative form, or allele, identified as A1. Researchers have found that subjects with this uncommon gene have a higher than average rate of alcoholism. For example, one study found this gene in the brains of 69 percent of alcoholics compared to 24 percent of nonalcoholics.

In Chapter 1, I explained that dopamine plays an extremely important role in how neurotransmitters generate a sense of pleasure in the brain. When this "reward cascade" is working well, you have a sense of contentment and ease. When it is not working well, you experience anxiety, cravings, and a sense of discomfort. Researchers analyzed data from ten independent studies and found that those with the D2/A1 gene had one-third fewer dopamine receptors in their brains. This gene was significantly associated with severe alcoholism and other forms of drug abuse.

The implications are significant. One estimate is that the approximately 29 million children of alcoholics in the United States have at least a several times greater chance of developing alcoholism compared to children of nonalcoholics. This gene may also be involved in the expression of attention deficit hyperactivity disorder (ADHD) and posttraumatic stress disorder (PTSD). While research that is under way may ultimately decode and identify more alcohol-related genes, this does not mean that nutritional, lifestyle, or social factors are irrelevant to alcoholism. Even genetic researchers are careful to point out that although the genes themselves can't be altered, an individual's actions on a number of levels can influence their expression. For example, these genetic tendencies, which are the hard wiring of the computer, are significantly affected by the quality of the nutrition of both parents before conception; the effects of prenatal nutrition on the developing nervous system and brain in utero; and the effects of infant, childhood, and adult nutrition on the functioning brain.

I believe, however, that a holistic approach to the treatment of chronic alcoholism needs to go beyond diet to accomplish at least three main objectives, all of which are interrelated:

- repair the results of chronic mental stress
- increase endorphin and neurotransmitter levels
- provide optimal nutrition

Only then can we begin to bring an addictive neurochemistry back into harmony.

Stress and Addiction

Stress and alcohol are intertwined: drinking alcohol can change how the body responds to stress, and stress can affect when and how much alcohol you consume. When an individual is experiencing a sense of well-being, he or she is likely to have a healthy level of the natural opioid compounds known as endorphins and enkephalins present in the brain. Stress, however, especially if it is severe or chronic, can increase the release of enkephalinase, an enzyme that destroys the endorphins and causes their levels to drop significantly.

Releasing this enzyme is part of a normal coping mechanism because when opioid levels fall, you develop more of a sense of urgency. This can help to motivate you to respond to an emergency, fulfill an important task at work, or show more alertness, concentration, and focus. The low opioid output also has subtle effects on various neurotransmitters, tending to increase dopamine and noradrenaline and to reduce serotonin.

In a person with normal endorphin functioning, when the stress passes, the endorphins return to their normal levels and the sense of well-being returns. Some people, however, are not born with an efficiently working endorphin system. This may be due to poor prenatal nutrition or other factors. From the time they are born, they suffer from a low endorphin output and consequently a chronic sense of unease and discomfort. With the addition of modern levels of stress (which by one estimate is doubling every decade), their endorphin levels descend further.

Individuals with low opioid production and increasing levels of distress exhibit a tendency to enter into addictive habits because these addictive habits temporarily increase production of opioids, providing at least some temporary sense of well-being. The habit may be continuous heavy exercise, eating, gambling, smoking, or having sex. All of these activities can increase endorphins.

Alcohol also provides significant opioid relief but in a slightly different way. When alcohol is ingested, it is metabolized to tetrahydroisoquinolines (TIQs). These TIQs preferentially bind to one or more opioid receptor sites. They actually have the capacity to displace enkephalins and endorphins from these sites. The TIQs act like opioids and induce a sense of peace and ease. They also create a feedback loop that ultimately decreases enkephalin synthesis. In addition, alcohol increases the level of enkephalinase in the system and thus further decreases levels of natural opioids available to us.

Some research has shown that chronic alcoholics have lower than normal plasma beta-endorphin levels and thus reduced natural opioid activity. One study in the early 1980s found that beta-endorphin levels in the cerebrospinal fluid of twenty-nine chronic alcoholics were approximately two thirds less than that of the average nonalcoholic person. Low endorphin levels have even been found in alcoholics who have managed to abstain from drinking for ten years. (This study raised the difficult-to-answer question as to whether low endorphin levels are a cause or an effect of alcoholism. It also suggested why alcoholics whose biochemistry is not addressed are so predisposed to relapse.)

Research done on "alcohol-preferring" mice has shown that they have a lower level of enkephalins. Research also indicates that when normal mice are stressed, they tend to prefer alcohol to water immediately after the stress. Presumably this is to establish a sense of well-being by the production of TIQs. Animal studies have also found that unrelieved stress could cause a chronic deficiency of beta-endorphins in the pituitary and in a certain part of the brain called the corpus striatum.

Chronic stress in previously normal individuals seems to reset endorphin levels at a lower value. Without treatment like the five-step program to raise endorphins, people may experience chronic endorphin depletion and thus constant anxiety. In the battle of Stalingrad in 1942, Russian soldiers resisted block by block. The rate of hypertension in this group rose dramatically, from approximately one in twenty-five individuals to fifteen in twenty-five. This high rate did not drop after the battle ended, however, and the surviving soldiers ended up having some twenty years shaved off of their normal life expectancy. Other research has shown that soldiers who fought in Korea or Vietnam were twice as likely to become alcoholic compared to noncombat veterans. The rate of alcoholism increased proportionately to the time in combat.

Thus, a major concern for many alcoholics is that their bodies are not producing enough opioids and other neurotransmitters to keep their pleasure centers sufficiently activated. This is a primary reason why alcoholics are so much more likely to become ensnared by other drugs in addition to alcohol. Surveys suggest that as many as nine out of ten alcoholics are also addicted to nicotine. One recent study found that compared to nonalcoholics, over a lifetime, alcoholics are thirty-five times more likely to also use cocaine. They are also seventeen times more likely to use sedatives, thirteen times more likely to use opiates, and eleven times as likely to use stimulants. The five-step *Depression-Free for Life* program helps people to lose their strong cravings for alcohol as well as these other drugs because their endorphin receptors are filled with their own natural endogenous opiates.

The neurochemistry of the addictive brain and how it relates to mood and behavior is complex. Neurotransmitters and opioids in the brain interact in synergistic patterns that produce a variety of mental and emotional states. It is an oversimplification to reduce addiction to a few biochemicals being released in a linear sequence. The broad-stroke picture is only a first step toward fashioning a practical model for how to create a state of well-being, nonstress, ease, peace, and inner contentment.

Sister Conditions

In essence, if you can balance your neurotransmitters and create an efficient supply of endorphins, you'll be able to naturally activate your body's pleasure centers. You'll thus be much less likely to compulsively turn to substances such as alcohol or to behaviors such as overeating or gambling for the same purpose. You'll also be less likely to suffer from depression as well as what I consider to be other forms of a breakdown in this reward synergy. These other related conditions may include ADHD, eating disorders such as bulimia, and posttraumatic stress disorders.

ADHD is the most common childhood behavior disorder. It affects 5 to 8 percent of boys and 2 to 4 percent of girls. About half of these children have significant symptoms into adulthood. Children with ADHD have a higher percentage of learning disorders and anxiety. Studies suggest that a significant number of children with ADHD develop problems with drugs and alcohol. One Swedish study showed that those children with more severe ADHD symptoms had a higher percentage of alcoholism than those ADHD children who had fewer symptoms. Alternatively, an estimated one third of alcoholics meet the criteria defining ADHD, and alcoholics have a history of a higher rate of childhood ADHD.

Bulimia is most common among adolescent girls and young women. In many ways it is an addictive disorder, in that bulimics lack control over their food behavior and sacrifice long-term health for the short-term gratification of bingeing on high-sugar and high-fat foods.

Researchers have established that bulimics' abusive approach to food often extends to drugs. Bulimics have high rates of alcoholism. They also share with alcoholics a prominent tendency toward alcoholism in the immediate family.

Retuning the Neurotransmitters of Addiction

In my work with people with ADHD, bulimia, and posttraumatic stress disorder, serotonin deficiencies are common. Serotonin seems particularly related to the functioning of parts of the brain associated with concentration, thinking before acting, and motivation. It is no surprise that one researcher found a significant decrease in serotonin levels in a study of ADHD patients. He also found a significant decrease in tryptophan levels in these patients.

Serotonin deficiencies are also common in drug addiction and alcoholism. Research shows that chronic alcohol use decreases hypothalamic serotonin output in rodents. Serotonin dysfunction has also been linked to decreased enkephalin utilization and release in rat studies. Another study done on monkeys found that one of the serotonin reuptake inhibitor antidepressants could reduce alcohol consumption, although it was not very effective if the monkeys were being exposed to a source of stress (in this case, social separation) during the treatment. (Other animal studies have also found that the increase in alcohol intake as a result of stress is more likely to occur after the stress than during it.) Among the patients I have treated, a high percentage with "addictive brains" benefit tremendously from supplementation with tryptophan and 5-HTP.

Alcohol also induces dopamine release on an acute basis, especially in the nucleus accumbens, the part of the brain associated with pleasure generation. Other addictive drugs like amphetamines also target dopamine and the nucleus accumbens. The chronic use of alcohol and other drugs, however, leads to a decrease in dopamine content in the brain tissue. Alcohol can affect noradrenaline release as well. Alcohol's ability to reduce tension, anxiety, and fear may be linked to an inhibiting effect on noradrenaline in parts of the brain. So I find that many of these people are deficient in phenylalanine or tyrosine, the precursors to dopamine and noradrenaline.

Finally, alcohol can affect GABA function. Short-term use of alcohol stimulates GABA activity and transmission in the brain. As with dopamine, however, chronic alcohol use diminishes GABA function. It decreases GABA binding and reduces the firing of certain neurons in a part of the brain especially affected by GABA.

As you might have guessed, attempting to balance the neurotransmitters usually involves almost all of the amino acid neurotransmitter precursors. DL-phenylalanine is particularly important because D-phenylalanine blocks the breakdown activity of enkephalinase and thus indirectly raises endorphin levels; L-phenylalanine increases the amount of dopamine and noradrenaline in the system and also seems to increase the number of dopamine receptors.

Taking various amino acids can significantly improve neurotransmitter levels and positively affect the healing of addictive syndromes. Each neurotransmitter has a specific function and is affected by a variety of foods and drugs. I use them synergistically because I have found that in cases of alcoholism, recovery from drug usage, ADHD, and bulimia, people are often deficient in most if not all of them. Of course, they are not taken in a vacuum. Various factors can affect how amino acids cross the blood-brain barrier to alter mind and mood, including such dietary issues as the ratio of fat, protein, and carbohydrates, blood sugar levels, and nutrients.

Foods and Supplements to Fight Addiction

Nutrient deficiencies are much more common among alcoholics than the general population. Problems may arise from a combination of insufficient intake, poor absorption, disturbed metabolism, or increased rate of bodily loss through excretion. Anyone who drinks even moderately would benefit greatly by taking optimal doses of the nutrients I listed in Chapter 6.

Alcohol in large quantities is first a drug and then a food. As a drug it is initially a mild social stimulant and then, over time and in increasing quantities, a potent bodywide depressant. Even relatively small doses can fairly be classified as toxic. Alcohol interferes prominently with brain function and memory. It has been known to cause diseases in virtually every part of the body. It influences all the organs and alters the metabolism of most tissues of the body, with especially dramatic effects on carbohydrate energy metabolism and glucose balance.

As a food, alcohol is a highly refined carbohydrate. It is a concentrated energy source that can be burned as a fuel but is otherwise a totally nonessential nutrient. It provides many calories to the diet—one estimate is that it contributes about 5 percent of Americans' per capita energy consumption. Users of alcohol may or may not gain weight from drinking it.

That's because people tend to eat less when they drink because they don't need as much food. This can have dramatic effects on nutrient intake, since alcohol is devoid of vitamins, minerals, or other nutrients. Chronic alcoholics can tend to gain weight around the middle of the body. This can be accompanied by a wasting away of the muscles in the arms and legs. Men may develop flabby breasts because alcohol inhibits their ability to break down estrogen, thus promoting its accumulation in the body.

Alcohol intake also seems to affect the balance of carbohydrate and protein intake. At the most extreme intakes, severe alcoholics and drug addicts can suffer from actual deficiencies in protein (or even total calories) otherwise more common to developing countries than to Western industrialized countries. At more common levels of intake, studies have found that alcohol tends to encourage the consumption of protein at the expense of carbohydrates. A high carbohydrate/low protein diet may reduce alcohol consumption, and a low carbohydrate/high protein diet may increase alcohol consumption in the body's attempt to balance the protein with higher intake of sugar.

Regardless of this effect on dietary carbohydrates, alcohol addiction often leads to hypoglycemia. Studies have found that hypoglycemia exists in more than four out of every five alcoholics, often causing mood swings, mental confusion, and fatigue. Stress is likely to enhance the effect.

Among the most common nutrient deficiencies in alcoholics are

- thiamine
- niacin
- pyridoxine
- vitamin B_{12}
- folic acid
- magnesium
- calcium
- zinc

I've found that treatment involves replacing all the nutritional deficiencies caused by chronic alcohol intake with a special focus on the B vitamins and zinc (most people benefit from taking approximately 50 mg of most B vitamins and 15 mg of zinc per day). It is likely that alcohol and nutrient deficiencies act synergistically in the nervous system. In general, the list of optimal nutrient levels in Chapter 6 will work well to address nutritional imbalances in alcoholics.

Some evidence exists that alcohol may increase the intestines' ability to absorb iron, and that iron has an exacerbating effect on cirrhosis. Alcoholics may therefore need to approach this one nutrient with some caution.

The omega-3 essential fatty acid DHA is absolutely critical for normal brain tissue development. DHA is depleted by alcohol usage. Also, some alcoholics have a gene defect that inhibits the conversion of essential fatty acids to series 1 prostaglandins. This defect seems to appear mostly in certain people from Ireland, Scotland, and the Netherlands. The series 1 prostaglandins have specific antidepressant effects. By helping the conversion to series 1 prostaglandins take place, alcohol serves as a type of treatment for the related depression. The long-term problem is that alcoholics do not absorb the essential fatty acids well, so with chronic alcohol use, they become deficient in essential fatty acids because the conversion of essential fatty acids is outpacing intake of same. The omega-6 essential fatty acid GLA in evening primrose oil is helpful in solving this problem. One study conducted in Scotland on two groups with this defect, both with a 50 percent lower essential fatty acid level, showed an 83 percent success rate in sobriety in those given primrose oil compared to 28 percent in the control group.

The adverse effects of alcoholic beverages are not limited to nutrient deficiencies. A high consumption of alcohol decreases the body's production of natural opioids. Their production may be further decreased as a result of the poor nutrition (and thus an insufficient supply of endorphin neurotransmitter precursors and cofactors) from which a chronic alcoholic often suffers.

Finally there is the issue of food allergies and sensitivity to the chemicals in alcoholic beverages. Heavy drinkers are especially vulnerable to the adverse effects of toxic chemicals in alcoholic beverages. Various potentially toxic and illness-inducing ingredients beyond alcohol (ethanol) are found in many alcoholic beverages. Yeast is needed to ferment alcoholic beverages and many people suffer from headaches, food cravings, skin rashes, and other allergic symptoms to yeast. The actual grains and fruits from which alcoholic beverages are made can be allergy-inducing. Some people are sensitive to other chemicals in alcoholic beverages, including the following:

- tyramine, a nonessential amino acid that is found especially in red wines and beer (as well as common foods such as cheddar cheese and chocolate). Taken in excess, tyramine can cause high blood pressure, anxiety, headache, and confusion. Consuming high amounts of tyramine while taking antidepressant drugs that inhibit the enzyme monoamine oxidase (MAO inhibitors) can cause a potentially fatal reaction.

- sulfites, common disinfectants and fermentation-stoppers in wine
- pesticides, from spraying of grapes or other crops used to make alcoholic beverages

Studies have suggested that approximately three out of five alcoholics have allergies, especially to wheat, dairy, rye, potatoes, and grapes—all substances from which popular alcoholic beverages are made. Another one in two has chemical allergies, especially to gasoline, plastics, paints, and art supplies. When susceptible individuals are exposed to these, they tend to drink alcohol as a way to cope with the allergies. Alcohol can activate compounds known as xenobiotics, which are foreign to the body, such as are found in industrial chemicals and prescription and over-the-counter medications. Xenobiotics may be carcinogenic.

Studies have furthermore shown that alcohol generates harmful free radicals in the body. It also depletes glutathione, a chemical important to the body's natural antioxidant defenses. Taking the amino acid metabolite SAM (see Chapter 1) can promote glutathione activity.

Going All the Way

Like depression, alcoholism and other addictive disorders have both psychological and physical elements. I have emphasized the physical and biochemical elements in part because they are so often ignored. Counseling is important, both for depression and for alcoholism. But I don't believe it will be as effective on its own, just as I wouldn't expect a counseling-only approach to heart disease or cancer to be especially worthwhile without the concomitant biological treatment. When biochemical imbalances are addressed and nutrients are provided to restore optimal mind and body function, a person's chances of recovering from alcohol and other drug addictions are greatly enhanced.

11

A Plan in Full:
Depression-Free for Life

Doctors have all sorts of reasons, both lofty and banal, for pursuing their calling. For me, the experience of helping to guide a person who is depressed to a newfound sense of happiness and connection to life and to spirit is deeply rewarding. Nothing else even comes close to providing the satisfaction of seeing people become free of all addictions and better able to express the ultimate joy in life that is a birthright for all of us. The endeavor may often appear hopeless at first to the patient, but when the effort is made and the natural program succeeds to its fullest extent, the result is a blessing to behold.

I'm reminded of Pauline, one of my most recent patients. A mother and homemaker in her early fifties, Pauline had a long history of depression. She was overweight, looked tired, and was difficult to engage. Even the simplest questions would elicit deep sighs and spells of staring vacantly into space. She was taking three prescription drugs for depression, a combination that didn't seem to be working much better than a half-dozen other combinations she had already tried. Food allergies, chronic fatigue, sugar cravings, and various other problems complicated her condition. Repeated thoughts about suicide and extreme variations in mood actually made her a potential candidate for hospitalization. I soon realized that she would be a challenging test case for the natural method.

Pauline didn't turn into a self-actualized supermom overnight, but she did gradually improve and within six months was almost a new person. I wish I had a set of before and after photos, like the ones they use in ads for weight-loss products, because her physical makeover was almost as dramatic as those that portray slim and trim former-four-hundred-pounders. She went from a gaunt and haunted look that clearly showed every one of her years to regaining a sparkle in her eyes and a softer, more youthful appearance. All of the steps I've described in Part Two of this book, as well as regular counseling sessions, were necessary to wean her off the prescription antidepressants, boost her overall health, and improve her outlook. She lost fat, put on muscle, and gained energy. She adjusts to life's highs and lows. In fact, she reported feeling as good as she had in her whole life.

Talking with the new Pauline was like meeting someone you knew who'd been transported back in time, to the days when she was younger, more resilient, more optimistic about the future. In a way, I realized, her depression and the prescription drugs she'd been taking had been artificially aging her, and the natural treatment was not only a cure for her depression but a sort of youth serum for body, mind, and spirit. Her transformation took time and work, but the result was something that no exotic admixture of prescription drugs ever could have accomplished.

One aspect of Pauline's treatment that I haven't talked much about is counseling. I don't want you to finish this book with the impression that I think that psychotherapy is unhelpful. On the contrary, it is quite frequently an invaluable component of full recovery. In my work I've refined a psychospiritual approach that empowers people to heal themselves. I also use couple and family therapy whenever possible to involve a depressed person's mate or loved ones in the healing process. As with alcoholism and drug addiction, you need to consider the entire social setting for true healing. This type of psychotherapy is especially important when a person is undergoing a psychological crisis, such as from a failed relationship, a divorce, a midlife crisis, or some other source of immediate distress. These crises depress people's neurotransmitters and endorphins and plunge their emotions into despair, often for months or years. Biological and lifestyle support, such as supplements, homeopathy, diet, exercise, and spiritual work, promote a necessary rebalancing of the body/mind response to activate the pleasure centers. That response can be notably encouraged and supported by the empathy and insight that comes during effective psychospiritual work.

Sometimes just one key session can break the emotional logjam. I try to go right to the critical issue and help the person resolve it. If he or she is willing to be open and to work, it is amazing what can be done. For example, I treated a lawyer from New York City who had become progressively depressed for more than a year. With one session he made a major breakthrough and over the next six weeks, with the help of the five-step program, his long-standing depression faded away. Today he remains free of depression and enjoys life fully. On the other hand, it is not uncommon for people with major chronic depression to need long-term therapy.

Making the Transition from Prozac

Another aspect of Pauline's inspiring recovery from depression was how we weaned her from a number of potent prescription drugs before she really gained the full benefits of the five-step program. This part of the program needs to be approached with patience and care. I want to emphasize that you should never abruptly discontinue psychotropic medication nor make changes to your drug program without obtaining the advice of your physician. I realize that in many cases this will present difficulties. Conventional physicians are thoroughly trained in drug therapy. Many consider it the only reliable treatment for medical conditions, including depression. If your doctor is typical, he or she will probably advise you not to attempt to end medication in favor of trying a more natural approach to your mood disorder.

I suggest that you gently but firmly try to educate your physician about the potential benefits you expect to gain by switching from drugs to reactivating your brain's pleasure centers. Tell her that if in fact after six months or so the natural method has failed, you will reconsider the value of drug therapy. Tell her what you dislike about the drugs you are taking, and admit that you need her help and expertise in trying another option. If a reasoned approach is impossible, you may need to switch physicians.

In my experience, doctors' resistance is only one of two main obstacles you're going to face in trying to get off Prozac and similar drugs. The second is your own fears of what will happen. I've found that one of the most important roles I play is to encourage people to empower themselves. The longer you've been taking antidepressant medications, in many cases the more fearful you are likely to be about the consequences of coming off these drugs. Many people I've treated have managed to successfully stop taking prescription drugs, not only for their depression but for a host of other accompanying ailments, but it takes an effort to overcome their fear of what will happen.

Tina is a former patient who successfully made the transition from Prozac to the five-step, drug-free program. A fifty-nine-year-old real estate developer without any history of major depression, she was prescribed Prozac for a situational depression (she became despondent over the death of a sister she'd been especially close to) and had been taking it for almost two years when she first came to see me. Tina's inability, even on Prozac, to regain her former confident self had caused her to become tentative and had reduced her sense of self-esteem. With the help of some amino acid and nutritional supplements, her lingering low mood dissipated within two weeks. It took another two months, however, before we could slowly end the prescription for Prozac and she could return to her happy and vivacious self.

Work with your prescribing doctor to reduce the dosage you are taking of your antidepressant medication over a graduated time period. For example, if you are taking 20 mg per day, you may be able to reduce the dosage by 5 mg every two to four weeks as you replace the drug with combinations of dietary supplements and lifestyle changes specific to your biochemical imbalance. Adjust your substitution pattern over time by watching for symptoms such as fatigue and restlessness to obtain the best long-term results.

Highlights of the Five-Step Program for Specific Biochemical Imbalances

In the first part of this book I identified seven types of often ignored biochemical imbalances or bodily conditions that can cause or contribute to your depression:

1. an imbalance in various natural brain chemicals, especially a deficiency in serotonin, dopamine, noradrenaline, glutamine, GABA, or the endorphins

2. underlying conditions, especially side effects from prescription, over-the-counter, and recreational drugs; the consequences of nutritional deficiencies; and allergies to foods, chemicals, and metals
3. gender and seasonal-related factors, which may be complicated by an imbalance in melatonin or other hormones
4. a blood sugar imbalance, which can be expressed differently depending upon whether you are a fast or slow oxidizer
5. a thyroid imbalance, usually from a deficiency but sometimes from an overabundance of thyroid hormone activity
6. a stress hormone imbalance
7. a dietary fat/essential fatty acid imbalance

In Part Two we looked at how various nutritional supplements, dietary adjustments, and lifestyle factors could help to address these imbalances and conditions. We saw that amino acids could dramatically boost neurotransmitter activity, that vitamins and essential fatty acids could help to balance hormones, and that diet has a major effect on everything from biochemicals to blood sugar. Here I'd like to pull together the diagnostic elements from Part One and the prescriptive recommendations from Part Two into a series of mini-plans for various individuals.

These mini-plans are meant to provide guidelines for treatment rather than be comprehensive plans for any one person. The amino acids, nutrients, and dietary and lifestyle advice included in these lists are among the most important elements you should consider. I caution you, however, not to treat these lists as "magic bullet" prescriptions for your depression. These are good starting points, but you need to make an effort to include the broader elements of the five-step program. Also, many individuals need to combine elements from several mini-plans because, for example, they suffer from a serotonin deficiency, an inappropriate diet, and poor stress control. (See the relevant chapters in Part Two for dosage recommendations.)

Serotonin Deficiency

STEP ONE/AMINO ACIDS
- tryptophan (for insomnia/depression) or 5-HTP (for depression/anxiety)

- SAM
- glutamine

STEP TWO/NUTRIENTS
- vitamin E
- B-complex vitamins, especially niacin, pyridoxine, and folic acid
- vitamin C
- magnesium

STEP THREE/DIET
- foods relatively high in tryptophan content

STEP FOUR/ESSENTIAL FATTY ACIDS
- flaxseed

STEP FIVE/LIFESTYLE
- exercise/physical activity
- meditation
- breathing

Dopamine Deficiency

STEP ONE/AMINO ACIDS
- phenylalanine or tyrosine
- SAM

STEP TWO/NUTRIENTS
- NADH
- B-complex vitamins, especially niacin, pyridoxine, and folic acid
- copper
- iron
- vitamin C

STEP THREE/DIET
- foods relatively low in tryptophan content
- predominantly vegetarian diet

STEP FOUR/ESSENTIAL FATTY ACIDS
- flaxseeds
- evening primrose or borage oil

STEP FIVE/LIFESTYLE
- exercise/physical activity
- meditation
- breathing

Noradrenaline Deficiency

STEP ONE/AMINO ACIDS
- phenylalanine or tyrosine
- SAM

STEP TWO/NUTRIENTS
- NADH
- B-complex vitamins, especially niacin and pyridoxine
- vitamin C
- vitamin E
- Siberian ginseng and licorice root

STEP THREE/DIET
- foods relatively low in tryptophan content
- primarily vegetarian diet

STEP FOUR/ESSENTIAL FATTY ACIDS
- flaxseeds
- evening primrose or borage oil

STEP FIVE/LIFESTYLE
- exercise/physical activity
- meditation
- breathing

Glutamine Deficiency

STEP ONE/AMINO ACIDS
- glutamine

STEP TWO/NUTRIENTS
- NADH
- B-complex vitamins, especially niacin, B_5, and pyridoxine
- vitamin C
- vitamin E

- chromium
- ginkgo

STEP THREE/DIET
- low glycemic index foods
- primarily vegetarian diet

STEP FOUR/ESSENTIAL FATTY ACIDS
- flaxseeds
- borage oil
- DHA

STEP FIVE/LIFESTYLE
- exercise/physical activity
- meditation
- breathing

GABA Deficiency

STEP ONE/AMINO ACIDS
- GABA
- glutamine

STEP TWO/NUTRIENTS
- NADH
- B-complex vitamins, especially niacin, B_5, and pyridoxine
- vitamin C
- vitamin E
- chromium
- ginkgo

STEP THREE/DIET
- low glycemic index foods
- primarily vegetarian diet

STEP FOUR/ESSENTIAL FATTY ACIDS
- flaxseeds
- borage oil
- DHA

STEP FIVE/LIFESTYLE
- exercise/physical activity
- breathing

Endorphin Deficiency

STEP ONE/AMINO ACIDS
- D-phenylalanine
- SAM

STEP TWO/NUTRIENTS
- NADH
- B-complex vitamins, especially niacin and pyridoxine
- vitamin C
- vitamin E
- Siberian ginseng

STEP THREE/DIET
- foods relatively low in tryptophan content

STEP FOUR/ESSENTIAL FATTY ACIDS
- flaxseeds
- borage oil
- DHA

STEP FIVE/LIFESTYLE
- exercise/physical activity
- humor
- breathing

Underlying Ailments, Including Side Effects from Drugs, Nutritional Deficiencies, and Allergies

STEP ONE/AMINO ACIDS
- tyrosine
- glutamine (especially for alcohol and food allergies)

STEP TWO/NUTRIENTS
- vitamin A/mixed carotenoids
- vitamin E

- coenzyme Q10
- ginkgo
- iron (if iron deficiency)

STEP THREE/DIET
- low glycemic index foods
- primarily vegetarian diet

STEP FOUR/ESSENTIAL FATTY ACIDS
- flaxseeds
- borage oil
- DHA

STEP FIVE/LIFESTYLE
- exercise/physical activity
- meditation
- breathing

Gender/Seasonal Imbalance

STEP ONE/AMINO ACIDS
- tryptophan or 5-HTP

STEP TWO/NUTRIENTS
- melatonin
- vitamin D
- thyroid extracts (if deficiency)

STEP THREE/DIET
- foods relatively high in tryptophan content
- primarily vegetarian diet

STEP FOUR/ESSENTIAL FATTY ACIDS
- DHA or omega-3 essential fatty acids, if history of postpartum depression

STEP FIVE/LIFESTYLE
- exposure to at least one half-hour of sunlight per day
- sleep

- exercise/physical activity
- relaxation/meditation
- breathing

Blood Sugar Imbalance/Fast Oxidizer

STEP ONE/AMINO ACIDS
- glutamine

STEP TWO/NUTRIENTS
- vitamin A/mixed carotenoids
- pantothenic acid
- vitamin B_{12}
- boron, copper, and zinc
- coenzyme Q10
- calcium
- chromium

STEP THREE/DIET
- high-protein, moderate-fat foods
- five to six meals per day
- rich in calcium and iodine
- moderate to low on glycemic index
- high in purines
- primarily vegetarian diet

STEP FOUR/ESSENTIAL FATTY ACIDS
- flaxseeds
- evening primrose or borage oil

STEP FIVE/LIFESTYLE
- exercise/physical activity

Blood Sugar Imbalance/Slow Oxidizer

STEP ONE/AMINO ACIDS
- glutamine

STEP TWO/NUTRIENTS
- thiamine
- riboflavin

- niacin
- pyridoxine
- magnesium
- chromium
- copper and zinc
- coenzyme Q10

STEP THREE/DIET
- high complex carbohydrates, low-fat
- rich in potassium
- moderate to high on glycemic index
- primarily vegetarian diet

STEP FOUR/ESSENTIAL FATTY ACIDS
- flaxseeds

STEP FIVE/LIFESTYLE
- exercise/physical activity

Balanced Oxidizer

STEP ONE/AMINO ACIDS
- glutamine

STEP TWO/NUTRIENTS
- thiamine
- riboflavin
- niacin
- pyridoxine
- magnesium
- chromium
- copper and zinc
- coenzyme Q10
- vitamin B_{12}
- folic acid
- calcium

STEP THREE/DIET
- moderate amounts of carbohydrates, fat, and protein
- moderate to low on glycemic index

STEP FOUR/ESSENTIAL FATTY ACIDS
- flaxseeds

STEP FIVE/LIFESTYLE
- exercise/physical activity

Thyroid Imbalance (Deficiency)

STEP ONE/AMINO ACIDS
- tyrosine

STEP TWO/NUTRIENTS
- thyroid extracts

STEP THREE/DIET
- rich in iodine
- sea vegetables
- primarily vegetarian diet

STEP FOUR/ESSENTIAL FATTY ACIDS
- flaxseeds
- evening primrose or borage oil

STEP FIVE/LIFESTYLE
- exercise/physical activity
- breathing
- meditation

Stress Hormone Imbalance

STEP ONE/AMINO ACIDS
- GABA
- glutamine

STEP TWO/NUTRIENTS
- vitamin C
- vitamin E
- chromium
- magnesium

STEP THREE/DIET
- primarily vegetarian diet

STEP FOUR/ESSENTIAL FATTY ACIDS
- flaxseeds

STEP FIVE/LIFESTYLE
- exercise/physical activity
- sleep
- relaxation
- touch

Dietary Fat/Essential Fatty Acid Imbalance

STEP ONE/AMINO ACIDS
- tryptophan or 5-HTP

STEP TWO/NUTRIENTS
- vitamin A/mixed carotenoids
- niacin
- pyridoxine
- vitamin C
- vitamin E
- magnesium
- selenium
- melatonin

STEP THREE/DIET
- eat more nuts, seeds (especially ground flaxseeds), beans, and other sources of natural fats (for meat-eaters, cold-water fish are an alternate source)
- avoid sugary, fatty diet rich in processed foods and omega-6-rich cooking oils

STEP FOUR/ESSENTIAL FATTY ACIDS
- omega-balanced seed oils
- omega-6 supplements, if symptoms of deficiency exist
- DHA

STEP FIVE/LIFESTYLE
- exercise/physical activity
- relaxation
- breathing

Eyes on the Prize

Being a psychiatrist and holistic physician is a humbling position. I am reminded daily of how much I still don't know, of how new studies are constantly adding to our knowledge. Even though scientists and practitioners have made tremendous strides in understanding the cause and cure of depression and other mood disorders in recent years, much still needs to be learned. The human organism is a mystery and perhaps always will be. As we've seen, a variety of bodily systems in addition to the nervous system can affect mood, and these systems can be fine-tuned using a whole host of substances and activities. The brain is enormously complex, and human behavior has more quirks than the universe has quarks.

Researchers promise to answer many of the important questions still outstanding in the field. Yet the prevailing scientific focus in many ways is misdirected. Yes, some people will benefit when scientists discover genetic links to depression, or when pharmaceutical researchers develop new drugs that adjust one or another neurotransmitter. A huge investment in time and money toward these ends, however, can also unfortunately distance individuals and society from the ultimate goal.

As difficult as it is to alleviate depression, is it enough? That is, is the goal to be able to say, "Sheila no longer suffers from seasonal affective disorder," or is a greater prize within reach? Certainly modern psychiatry has in recent years focused on formulating diagnostic criteria for a dizzying number of personality- and mood-related conditions. In the three decades I've been a practicing psychiatrist, the number of conventionally accepted personality and mood disorders has increased almost exponentially. The bible of the psychiatric profession, the *DSM-IV: Diagnostic and Statistical Manual of Mental Disorders* (fourth edition), now lists more than 350 disorders, from low sex desire to pathological gambling.

Often, the next step after labeling a disorder is to find a drug to alleviate the symptoms. Look at what has happened in recent years with attention deficit disorder (ADD) and attention deficit hyperactivity disorder (ADHD). The number of children and adults being treated for these conditions has skyrocketed. This may be due to various factors, from the effects of diet to an increasingly narrow interpretation of what amounts to creative, impulsive, and exploratory behavior in an increasingly regimented and controlled society. What no one can dispute is the explosion in use of methylphenidate (Ritalin) and related amphetamine-like controlled substances to treat these conditions. The manufacturer of Ritalin is producing seven times as much of the drug as it was at the beginning of the 1990s, the bulk of it for United States consumption.

A similar case can be made against Prozac and depression. Its use has multiplied wildly since its introduction a dozen years ago. Conditions that probably have complex underpinnings are labeled and said to be improved by taking Prozac, perhaps indefinitely. Too frequently doctors and their patients think of Prozac or Ritalin first instead of trying to identify underlying factors in the person's biochemical makeup, environment, dietary practices, and lifestyle. No one is born with a Ritalin deficiency or a Prozac deficiency, and using such compounds to treat mind- and mood-related disorders is rarely a long-term solution.

Whether it is Ritalin for hyperactivity or Prozac for depression, we need to rethink the model for what it means to feel alive and well, and what it means to be a fully functioning and emotionally integrated human being. I believe that we need to shift the focus from drugs that merely have a leveling effect on mind and mood to strategies for actually optimizing the innate powers of body and mind, for extending longevity and promoting better overall health and human fulfillment. What constitutes optimal health for the body and mind, for the brain and the other organs, is interconnected.

The process of alleviating depression thus goes beyond helping people to no longer feel blue. A true recovery from depression re-energizes the body and opens your eyes to new possibilities and greater self-awareness. It offers the possibility for a spiritual rebirth, for opening up to your full potential. Sometimes these changes happen within a day and sometimes these shifts take a few months to manifest. It is a wonderful process to experience and to observe, one that I always feel privileged to be a part of. Whenever someone asks me about how difficult it must be to work all the time with sad and distant patients, I think about Phillip, one of my most successful clients. An investment banker, he came to see me complaining of depression as well as decreased sex drive, fatigue, high blood pressure, headaches, and chronic constipation. Within a month of incorporating various elements of the five-step program, he had recovered from the depression. But I would hardly have felt successful if he had still been plagued by fatigue, high blood pressure, headaches, and chronic constipation. He wasn't, and he knew it and felt the difference. He told me, "My life has been completely turned around. My physical and emotional state was ruining my career, it was threatening my marriage, and it was disrupting my relationship with my friends. I feel as if I've discovered a new self, one that is healthier and better able to face the future than not only my depressed self but my self before I was depressed."

I believe that just as every person has unique biochemical and personal characteristics, so every person can reach an optimal zone in which his or her physical and mental energies operate at their peak. This zone is one in which the sweetness of the divine is expressed in every moment. You live with a continual sense of well-being. No matter what happens in the external world, you feel physically, emotionally, mentally, and spiritually rejuvenated. Yes, the process may be difficult, and you may never know all of the variables that affect your mind and mood, but you already know enough to take the basic steps necessary. You can attain that optimal state of feeling energized yet calm, emotionally well balanced yet glowing with vitality. You can reach the point where you are able to fully love yourself, to love and accept others, and to love and honor the planet, and join the sacred and joyful dance of being fully awake, free, and alive. It is this natural birthright that is the ultimate prize for anybody who wishes to become depression-free for life.

Supplement Resources

Most of the depression-busting nutritional substances mentioned in the text are widely available in natural food stores, health food stores, and even supermarkets and pharmacies. A few, such as SAM, 5-HTP and other amino acids, flax and hemp seed products, DHA, and NADH, are relatively new to the market and harder to locate. Also, the FDA has prohibited the sale of tryptophan supplements in the United States since 1990. Tryptophan can be obtained with a prescription from some compounding pharmacies.

The following mail-order listings are, by necessity, representative rather than comprehensive. I list their difficult-to-find products, but many also offer a wide range of vitamins, minerals, and specialized nutritional formulas.

Barlean's Organic Oils
4936 Lake Terrell Rd.
Ferndale, WA 98248
(800) 445-3529
www.barleans.com
flaxseed oil

Life Enhancement Products
P. O. Box 751390
Petaluma, CA 94975
(800) 543-3873; (707) 762-6144;
(707) 769-8016 (fax)

www.life-enhancement.com
*5-HTP capsules, 5-HTP formula
("5-HTP SeroTonic," a combination of
5-HTP, St. John's wort, and four
nutrients); glutamine capsules*

LifeLink
P. O. Box 1299
Grover Beach, CA 93483
(805) 473-1389; (888) 433-5266
(toll-free); (805) 473-2803 (fax)
www.lifelinknet.com
*5-HTP capsules, sublingual; methylcobal-
amin capsules*

Life Services Supplements
3535 Highway 66
Neptune, NJ 07753
(800) 542-3230; (732) 922-0009;
(732) 922-5329 (fax)
www.lifeservices.com
*glutamine capsules and powder; tyrosine
capsules*

Martek Biosciences
6480 Dobbin Rd.
Columbia, MD 21045
(410) 740-0081; (410) 740-2985 (fax)
www.martekbio.com
*for more information on Neuromins
microalgae-derived DHA products*

Omega Nutrition USA
6515 Aldrich Rd.
Bellingham, WA 98226
(800) 661-3529
www.omegaflo.com
flaxseed oil

Peggy's Health Center
151 First St.
Los Altos, CA 94022
(800) 862-9191; (650) 948-9191;
(650) 941-9512 (fax)
www.peggyshealth.com
NADH tablets; 5-HTP capsules

Smart Basics
1626 Union St.
San Francisco, CA 94123
(800) 878-6520; (415) 749-3990;
(415) 351-1348 (fax)
www.smartbasic.com
*5-HTP capsules; tyrosine capsules; gluta-
mine capsules and powder; flaxseed oil
capsules; NADH*

Vitamin Research Products
3579 Highway 50 East
Carson City, NV 89701

(800) 877-2447; (775) 884-1300;
(800) 877-3292 (fax);
(775) 884-1331 (fax)
www.vrp.com
*5-HTP capsules; L-phenylalanine cap-
sules; DL-phenylalanine capsules; tyrosine
capsules; glutamine capsules; flaxseeds,
flaxseed starter kit (with electric grinder);
adrenal stress index test kit (salivary test)*

Mail-Order and Internet Supplement Discounters

The following companies offer discounted prices on nutritional supplements
from a variety of producers.

MotherNature.com
490 Virginia Road
Concord, MA 01742
(800) 517-9020; (978) 929-2000;
(978) 929-2001 (fax)
www.MotherNature.com

Nutrition Express
P.O. Box 4076
Torrance, CA 90510
(800) 338-7979; (310) 370-6365;
(310) 784-8522 (fax)

Nutrition Plus
4747 E. Elliot Rd., #29
Phoenix, AZ 85044
(800) 241-9236; (970) 872-8664;
(970) 872-3862 (fax)

Sunburst Biorganics
832 Merrick Rd.
Baldwin, NY 11510
(800) 645-8448; (516) 623-8478;
(516) 623-2413 (fax)
www.sunburstbiorganics.com

Vitamin Discount Connection
35 N. 8th St.
P. O. Box 1431
Indiana, PA 15701
(800) 848-2990; (412) 349-2367;
(412) 349-3711 (fax)

Vitamin Express
1428 Irving St.
San Francisco, CA 94122
(800) 500-0733; (800) 218-7900 (fax)
www.vitaminexpress.com

The Vitamin Shoppe
4700 Westside Ave.
North Bergen, NJ 07047
(800) 223-1216; (201) 866-7711;
(800) 852-7153 (fax);
(201) 866-9513 (fax)
www.vitaminshoppe.com

Vitamin Specialties
8200 Ogontz Ave.
Wyncote, PA 19095
(800) 365-8482;
(215) 885-1310 (fax)

The Vitamin Trader
6501 Fourth St. NW
Albuquerque, NM 87107
(800) 334-9310; (505) 344-6060;
(800) 334-9320 (fax)

Wellness Health & Pharmacy
2800 South 18th St.
Birmingham, AL 35209
(800) 227-2627;
(800) 369-0302 (fax)

Wholesale Nutrition
Box 3345
Saratoga, CA 95070
(800) 325-2664; (800) 858-6520

References

For each chapter, I list citations for scientific studies mentioned in the text, as well as for important journal articles that may not be directly mentioned.

1. Natural Drugs of the Brain

Serotonin

Meltzer, C. C., et al. "Serotonin in aging, late-life depression, and Alzheimer's disease: the emerging role of functional imaging." *Neuropsychopharmacol* (1998), 18(6):407–30.

Moore, P., et al. "Rapid tryptophan depletion, sleep electroencephalogram, and mood in men with remitted depression on serotonin reuptake inhibitors." *Arch Gen Psychiatry* (1998), 55(6):534–39.

Mourilhe, P., and P. E. Stokes. "Risks and benefits of selective serotonin reuptake inhibitors in the treatment of depression." *Drug Saf* (1998), 18(1):57–82.

Panzer, A. "Depression or cancer: the choice between serotonin or melatonin?" *Med Hypotheses* (1998), 50(5):385–87

Stockmeier, C. A. "Neurobiology of serotonin in depression and suicide." *Ann N Y Acad Sci* (1997), 836:220–32.

Dopamine

Bowden, C., et al. "Reduced dopamine turnover in the basal ganglia of depressed suicides." *Brain Res* (1997), 769(1):135–40

Cabib, S., and S. Puglisi-Allegra. "Stress, depression and the mesolimbic dopamine system," *Psychopharmacol* (1996), 128(4):331–42.

Diehl, D. J., and S. Gershon. "The role of dopamine in mood disorders." *Compr Psychiatry* (1992), 33(2):115–20.

Muscat, R., et al. "Antidepressant-like effects of dopamine agonists in an animal model of depression." *Biol Psychiatry* (1992), 31(9):937–46.

Roy, A., et al. "Marked reduction in indexes of dopamine metabolism among patients with depression who attempt suicide." *Arch Gen Psychiatry* (1992), 49(6):447–50.

Yehuda, R., et al. "Plasma norepinephrine and 3-methoxy-4-hydroxyphenylglycol concentrations and severity of depression in combat posttraumatic stress disorder and major depressive disorder." *Biol Psychiatry* (1998), 44(1):56–63.

Noradrenaline

Kelly, C. B., and S. J. Cooper. "Plasma noradrenaline response to electroconvulsive therapy in depressive illness." *Br J Psychiatry* (1997), 171:182–86.

Leonard, B. E. "Noradrenaline in basic models of depression." *Eur Neuropsychopharmacol* (1997), 7 Suppl 1:S11–6; discussion S71–73.

———. "The role of noradrenaline in depression: a review." *J Psychopharmacol* (1997), 11(4 Suppl):S39–47.

Nutt, D. J. "Noradrenaline in depression: half a century of progress." *J Psychopharmacol* (1997), 11(4 Suppl):S3.

Palazidou, E., et al. "Noradrenaline uptake inhibition increases melatonin secretion, a measure of noradrenergic neurotransmission, in depressed patients." *Psychol Med* (1992), 22(2):309–15.

Plaznik, A., and W. Kostowski. "The involvement of serotonin and noradrenaline in the psychopathological processes of stress and depression: animal models and the effect of antidepressant drugs." *Pol J Pharmacol Pharm* (1991), 43(4):301–22.

Endorphins

Brambilla, F., et al. "Beta-endorphin concentration in peripheral blood mononuclear cells of elderly depressed patients—effects of phosphatidylserine therapy." *Neuropsychobiol* (1996), 34(1):18–21.

Darko, D. F., et al. "Plasma beta-endorphin and natural killer cell activity in major depression: a preliminary study." *Psychiatry Res* (1992), 43(2):111–19.

———. "Association of beta-endorphin with specific clinical symptoms of depression." *Am J Psychiatry* (1992), 149(9):1162–67.

France, R. D., and B. J. Urban. "Cerebrospinal fluid concentrations of beta-endorphin in chronic low back pain patients. Influence of depression and treatment." *Psychosom* (1991), 32(1):72–7.

Krittayaphong, R., et al. "Relationship among depression scores, beta-endorphin, and angina pectoris during exercise in patients with coronary artery disease." *Clin J Pain* (1996), 12(2):126–33.

Light, K. C., et al. "Depression and type A behavior pattern in patients with coronary artery disease: relationships to painful versus silent myocardial ischemia and beta-endorphin responses during exercise." *Psychosom Med* (1991), 53(6):669–83.

Lobstein, D. D., and C. L. Rasmussen. "Decreases in resting plasma beta-endorphin and depression scores after endurance training." *J Sports Med Phys Fitness* (1991), 31(4):543–51.

Maes, M., et al. "Stimulatory effects of L-5-hydroxytryptophan on postdexamethasone beta-endorphin levels in major depression." *Neuropsychopharmacol* (1996), 15(4):340–48.

Nemeroff, C. B., et al. "Neuropeptide concentrations in the cerebrospinal fluid of depressed patients treated with electroconvulsive therapy. Corticotrophin-releasing factor, beta-endorphin and somatostatin." *Br J Psychiatry* (1991), 158:59–63.

2. From Lithium to Prozac

Alexopoulos, G. S., et al. "Vascular depression hypothesis." *Arch Gen Psychiatry* (1997), 54:915–22.

Bouhassira, M., et al. "Which patients receive antidepressants? A 'real world' telephone study." *J Affect Disord* (1998), 49(1):19–26.

Buckley, N. A., and P. R. McManus. "Can the fatal toxicity of antidepressant drugs be predicted with pharmacological and toxicological data?" *Drug Saf* (1998), 18(5):369–81.

Kendler, K. S., et al. "Sources of individual differences in depressive symptoms: analysis of two samples of twins and their families." *Am J Psychiatry* (1994), 51:1605–14.

Montgomery, S. A. "Reboxetine: additional benefits to the depressed patient." *J Psychopharmacol* (1997), 11:4(Suppl, S9–15).

Olfson, M., et al. "Antidepressant prescribing practices of outpatient psychiatrists." *Arch Gen Psychiatry* (1998), 55(4):310–16.

Segraves, R. T. "Antidepressant-induced sexual dysfunction." *J Clin Psychiatry* (1998), 59 Suppl 4:48–54.

Stahl, S. M. "Basic psychopharmacology of antidepressants, part 1: Antidepressants have seven distinct mechanisms of action." *J Clin Psychiatry* (1998), 59 Suppl 4:5–14.

Thapa, P. B., et al. "Antidepressants and the risk of falls among nursing home residents." *N Engl J Med* (1998), 339(13):875–82.

3. The Gender Factor
Gender

Ahnlund, K., and A. Frodi. "Gender differences in the development of depression." *Scand J Psychol* (1996), 37(3):229–37.

Bagdy, G. "Serotonin, anxiety, and stress hormones. Focus on 5-HT receptor subtypes, species and gender differences." *Ann N Y Acad Sci* (1998), 851:357–63.

Betrus, P. A., et al. "Women and depression." *Health Care Women* (1995), 16(3):243–52.

Dorn, L. D., et al. "Response to oCRH in depressed and nondepressed adolescents: does gender make a difference?" *J Am Acad Child Adolesc Psychiatry* (1996), 35(6):764–73.

Fava, M., et al. "Gender differences in hostility among depressed and medical outpatients." *J Nerv Ment Dis* (1995), 183(1):10–14.

Gelfin, Y., et al. "Complex effects of age and gender on hypothermic, adrenocorticotrophic hormone and cortisol responses to ipsapirone challenge in normal subjects." *Psychopharmacol* (1995), 120(3):356–64.

Halbreich, U., et al. "Sex differences in biological factors putatively related to depression." *J Affect Disord* (1984), 7(3–4):223–33.

Hankin, B. L., et al. "Development of depression from preadolescence to young adulthood: emerging gender differences in a 10–year longitudinal study." *J Abnorm Psychol* (1998), 107(1):128–40.

Kellner, M., et al. "Corticotropin-releasing hormone inhibits melatonin secretion in healthy volunteers—a potential link to low-melatonin syndrome in depression?" *Neuroendocrinol* (1997), 65(4):284–90.

Kessler, R. C., et al. "Sex and depression in the National Comorbidity Survey: I: Lifetime prevalence, chronicity, and recurrence." *J Affect Disord* (1993), 29:85–96.

Klerman, G. L., and M. M. Weissman. "Increasing rates of depression." *JAMA* (1989), 261(15):2229–35.

Loewenthal, K., et al. "Gender and depression in Anglo-Jewry." *Psychol Med* (1995), 25(5):1051–63.

Merikangas, K. R., et al. "Genetic factors in the sex ratio of major depression." *Psychol Med* (1985), 15(1):63–69.

Mitchell, S., and S. Abbott. "Gender and symptoms of depression and anxiety among Kikuyu secondary school students in Kenya." *Soc Sci Med* (1987), 24(4):303–16.

Musante, G. J., et al. "The comorbidity of depression and eating dysregulation processes in a diet-seeking obese population: a matter of gender specificity." *Int J Eat Disord* (1998), 23(1):65–75.

Nishizawa, S., et al. "Differences between males and females in rates of serotonin synthesis in the human brain." *Proc Natl Acad Sci USA* (1997), 94(10):5308–13.

Page, C., and N. Ricard. "[A comparative study on the self-care needs as perceived by women treated for depression]." *Can J Nurs Res* (1995), 27(3):87–109.

Reynolds, C. F. 3rd, et al. "Sleep, gender, and depression: an analysis of gender effects on the electroencephalographic sleep of 302 depressed outpatients." *Biol Psychiatry* (1990), 28(8):673–84.

Rybakowski, J., and M. Plocka. "Seasonal variations of the dexamethasone suppression test in depression compared with schizophrenia: a gender effect." *J Affect Disord* (1992), 24(2):87–91.

Shaw, D., and B. D. Goldman. "Gender differences in influence of prenatal photoperiods on postnatal pineal melatonin rhythms and serum prolactic and follicle-stimulating hormone in the Siberian hamster (*Phodopus sungorus*)." *Endocrinol* (1995), 136(10):4237–46.

Shear, M. K. "Anxiety disorders in women: gender-related modulation of neurobiology and behavior." *Semin Reprod Endocrinol* (1997), 15(1):69–76.

Spangler, D. L., et al. "Gender differences in cognitive diathesis-stress domain match: implications for differential pathways to depression." *J Abnorm Psychol* (1996), 105(4):653–57.

Suhail, K., and R. Cochrane. "Seasonal variations in hospital admissions for affective disorders by gender and ethnicity." *Soc Psychiatry Psychiatr Epidemiol* (1998), 33(5):211–17.

Weissman, M. M., et al. "The epidemiology of depression: An update on sex differences in rates." *J Affect Disord* (1984), 7(3–4):179–88.

———. "Cross-national epidemiology of major depression and bipolar disorder." *JAMA* (1996), 276(4):293–99.

Weissman, M. M., and G. L. Klerman. "Sex differences and the epidemiology of depression." *Arch Gen Psychiatry* (1977), 34(1):98–111.

Whiffen, V. E., and S. E. Clark. "Does victimization account for sex differences in depressive symptoms?" *Br J Clin Psychol* (1997), 36(Pt. 2):185–93.

Zunzunegui, M. V., et al. "Gender differences in depressive symptoms among Spanish elderly." *Soc Psychiatry Psychiatr Epidemiol* (1998), 33(5):195–205.

Season/Melatonin

Bozhko, G. K., et al. "[Melatonin excretion in patients with depression under the action of light of increased intensity]." *Zh Nevropatol Psikhiatr Im S S Korsakova* (1995), 95(4):51–53.

Dollins, A. B., et al. "Effect of inducing nocturnal serum melatonin concentrations in daytime on sleep, mood, body temperature, and performance." *Proc Natl Acad Sci USA* (1994), 91(5):1824–28.

Kellner, M., et al. "Corticotropin-releasing hormone inhibits melatonin secretion in healthy volunteers—a potential link to low-melatonin syndrome in depression?" *Neuroendocrinol* (1997), 65(4):284–90.

Maurizi, C. P. "The therapeutic potential for tryptophan and melatonin: possible roles in depression, sleep, Alzheimer's disease and abnormal aging." *Med Hypotheses* (1990), 31(3):233–42.

Peschke, E., et al. "Influence of melatonin and serotonin on glucose-stimulated insulin release from perifused rat pancreatic islets in vitro." *J Pineal Res* (1997), 23(3):156–63.

Rao, M. L., et al. "Blood serotonin, serum melatonin and light therapy in healthy subjects and in patients with nonseasonal depression." *Acta Psychiatr Scand* (1992), 86(2):127–32.

Rao, M. L., et al. "The influence of phototherapy on serotonin and melatonin in non-seasonal depression." *Pharmacopsychiatry* (1990), 23(3):155–58.

Rubin, R. T., et al. "Neuroendocrine aspects of primary endogenous depression. XI. Serum melatonin measures in patients and matched control subjects." *Arch Gen Psychiatry* (1992), 49(7):558–67.

Sekula, L. K., et al. "Neuroendocrine aspects of primary endogenous depression. XV: Mathematical modeling of nocturnal melatonin secretion in major depressives and normal controls." *Psychiatry Res* (1997), 69(2–3):143–53.

Shafii, M., et al. "Nocturnal serum melatonin profile in major depression in children and adolescents." *Arch Gen Psychiatry* (1996), 53(11):1009–13.

Shaji, A. V., and S. K. Kulkarni. "Evidence of GABAergic modulation in melatonin-induced short-term memory deficits and food consumption." *Methods Find Exp Clin Pharmacol* (1998), 20(4):311–19.

Tarquini, B., et al. "[Melatonin and seasonal depression]." *Recenti Prog Med* (1998), 89(7–8):395–403.

Wetterberg, L., et al. "Age, alcoholism and depression are associated with low levels of urinary melatonin." *J Psychiatry Neurosci* (1992), 17(5): 215–24.

4. *Your Personal Biochemistry*

Blood Sugar

Drevets, W. C. "Functional neuroimaging studies of depression: the anatomy of melancholia." *Annu Rev Med* (1998), 49:341–61.

Gold, A. E., et al. "Changes in mood during acute hypoglycemia in healthy participants." *J Pers Soc Psychol* (1995), 68(3):498–504.

Soares, J. C., and J. J. Mann. "The functional neuroanatomy of mood disorders." *J Psychiatr Res* (1997), 31(4):393–432.

Thyroid

Aufmkolk, M., et al. "Extracts and auto-oxidized constituents of certain plants inhibit the receptor-binding and the biological activity of Graves' immunoglobulins." *Endocrinol* (1985), 116(5):1687–93.

Brown, G. M., et al. "Lack of association between thyroid and pineal responses to antidepressant treatment." *Depression* (1996), 4(2):73–76.

Chen, M. D., et al. "[Influence of yang-restoring herb medicines upon metabolism of thyroid hormone in normal rats and a drug administration schedule]." *Chung Hsi I Chieh Ho Tsa Chih* (1989), 9(2):93–95.

Duval, F., et al. "Effect of antidepressant medication on morning and evening thyroid function tests during a major depressive episode." *Arch Gen Psychiatry* (1996), 53(9):833–40.

Esposito, S., et al. "The thyroid axis and mood disorders: overview and future prospects." *Psychopharmacol Bull* (1997), 33(2):205–17.

Harris, S., and B. Dawson-Hughes. "Seasonal mood changes in 250 normal women." *Psychiatry Res* (1993), 49(1):77–87.

Kadono, Y., et al. "Effects of antidepressants on thyroid stimulating hormone release in rats under ether stress." *Psychiatry Clin Neurosci* (1995), 49(4): 231–36.

Mason, G. A., et al. "GABA intake is inhibited by thyroid hormones: Implications for depression." *Psychoneuroendocrinol* (1987), 12:53–59.

Nakamura, T., and J. Nomura. "Comparison of thyroid function between responders and nonresponders to thyroid hormone supplementation in depression." *Jpn J Psychiatry Neurol* (1992), 46(4):905–09.

Rao, M. L., et al. "Low plasma thyroid indices of depressed patients are attenuated by antidepressant drugs and influence treatment outcome." *Pharmacopsychiatry* (1996), 29(5):180–86.

Zhang, J. Q., and M. Zhao. "[Effects of yin-tonics and yang-tonics on serum thyroid hormone levels and thyroid hormone receptors of hepatic cell nucleus in hyperthyroxinemic and hypothyroxinemic rats]." *Chung Hsi I Chieh Ho Tsa Chih* (1991), 11(2):105–06.

Stress

Birmaher, B., et al. "Neuroendocrine response to 5-hydroxy-L-tryptophan in prepubertal children at high risk of major depressive disorder." *Arch Gen Psychiatry* (1997), 54(12):1113–19.

Catalan, R., et al. "Plasma corticotropin-releasing factor in depressive disorders." *Biol Psychiatry* (1998), 44(1):15–20.

Fassbender, K., et al. "Mood disorders and dysfunction of the hypothalamic-pituitary-adrenal axis in multiple sclerosis: association with cerebral inflammation." *Arch Neurol* (1998), 55(1):66–72.

Goodwin, G. M., et al. "The effects of cortisol infusion upon hormone secretion from the anterior pituitary and subjective mood in depressive illness and in controls." *J Affect Disord* (1992), 26(2):73–83.

Goodyer, I. M., et al. "Adrenal steroid secretion and major depression in 8- to 16-year-olds. III. Influence of cortisol/DHEA ratio at presentation on subsequent rates of disappointing life events and persistent major depression." *Psychol Med* (1998), 28(2):265–73.

Harte, J. L., et al. "The effects of running and meditation on beta-endorphin, corticotropin-releasing hormone and cortisol in plasma, and on mood." *Biol Psychol* (1995), 40(3):251–65.

Markus, C. R., et al. "Does carbohydrate-rich, protein-poor food prevent a deterioration of mood and cognitive performance of stress-prone subjects when subjected to a stressful task?" *Appetite* (1998), 31(1):49–65.

Mokrani, M. C., et al. "HPA axis dysfunction in depression: correlation with monoamine system abnormalities." *Psychoneuroendocrinol* (1997), 22 Suppl 1:S63–68.

Odagiri, Y., et al. "Relationships between exhaustive mood state and changes in stress hormones following an ultraendurance race." *Int J Sports Med* (1996), 17(5):325–31.

Thakore, J. H., et al. "Effects of antidepressant treatment on corticotropin-induced cortisol responses in patients with melancholic depression." *Psychiatry Res* (1997), 73(1–2):27–32.

Fat Balance

Adams, P. B., et al. "Arachidonic acid to eicosapentaenoic acid ratio in blood correlates positively with clinical symptoms of depression." *Lipids* (1996), 31 Suppl:S157–61.

Horsten, M., et al. "Depressive symptoms, social support, and lipid profile in healthy middle-aged women." *Psychosom Med* (1997), 59(5):521–28.

Maes, M., et al. "Fatty acid composition in major depression: decreased omega 3 fractions in cholesteryl esters and increased C20: 4 omega 6/C20:5 omega 3 ratio in cholesteryl esters and phospholipids." *J Affect Disord* (1996), 38(1):35–46.

Olusi, S. O., and A. A. Fido. "Serum lipid concentrations in patients with major depressive disorder." *Biol Psychiatry* (1996), 40(11): 1128–31.

5. Step One: Take Mood-Boosting Amino Acids

Tryptophan

Belongia, E. A., et al. "An investigation of the cause of the eosinophilia-myalgia syndrome associated with tryptophan use." *N Engl J Med* (1990), 323:357–65.

Bhatti, T., et al. "Effects of a tryptophan-free amino acid drink challenge on normal human sleep electroencephalogram and mood." *Biol Psychiatry* (1998), 43(1):52–59.

Boman, B. "L-tryptophan: A rational antidepressant and a natural hypnotic?" *Aust NZ J Psychiatry* (1988), 22:83–97.

Buist, R. "The therapeutic predictability of tryptophan and tyrosine in the treatment of depression." *Int J Clin Nutr Rev* (1983), 3:1–3.

Chouinard, G., et al. "Tryptophan in the treatment of depression and mania." *Adv Biol Psychiatry* (1983), 10:47–66.

Delgado, P. D., et al. "Serotonin function and the mechanism of antidepressant action." *Arch Gen Psychiatry* (1990), 47:411–18.

Huether, G., et al. "Effect of tryptophan administration on circulating melatonin levels in chicks and rats: Evidence for stimulation of melatonin synthesis and release in the gastrointestinal tract." *Life Sci* (1992), 51:945–53.

Kitahara, M. "Dietary tryptophan ratio and suicide in the United Kingdom, Ireland, the United States, Canada, Australia, and New Zealand." *Omega J Death Dying* (1987), 18:71–76.

Lam, R. W., et al. "L-tryptophan augmentation of light therapy in patients with seasonal affective disorder." *Can J Psychiatry* (1997), 42(3):303–06.

Lucca, A., et al. "Plasma tryptophan levels and plasma tryptophan/neutral amino acids ratio in patients with mood disorder, patients with obsessive-compulsive disorder, and normal subjects." *Psychiatry Res* (1992), 44(2):85–91.

Moller, S., et al. "Tryptophan availability in endogenous depression: relation to efficacy of L-tryptophan treatment." *Adv Biol Psychiatry* (1983), 10:30–46.

Neumeister, A., et al. "Effects of tryptophan depletion on drug-free patients with seasonal affective disorder during a stable response to bright light therapy." *Arch Gen Psychiatry* (1997), 54:133–38.

Quadbeck, H., et al. "Comparison of the antidepressant action of tryptophan, tryptophan/5-hydroxytryptophan combination and nomifensine." *Neuropsychobiology* (1984), 11(2):111–15.

Sandyk, R. "L-tryptophan in neuropsychiatric disorder: a review." *Int J Neurosci* (1992), 67(1–4):127–44.

Schneider-Helmet, D., et al. "Evaluation of L-tryptophan for treatment of insomnia: a review." *Psychopharmacol* (1986), 89(1):1–7.

Schweiger, U., et al. "Macronutrient intake, plasma large neutral amino acids and mood during weight-reducing diets." *J Neural Transm* (1986), 67(1–2): 77–86.

Slutsker, L., et al. "Eosinophilia-myalgia syndrome associated with exposure to tryptophan from a single manufacturer." *JAMA* (1990), 264:213–17.

Young, S. N. "The 1989 Borden Award Lecture. Some effects of dietary components (amino acids, carbohydrate, folic acid) on brain serotonin synthesis, mood, and behavior." *Can J Physiol Pharmacol* (1991), 69(7):893–903.

———. "Use of tryptophan in combination with other antidepressant treatments: a review." *J Psychiatry Neuroscience* (1991), 16(5):241–46.

Young, S. N., et al. "Tryptophan depletion causes a rapid lowering of mood in normal males." *Psychopharmacol* (1985), 87:173–77.

5-HTP

Agren, H., et al. "Low brain uptake of L-(11C)5-hydroxytryptophan in major depression: A positron emission tomography study on patients and healthy volunteers." *Acta Psychiatr Scand* (1991), 83:449–55.

Alino, J. J., et al. "5-hydroxytryptophan (5-HTP) and a MAOI (nialamide) in the treatment of depressions. A double-blind controlled study." *Int Pharmacopsychiatry* (1976), 11(1):9–15.

Angst, J., et al. "The treatment of depression with L-5-hydroxytryptophan versus imipramine: Results of two open and one double-blind study." *Arch Psychiatr Nervenkr* (1977), 224:175–86.

Byerley, W. F., et al. "5-Hydroxytryptophan: A review of its antidepressant efficacy and adverse effects." *J Clin Psychopharm* (1987), 7(3):127–37.

Kahn, R. S., and H. Westenberg. "L-5-hydroxytryptophan in the treatment of anxiety disorders." *J Affect Disord* (1985), 8:197–200.

Kahn, R. S., et al. "Effect of a serotonin precursor and uptake inhibitor in anxiety disorders: A double-blind comparison of 5-hydroxytryptophan, clomipramine and placebo." *Int Clin Psychopharmacol* (1987), 2(1):33–45.

Li Kam Wa, T., et al. "Blood and urine 5-hydroxytryptamine [serotonin] levels after administration of two 5-hydroxytryptophan precursors in normal man." *Br J Clin Pharmacol* (1995), 39:327–29.

Maes, M., et al. "Stimulatory effects of L-5-hydroxytryptophan on postdexamethasone beta-endorphin levels in major depression." *Neuropsychopharmacol* (1996), 15:340–48.

Nardini, M., et al. "Treatment of depression with L-5-hydroxytryptophan combined with chlorimipramine: A double blind study." *J Clin Pharmacolog Res* (1983), 3:239–250.

Nolen, W. A., et al. "Treatment strategy in depression. II. MAO inhibitors in depression resistant to cyclic antidepressants: two controlled crossover studies with tranylcypromine versus L-5-hydroxy-tryptophan and nomifensine." *Acta Psychiat Scand* (1988), 78(5):676–83.

Pöldinger, W., et al. "A functional-dimensional approach to depression: Serotonin deficiency as a target syndrome in a comparison of 5-hydroxytryptophan and fluvoxamine." *Psychopathol* (1991), 24(2):53–81.

Takahashi, S., et al. "Effect of L-5-hydroxytryptophan on brain monoamine metabolism and evaluation of its clinical effect in depressed patients." *J Psychiatric Res* (1975), 12:177–87.

Ursin, R. "The effect of 5-hydroxytryptophan and L-tryptophan on wakefulness and sleep patterns in the cat." *Brain Res* (1976), 106:106–15.

Van Praag, H. M. "Studies in the mechanism of action of serotonin precursors in depression." *Psychopharmacol Bull* (1984), 20:599–602.

Van Praag, H. M., et al. "5-Hydroxytryptophan in combination with clomipramine in 'therapy-resistant' depression." *Psychopharmacol* (1974), 38:267–69.

Van Praag, H. M., and H. G. Westenberg. "The treatment of depressions with L-5-hydroxytryptophan: Theoretical backgrounds and practical application." *Adv Biol Psychiatry* (1983), 10:94–128.

Zmilacher, K., et al. "L-5-hydroxytryptophan alone and in combination with a peripheral decarboxylase inhibitor in the treatment of depression." *Neuropsychobiol* (1988), 20:28–35.

Phenylalanine

Beckmann, H. "Phenylalanine in affective disorders." *Adv Biol Psychiatry* (1983), 10:137–47.

Beckmann, H., et al. "DL-phenylalanine versus imipramine: A double-blind controlled study." *Archiv fur Psychiatrie und Nervenkrankheiten* (1979), 227(1): 49–58.

Beckmann, H., and E. Ludolph. "[DL-phenylalanine as an antidepressant: Open study]." *Arzneimittelforschung* (1978), 28(8):1283–84.

Beckmann, H., et al. "DL-phenylalanine in depressed patients: an open study." *J Neural Transm* (1977), 41(2–3):123–34.

Ehrenpreis, S. "D-phenylalanine and other enkephalinase inhibitors as pharmacological agents: implications for some important therapeutic application." *Subst Alcohol Actions Misuse* (1982), 3(4):231–39.

Ehrenpreis, S. "D-phenylalanine and other enkephalinase inhibitors as pharmacological agents: implications for some important therapeutic application." *Acupunct Electrother Res* (1982), 7(2–3):157–72.

Halpern, L. M., and W. K. Dong. "D-phenylalanine: a putative enkephalinase inhibitor studied in a primate acute pain model." *Pain* (1986), 24(2):223–37.

Hashimoto, H., et al. "Metabolism of D-phenylalanine and its effects on concentrations of brain monoamines and amino acids in rats—a basic study on possibility of clinical use of D-phenylalanine as an antidepressant." *Folia Psychiatr Neurol Jpn* (1983), 37(2):137–44.

Kravitz, H. M., et al. "Dietary supplements of phenylalanine and other amino acid precursors of brain neuroamines in the treatment of depressive disorders." *J Am Osteo Assoc* (1984), 84:119.

Sabelli, H. C. "Clinical antidepressant effects of selegiline and L-phenylalanine support mood regulating role for brain 2-phenylethylamine." Paper presented at 75th annual meeting of the Federation of American Societies for Experimental Biology, Atlanta, 1991.

Sabelli, H. C., et al. "Antidepressant effects of L-phenylalanine." Paper presented at second world conference, Clinical Pharmacology and Therapeutics, Washington, D.C., August 1983.

———. "Clinical studies on the phenylethylamine hypothesis of affective disorder: Urine and blood phenylacetic acid and phenylalanine dietary supplements." *J Clin Psychiatry* (1986), 47(2):66–70.

Spatz, H., et al. "Effects of D-phenylalanine on clinical picture and phenylethylaminuria in depression." *Biol Psychiatry* (1975), 10:235.

Tyrosine

Gibson, C., and A. J. Gelenberg. "Tyrosine for depression," *Adv Biol Psychiatry* (1983), 10:148–59.

Gelenberg, A. J., et al. "Tyrosine for the treatment of depression." *Am J Psychiatry* (1980), 137(5):622–23.

———. "Tyrosine for depression." *J Psychiatr Res* (1982–83), 17(2):175–80.

———. "Tyrosine for depression: a double-blind trial." *J Affect Disord* (1990), 19(2):125–32.

Leonard, B. E. "The role of noradrenaline in depression: a review." *J Psychopharmacol* (Oxf) (1997), 11(4 Suppl):S39–47.

Serretti, A., et al. "Tyrosine hydroxylase gene associated with depressive symptomatology in mood disorder." *Am J Med Genet* (1998), 81(2):127–30.

Mouret, J., et al. "[L-tyrosine cures, immediate and long term, dopamine-dependent depressions. Clinical and polygraphic studies]." *C R Acad Sci III* (1988), 306(3):93–98.

Glutamine

Paslawski, T. M., et al. "Effects of the MAO inhibitor phenelzine on glutamine and GABA concentrations in rat brain." *Prog Brain Res* (1995), 106:181–86.

Vargas, C., et al. "Dissimilar effects of lithium and valproic acid on GABA and glutamine concentrations in rat cerebrospinal fluid." *Gen Pharmacol* (1998), 30(4):601–04.

GABA

Bartholini, G., et al. "The GABA hypothesis of depression and antidepressant drug action." *Psychopharmacol Bull* (1985), 21(3):385–88.

Monteleone, P. "GABA, depression and the mechanism of action of antidepressant drugs: a neuroendocrine approach." *J Affect Disord* (1990), 20(1):1–5.

Petty, F. "GABA and mood disorders: a brief review and hypothesis." *J Affect Disord* (1995), 34(4):275–81.

Petty, F., et al. "Plasma GABA in mood disorders." *Psychopharmacol Bull* (1990), 26(2):157–61.

———. "Benzodiazepines as antidepressants: does GABA play a role in depression?" *Biol Psychiatry* (1995), 38(9):578–91.

Prosser, J., et al. "Plasma GABA in children and adolescents with mood, behavior, and comorbid mood and behavior disorders: a preliminary study." *J Child Adolesc Psychopharmacol* (1997), 7(3):181–99.

Zhang, S. S., et al. "Effects of cerebral GABA level on learning and memory." *Acta Pharmacologica Sinica* (1989), 10(1):10–12.

SAM

Abou-Saleh, M. T., and A. Coppen. "The biology of folate in depression: implications for nutritional hypotheses of the psychoses." *J Psychiatr Res* (1986), 20(2):91–101.

Anon. "A new treatment for depression: S-adenosylmethionine. An international symposium. Trieste, Italy, June 18, 1987, Proceedings." *Ala J Med Sci* (1988), 25(3):291–319.

Bell, K. M., et al. "S-adenosylmethionine treatment of depression: a controlled clinical trial." *Am J Psychiatry* (1988), 145(9):1110–14.

Bottiglieri, T., et al. "Cerebrospinal fluid S-adenosylmethionine in depression and dementia: effects of treatment with parenteral and oral S-adenosylmethionine." *J Neurol Neurosurg Psychiatry* (1990), 53(12):1096–98.

Bressa, G. M. "S-adenosyl-l-methionine (SAMe) as antidepressant: meta-analysis of clinical studies." *Acta Neurol Scand Suppl* (1994), 154:7–14.

Cantoni, G. L., et al. "Affective disorders and S-adenosylmethionine: a new hypothesis." *Trends Neurosci* (1989), 12(9):319–24.

Carney, M. W., et al. "S-adenosylmethionine and affective disorder." *Am J Med* (1987), 83(5A):104–06.

Charlton, C. G. "Depletion of nigrostriatal and forebrain tyrosine hydroxylase by S-adenosylmethionine: a model that may explain the occurrence of depression in Parkinson's disease." *Life Sci* (1997), 61(5):495–502.

DeLeo, D. "S-adenosylmethionine as an antidepressant: A double-blind trial versus placebo." *Curr Ther Res* (1987), 41(6):865–70.

Janicak, P. G., et al. "S-adenosylmethionine in depression. A literature review and preliminary report." *Ala J Med Sci* (1988), 25(3):306–13.

———. "Parenteral S-adenosyl-methionine (SAMe) in depression: literature review and preliminary data." *Psychopharmacol Bull* (1989), 25(2): 238–42.

Kagan, B. L., et al. "Oral S-adenosylmethionine in depression: a randomized, double-blind, placebo-controlled trial." *Am J Psychiatry* (1990), 147(5):591–95.

Rosenbaum, J. F., et al. "The antidepressant potential of oral S-adenosyl-l-methionine." *Acta Psychiatr Scand* (1990), 81(5):432–36.

Vahora, S. A., and P. Malek-Ahmadi. "S-adenosylmethionine in the treatment of depression." *Neurosci Biobehav Rev* (1988), 12(2):139–41.

6. Step Two: Optimize Your Supplements

Abou-Saleh, M. T., and A. Coppen. "The biology of folate in depression: Implications for nutritional hypotheses of the psychoses." *J Psychiatr Res* (1986), 20(2):91–101.

Bell, I. R., et al. "B-complex vitamin patterns in geriatric and young adult inpatients with major depression." *J Am Ger Soc* (1991), 39(3):252–57.

————. "Brief communication. Vitamin B_1, B_2, and B_6 augmentation of tricyclic antidepressant treatment in geriatric depression with cognitive dysfunction." *J Am Coll Nutr* (1992), 11(2):159–63.

————. "Relationship of normal serum vitamin B_{12} and folate levels to cognitive test performance in subtypes of geriatric major depression." *J Geriatr Psychiatry Neurol* (1990), 3(2):98–105.

Ben-Hur, E., and S. Fulder. "Effect of *Panax ginseng* saponins and *Eleutherococcus senticosus* on survival of cultured mammalian cells after ionizing radiation." *Am J Chinese Med* (1981), 9(1):48–56.

Benton, D., et al. "Thiamine supplementation mood and cognitive functioning." *Psychopharmacol* (1997), 129(1):66–71.

Bespalov, V. G., et al. "The inhibiting effect of phytoadaptogenic preparations from bioginseng, *Eleutherococcus senticosus*, and *Rhaponticum carthamoides* on the development of nervous system tumors in rats induced by N-nitrosoethylurea." *Voprosy Onkologii* (1992), 38(9):1073–80.

Birkmayer, J. G. "Coenzyme nicotinamide adenine dinucleotide: New therapeutic approach for improving dementia of the Alzheimer type." *Ann Clin Lab Sci* (1996), 26(1):1–9.

Birkmayer, J. G., and P. Vank. "Reduced coenzyme 1 (NADH) improves psychomotoric and physical performance in athletes." White Paper Report, New York: Menuco Corp., 1996.

Birkmayer, J. G., and W. Birkmayer. "Stimulation of endogenous L-dopa biosynthesis—a new principle for the therapy of Parkinson's disease: The clinical effect of nicotinamide adenine dinucleotide (NADH) and nicotinamide adenine dinucleotidephosphate (NADPH)." *Acta Neurol Scand Suppl* (1989), 126:183–87.

Birkmayer, J. G., et al. "Nicotinamide adenine dinucleotide (NADH): A new therapeutic approach to Parkinson's disease: Comparison of oral and parenteral application." *Acta Neurol Scand* (1993), 87(Suppl 146):32–35.

Birkmayer, W., and J. G. Birkmayer. "Nicotinamideadenindinucleotide (NADH): the new approach in the therapy of Parkinson's disease." *Ann Clin Lab Sci* (1989), 19(1):38–43.

————. "The coenzyme nicotinamide adenine dinucleotide (NADH) as biological anti-depressive agent." *New Trends Clin Neuropharmacol* (1992), 5:19–25.

Birkmayer, W., et al. "The coenzyme nicotinamide adenine dinucleotide (NADH) improves the disability of Parkinsonian patients." *J Neural Transm Park Dis Dement Sect* (1989), 1(4):297–302.

Bohn, B., et al. "Flow cytometric studies with *Eleutherococcus senticosus* extract as an immunomodulatory agent." *Arzneimittel-Forschung* (1987), 37(10):1193–96.

Brekhman, I. I., and I. V. Dardymov. "Pharmacological investigation of glycosides from ginseng and *Eleutherococcus*." *Lloydia* (1969), 32(1):46–51.

Deijen, J. B., et al. "Vitamin B_6 supplementation in elderly men: Effects on mood, memory, performance and mental effort." *Psychopharmacol* (1992), 109(4):489–96.

Dowling, E. A., et al. "Effect of *Eleutherococcus senticosus* on submaximal and maximal exercise performance." *Med Sci Sports Exercise* (1996), 28(4):482–89.

Farnsworth, N. R., et al. "Siberian ginseng (*Eleutherococcus senticosus*): Current status as an adaptogen." *Econ Med Plant Res* (1985), 1:155–215.

Fava, M., et al. "Folate, vitamin B_{12}, and homocysteine in major depressive disorder." *Am J Psychiatry* (1997), 154(3):426–28.

Fujikawa, T., et al. "Protective effects of *Acanthopanax senticosus* [Harms] from Hokkaido and its components on gastric ulcer in restrained cold water stressed rats." *Biol Pharmaceut Bull* (1996), 19(9):1227–30.

Ghadirian, A. M., et al. "Folic acid deficiency and depression." *Psychosom* (1980), 21:926–29.

Kanowski, S., et al. "Proof of efficacy of the *Ginkgo biloba* special extract EGb 761 in outpatients suffering from mild to moderate primary degenerative dementia of the Alzheimer's type or multi-infarct dementia." *Phytomed* (1997), 4(1):3–13.

Kuhn, W., et al. "Parenteral application of NADH in Parkinson's disease: Clinical improvement partially due to stimulation of endogenous levodopa biosynthesis." *J Neural Transm* (1996), 103(10):1187–93.

LeBars, P. L., et al. "A placebo-controlled, double-blind, randomized trial of an extract of *Ginkgo biloba* for dementia." *JAMA* (1997), 278:1327–32.

Levine, J. "Controlled trials of inositol in psychiatry." *Eur Neuropsychopharmacol* (1997), 7(2):147–55.

———. "Follow-up and relapse analysis of an inositol study of depression." *Israel J Psychiatry Rel Sci* (1995), 32:14–21.

Levitt, A. J., and R. T. Joffe. "Folate, B_{12}, and life course of depressive illness." *Biol Psychiatry* (1989), 25(7):867–72.

Smith, P. F., et al. "The neuroprotective properties of the *Ginkgo biloba* leaf: a review of the possible relationship to platelet-activating factor (PAF)." *J Ethnopharmacol* (1996), 50(3):131–39.

Storga, D., et al. "Monoaminergic neurotransmitters: Their precursors and metabolites in brains of Alzheimer patients." *Neurosci Lett* (1996), 203(1):29–32.

Vrecko, K., et al. "NADH stimulates endogenous dopamine biosynthesis by enhancing the recycling of tetrahydrobiopterin in rat phaeochromocytoma cells." *Biochim Biophys Acta* (1997), 1361(1):59–65.

White, H. L., et al. "Extracts of *Ginkgo biloba* leaves inhibit monoamine oxidase." *Life Sci* (1996), 58:1315–21.

Wolfersdorf, M., and F. König. "Serum folic acid and vitamin B_{12} in depressed inpatients. A study of serum folic acid with radioimmunoassay in 121 depressed inpatients." *Psychiatr Prax* (1995), 22(4):162–64.

270   References

7. Step Three: Make the Fatty Acids Essential

Bjerve, K. S., et al. "Alpha-linolenic acid deficiency in man: effect of essential fatty acids on fatty acid composition." *Adv Prostaglandin Thromboxane Leukot Res* (1987), 17B:862–65.

Cadeddu, G., et al. "Relationship between cholesterol levels and depression in the elderly." *Minerva Med* (1995), 86(6):251–56.

Calabrese, J. R., et al. "Depression, immunocompetence, and prostaglandins of the E series." *Psychiatry Res* (1986), 17(1):41–47.

Clandinin, M. T., et al. "Docosahexaenoic acid increases thyroid-stimulating hormone concentration in male and adrenal corticotrophic hormone concentration in female weanling rats." *J Nutr* (1998), 128(8):1257–61.

Edwards, R., et al. "Depletion of docosahexaenoic acid in red blood cell membranes of depressive patients." *Biochem Soc Trans* (1998), 26(2):S142.

Engstrom, G., et al. "Serum lipids in suicide attempters." *Suicide and Life-Threatening Behavior* (1995), 25(3):393–400.

Gerster, H. "Can adults adequately convert alpha-linolenic acid (18:3n-3) to eicosapentaenoic acid (20:5n-3) and docosahexaenoic acid (22:6n-3)?" *Int J Vitam Nutr Res* (1998), 68(3):159–73.

Horwood, L. J., and D. M. Fergusson. "Breastfeeding and later cognitive and academic outcomes." *Pediatrics* (1998), 101(1):E9.

Kalmijn, S., et al. "Polyunsaturated fatty acids, antioxidants, and cognitive function in very old men." *Am J Epidem* (1997), 145:33.

Kanof, P. D., et al. "Prostaglandin receptor sensitivity in psychiatric disorders." *Arch Gen Psychiatry* (1986), 43(10):987–93.

Lanting, C. I., et al. "Neurological differences between 9-year-old children fed breast milk or formula as babies." *The Lancet* (1994), 344:1319–22.

Ohishi, K., et al. "Increased level of salivary prostaglandins in patients with major depression." *Biol Psychiatry* (1988), 23(4):326–34.

Simopoulos A. P., et al. "Common purslane: a source of omega-3 fatty acids and antioxidants." *J Am Coll Nutr* (1992), 11(4):374–82.

Simopoulos, A. P. "Omega-3 fatty acids in health and disease and in growth and development." *Am J Clin Nutr* (1991), 54(3):438–63.

8. Step Four: Diet for Mental Health

Barton, C., et al. "Differential effects of enterostatin, galanin and opioids on high-fat diet consumption." *Brain Res* (1995), 702(1–2):55–60.

Challet, E., et al. "Phase-advanced daily rhythms of melatonin, body temperature, and locomotor activity in food-restricted rats fed during daytime." *J Biol Rhythms* (1997), 12(1):65–79.

Domingue, B. M., et al. "Effects of subcutaneous melatonin implants during long daylength on voluntary feed intake, rumen capacity and heart rate of red deer (*Cervus elaphus*) fed on a forage diet." *Br J Nutr* (1992), 68(1):77–88.

Dubbels, R., et al. "Melatonin in edible plants identified by radioimmunoassay and by high performance liquid chromatography-mass spectrometry." *J Pineal Res* (1995), 18(1):28–31.

Ferrari, E., et al. "Hormonal circadian rhythms in eating disorders." *Biol Psychiatry* (1990), 27(9):1007–20.

Hattori, A., et al. "Identification of melatonin in plants and its effects on plasma melatonin levels and binding to melatonin receptors in vertebrates." *Biochem Mol Biol Int* (1995), 35(3):627–34.

Gordijn, M. C., et al. "Testing the hypothesis of a circadian phase disturbance underlying depressive mood in nonseasonal depression." *J Biol Rhythms* (1998), 13(2):132–47.

Hasegawa, T. "Depressive effects of lipid peroxides mediated via a purine receptor. Effect of lipid peroxide on the cortical synaptosomal GTPase activity." *Biochem Pharmacol* (1990), 40(7):1463–67.

Kars, M. E., et al. "Specific stimulation of brain serotonin mediated neurotransmission by dexfenfluramine does not restore growth hormone responsiveness in obese women." *Clin Endocrinol* (1996), 44(5):541–46.

Leibowitz, S. F. "The role of serotonin in eating disorders." *Drugs* (1990), 39 (Suppl 3):33–48.

Leibowitz, S. F., et al. "Obesity on a high-fat diet: role of hypothalamic galanin in neurons of the anterior paraventricular nucleus projecting to the median eminence." *J Neurosci* (1998), 18(7):2709–19.

Leibowitz, S. F., and T. Kim. "Impact of a galanin antagonist on exogenous galanin and natural patterns of fat ingestion." *Brain Res* (1992), 599(1):148–52.

Lidberg, L., and A. Daderman. "[Reduced serotonin levels are predisposing to violence. A simple blood test predicts dangerous character]. *Lakartidningen* (1997), 94(39):3385–88.

Lin, L., et al. "Comparison of Osborne-Mendel and S5B/PL strains of rat: central effects of galanin, NPY, beta-casomorphin and CRH on intake of high-fat and low-fat diets." *Obes Res* (1996), 4(2):117–24.

Peschke, E., et al. "Influence of melatonin and serotonin on glucose-stimulated insulin release from perifused rat pancreatic islets in vitro." *J Pineal Res* (1997), 23(3):156–63.

Rada, P., et al. "Galanin in the hypothalamus raises dopamine and lowers acetylcholine release in the nucleus accumbens: a possible mechanism for hypothalamic initiation of feeding behavior." *Brain Res* (1998), 798(1–2):1–6.

Rossi, R., et al. "Differential circadian eating patterns in two psychogenetically selected strains of rats fed low-, medium-, and high-fat diets." *Behav Genet* (1997), 27(6):565–72.

Shaji, A. V., and S. K. Kulkarni. "Evidence of GABAergic modulation in melatonin-induced short-term memory deficits and food consumption." *Methods Find Exp Clin Pharmacol* (1998), 20(4):311–19.

Venero, J. L., et al. "Changes in neurotransmitter levels associated with the deficiency of some essential amino acids in the diet." *Br J Nutr* (1992), 68(2):409–20.

Wolfe, B. E., et al. "The effects of dieting on plasma tryptophan concentration and food intake in healthy women." *Physiol Behav* (1997), 61(4):537–41.

Xu, Z. Q. and T. Hökfelt. "Expression of galanin and nitric oxide synthase in subpopulations of serotonin neurons of the rat dorsal raphe nucleus." *J Chem Neuroanat* (1997), 13(3):169–87.

Yeung, J. M., and E. Friedman. "Effect of aging and diet restriction on monoamines and amino acids in cerebral cortex of Fischer-344 rats." *Growth Dev Aging* (1991), 55(4):275–83.

9. Step Five: Eight Lifestyle Choices You Can Make to Help Beat Depression

Exercise

Aganoff, J. A., and G. J. Boyle. "Aerobic exercise, mood states and menstrual cycle symptoms." *J Psychosom Res* (1994), 38(3):183–92.

Byrne, A., and D. G. Byrne. "The effect of exercise on depression, anxiety and other mood states: a review." *J Psychosom Res* (1993), 37(6):565–74.

Choi, P. Y., et al. "Mood changes in women after an aerobics class: a preliminary study." *Health Care Women Int* (1993), 14(2):167–77.

Cockerill, I. M., et al. "Mood, mileage, and the menstrual cycle." *Br J Sports Med* (1992), 26(3):145–50.

Cramer, S. R., et al. "The effects of moderate exercise training on psychological well-being and mood state in women." *J Psychosom Res* (1991), 35(4–5):437–49.

Daniel, M., et al. "Opiate receptor blockade by naltrexone and mood state after acute physical activity." *Br J Sports Med* (1992), 26(2):111–15.

Head, A., et al. "Acute effects of beta blockade and exercise on mood and anxiety." *Br J Sports Med* (1996), 30(3):238–42.

Kraemer, R. R., et al. "Mood alteration from treadmill running and its relationship to beta-endorphin, corticotropin, and growth hormone." *J Sports Med Phys Fitness* (1990), 30(3):241–46.

Lennox, S. S., et al. "The effect of exercise on normal mood." *J Psychosom Res* (1990), 34(6):629–36.

Maroulakis, E., and Y. Zervas. "Effects of aerobic exercise on mood of adult women." *Percept Mot Skills* (1993), 76(3 Pt. 1):795–801.

McGowan, R. W., et al. "Beta-endorphins and mood states during resistance exercise." *Percept Mot Skills* (1993), 76(2):376–78.

Morris, M., and P. Salmon. "Qualitative and quantitative effects of running on mood." *J Sports Med Phys Fitness* (1994), 34(3):284–91.

Pronk, N. P., et al. "Maximal exercise and acute mood response in women." *Physiol Behav* (1995), 57(1):1–4.

Slaven, L., and C. Lee. "Mood and symptom reporting among middle-aged women: the relationship between menopausal status, hormone replacement therapy, and exercise participation." *Health Psychol* (1997), 16(3):203–08.

Steptoe, A., and S. Cox. "Acute effects of aerobic exercise on mood." *Health Psychol* (1988), 7(4):329–40.

Suter, E., et al. "[Effects of jogging on mental well-being and seasonal mood variations: a randomized study with healthy women and men]." *Schweiz Med Wochenschr* (1991), 121(35):1254–63.

Williams, P., and S. R. Lord. "Effects of group exercise on cognitive functioning and mood in older women." *Aust N Z J Public Health* (1997), 21(1):45–52.

Yeung, R. R. "The acute effects of exercise on mood state." *J Psychosom Res* (1996), 40(2):123–41.

Social Networks and Relations

Antonucci, T. C., et al. "Social relations and depressive symptomatology in a sample of community-dwelling French older adults." *Psychol Aging* (1997), 12(1):189–95.

Baker, F. M., et al. "Screening African-American elderly for the presence of depressive symptoms: a preliminary investigation." *J Geriatr Psychiatry Neurol* (1996), 9(3):127–32.

Braam, A. W., et al. "Religious involvement and depression in older Dutch citizens." *Soc Psychiatry Psychiatr Epidemiol* (1997), 32(5):284–91.

Burns, D. D., et al. "Intimate relationships and depression: Is there a causal connection?" *J Consult Clin Psychol* (1994), 62(5):1033–43.

Lee, M. S., et al. "Social support and depression among elderly Korean immigrants in the United States." *Int J Aging Hum Dev* (1996), 42(4):313–27.

Murberg, T. A., et al. "Social support, social disability and their role as predictors of depression among patients with congestive heart failure." *Scand J Soc Med* (1998), 26(2):87–95.

Creativity

Assael, M., and M. Popovici-Wacks. "Artistic expression in spontaneous paintings of depressed patients." *Isr J Psychiatry Relat Sci* (1989), 26(4):223–43.

Kleinke, C. L. "Comparing depression-coping strategies of schizophrenic men and depressed and nondepressed college students." *J Clin Psychol* (1984), 40(2):420–26.

Pöldinger, W. "The relation between depression and art." *Psychopathol* (1986), 19 (Suppl 2):263–68.

Post, F. "Verbal creativity, depression and alcoholism. An investigation of one hundred American and British writers." *Br J Psychiatry* (1996), 168(5):545–55.

Humor

Danzer, A., et al. "Effect of exposure to humorous stimuli on induced depression." *Psychol Rep* (1990), 66(3 Pt. 1):1027–36.

Moran, C. C. "Short-term mood change, perceived funniness, and the effect of humor stimuli." *Behav Med* (1996), 22(1):32–38.

Richman, J. "The lifesaving function of humor with the depressed and suicidal elderly." *Gerontologist* (1995), 35(2):271–73.

Sakamoto, S., et al. "Polygraphic evaluation of laughing and smiling in schizophrenic and depressive patients." *Percept Mot Skills* (1997), 85(3 Pt. 2): 1291–1302.

Schelde, J. T. "Major depression: behavioral markers of depression and recovery." *J Nerv Ment Dis* (1998), 186(3):133–40.

Sleep

Dolberg, O. T., et al. "Melatonin for the treatment of sleep disturbances in major depressive disorder." *Am J Psychiatry* (1998), 155(8):1119–21.

Orn, P. "[Risk of depression may be discovered by sleep. The sleep pattern is predictable and possible to manipulate]." *Lakartidningen* (1998), 95(11):1087.

Schechtman, K. B., et al. "Gender, self-reported depressive symptoms, and sleep disturbance among older community-dwelling persons. FICSIT group. Frailty and Injuries: Cooperative Studies of Intervention Techniques." *J Psychosom Res* (1997), 43(5):513–27.

Song, C., et al. "The inflammatory response system and the availability of plasma tryptophan in patients with primary sleep disorders and major depression." *J Affect Disord* (1998), 49(3):211–19.

Thase, M. E. "Depression, sleep, and antidepressants." *J Clin Psychiatry* (1998), 59 (Suppl 4):55–65.

Thase, M. E. "Electroencephalographic sleep profiles before and after cognitive behavior therapy of depression." *Arch Gen Psychiatry* (1998), 55(2):138–44.

Relaxation

Berger, B. G., et al. "Mood alteration with yoga and swimming: aerobic exercise may not be necessary." *Percept Mot Skills* (1992), 75(3 Pt. 2):1331–43.

Bowers, W. A. "Treatment of depressed in-patients. Cognitive therapy plus medication, relaxation plus medication, and medication alone." *Br J Psychiatry* (1990), 156:73–78.

DeVaney, S., et al. "Comparative effects of exercise reduction and relaxation training on mood states and Type A scores in habitual aerobic exercisers." *Percept Mot Skills* (1994), 79(3 Pt. 2):1635–44.

Holland, J. C., et al. "A randomized clinical trial of alprazolam versus progressive muscle relaxation in cancer patients with anxiety and depressive symptoms." *J Clin Oncol* (1991), 9(6):1004–11.

Murphy, G. E., et al. "Cognitive behavior therapy, relaxation training, and tricyclic antidepressant medication in the treatment of depression." *Psychol Rep* (1995), 77(2):403–20.

Rees, B. L. "Effect of relaxation with guided imagery on anxiety, depression, and self-esteem in primiparas." *J Holist Nurs* (1995), 13(3):255–67.

Taylor, D. N. "Effects of a behavioral stress-management program on anxiety, mood, self-esteem, and T-cell count in HIV positive men." *Psychol Rep* (1995), 76(2):451–57.

Teasdale, J. D., et al. "How does cognitive therapy prevent depressive relapse and why should attentional control (mindfulness) training help?" *Behav Res Ther* (1995), 33(1):25–39.

Thayer, R. E., et al. "Self-regulation of mood: strategies for changing a bad mood, raising energy, and reducing tension." *J Pers Soc Psychol* (1994), 67(5): 910–25.

Wood, C. "Mood change and perceptions of vitality: a comparison of the effects of relaxation, visualization and yoga." *J R Soc Med* (1993), 86(5):254–58.

Touch

Field, T., et al. "Massage and relaxation therapies' effects on depressed adolescent mothers." *Adolescence* (1996), 31(124):903–11.

Watson, S., and S. Watson. "The effects of massage: an holistic approach to care." *Nurs Stand* (1997), 11(47):45–47.

10. A New Approach to Alcoholism

Berman, J. D., et al. "Diminished adrenocorticotropin response to insulin-induced hypoglycemia in nondepressed, actively drinking male alcoholics." *J Clin Endocrinol Metab* (1990), 71(3):712–17.

Biery, J. R., et al. "Alcohol craving in rehabilitation: assessment of nutrition therapy." *J Am Diet Assoc* (1991), 91(4):463–66.

Blum, K., et al. "Association of the A1 allele of the D2 dopamine receptor gene with severe alcoholism." *Alcohol* (1991), 8(5):409–16.

————. "Allelic association of human dopamine D2 receptor gene in alcoholism." *JAMA* (1990), 263(15):2055–60.

Corrao, G., et al. "Alcohol consumption and micronutrient intake as risk factors for liver cirrhosis: a case-control study. The Provincial Group for the study of Chronic Liver Disease." *Ann Epidemiol* (1998), 8(3):154–59.

del Arbol, J. L., et al. "Plasma concentrations of beta-endorphin, adrenocorticotropic hormone, and cortisol in drinking and abstinent chronic alcoholics." *Alcohol* (1995), 12(6):525–29.

Forsander, O. A. "Dietary influences on alcohol intake: a review." *J Stud Alcohol* (1998), 59(1):26–31.

Genazzani, A. R., et al. "Central deficiency of beta-endorphin in alcohol addicts." *J Clin Endocrinol Metab* (1982), 55(3):583–86.

Gorwood, P., et al. "Lack of association between alcohol-dependence and D3 dopamine receptor gene in three independent samples." *Am J Med Genet* (1995), 60(6):529–31.

Higley, J., et al. "The serotonin reuptake inhibitor sertraline reduces excessive alcohol consumption in nonhuman primates: effect of stress." *Neuropsychopharmacol* (1998), 18(6):431–43.

Larue-Achagiotis, C., et al. "Does alcohol promote reactive hypoglycemia in the rat?" *Physiol Behav* (1990), 47(5):819–23.

Lieber, C. S. "Mechanisms of ethanol-drug-nutrition interactions." *J Toxicol Clin Toxicol* (1994), 32(6):631–81.

Marchesi, C., et al. "Abnormal plasma oxytocin and beta-endorphin levels in alcoholics after short- and long-term abstinence." *Prog Neuropsychopharmacol Biol Psychiatry* (1997), 21(5):797–807.

Marchesi, C., et al. "Beta-endorphin, adrenocorticotropic hormone and cortisol secretion in abstinent alcoholics." *Psychiatry Res* (1997), 72(3):187–94.

Manzo, L., et al. "Nutrition and alcohol neurotoxicity." *Neurotoxicol* (1994), 15(3):555–65.

Noble, E. P., et al. "Allelic association of the D2 dopamine receptor gene with receptor-binding characteristics in alcoholism." *Arch Gen Psychiatry* (1991), 48(7):648–54.

Preedy, V. R., et al. "Metabolic consequences of alcohol dependency." *Adverse Drug React Toxicol Rev* (1997), 16(4):235–56.

Santolaria-Fernandez, F. J., et al. "Nutritional assessment of drug addicts." *Drug Alcohol Depend* (1995), 38(1):11–18.

Tanaka, M. "[Stress and alcohol: research with experimental animals]." *Nihon Arukoru Yakubutsu Igakkai Zasshi* (1998), 33(1):31–43.

Varela, P., et al. "Nutritional status assessment of HIV-positive drug addicts." *Eur J Clin Nutr* (1990), 44(5):415–18.

Vescovi, P. P., et al. "Hormonal (ACTH, cortisol, beta-endorphin, and met-enkephalin) and cardiovascular responses to hyperthermic stress in chronic alcoholics." *Alcohol Clin Exp Res* (1997), 21(7):1195–98.

Bibliography

Natural Depression Treatments

Cleve, Jay. *Out of the Blues*. Minneapolis, Minn.: CompCare Publishers, 1989.

Hoffman, David. *An Herbal Guide to Stress Relief*. Rochester, Vt.: Healing Arts Press, 1986.

Marmorstein, Jerome, and Nanette Marmorstein. *The Psychometabolic Blues*. Santa Barbara, Calif.: Woodbridge Publishing Company, 1979.

Murray, Michael T. *Natural Alternatives to Prozac*. New York: William Morrow and Company, 1996.

Norden, Michael J. *Beyond Prozac: Brain-Toxic Lifestyles, Natural Antidotes and New Generation Antidepressants*. New York: ReganBooks, 1995.

Robertson, Joel, and Tom Monte. *Natural Prozac: Learning to Release Your Body's Own Antidepressants*. San Francisco: HarperSanFrancisco, 1997.

Sachs, Judith. *Nature's Prozac: Natural Therapies and Techniques to Rid Yourself of Anxiety, Depression, Panic Attacks and Stress*. New York: Prentice Hall, 1997.

Slagle, Priscilla. *The Way Up from Down: A Safe New Program That Relieves Low Moods and Depression with Amino Acids and Vitamin Supplements*. New York: Random House, 1987.

Zuess, Jonathan. *The Wisdom of Depression: A Guide to Understanding and Curing Depression Using Natural Medicine*. New York: Harmony Books, 1998.

Neurotransmitters and Mood

Appleton, William S. *Prozac and the New Antidepressants*. New York: Plume, 1997.

Breggin, Peter, and David Cohen. *Your Drug May Be Your Problem*. New York: HarperCollins, 1999.

Breggin, Peter R., and Ginger Ross-Breggin. *Talking Back to Prozac: What Doctors Won't Tell You About Today's Most Controversial Drug*. New York: St. Martin's Press, 1995.

Breggin, Peter R. *Toxic Psychiatry*. New York: St. Martin's Press, 1991.

Fieve, Ronald. *Prozac: Questions and Answers for Patients, Family, and Physicians*. New York: Avon, 1996.

Glenmullen, Joseph. *Prozac Backlash*. New York: Simon & Schuster, 2000.

Kramer, Peter. *Listening to Prozac*. New York: Viking, 1993.

Restak, Richard M. *Receptors*. New York: Bantam Books, 1994.

Wurtman, Judith J., and Susan Suffes. *The Serotonin Solution*. New York: Fawcett Columbine, 1996.

Gender

Jack, Dana Crowley. *Silencing the Self: Women and Depression*. Cambridge, Mass.: Harvard University Press, 1991.

Nolen-Hoeksema, Susan. *Six Differences in Depression*. Stanford, Calif.: Stanford University Press, 1990.

Real, Terrence. *I Don't Want to Talk About It: Overcoming the Secret Legacy of Male Depression*. New York: Scribner, 1997.

St. John's Wort

Bloomfield, Harold H., and Peter McWilliams. *Hypericum & Depression*. Los Angeles: Prelude Press, 1997.

Bratman, Steven. *Beat Depression with St. John's Wort*. Rocklin, Calif.: Prima Publishing, 1997.

Cass, Hyla. *St. John's Wort: Nature's Blues Buster*. Garden City Park, N.Y.: Avery, 1998.

Rosenthal, Norman. *Nature's Prozac*. New York: HarperCollins, 1998.

Turkington, Carol. *The Hypericum Handbook*. New York: M. Evans, 1998.

Upton, Roy. *St. John's Wort*. New Canaan, Ct.: Keats, 1997.

Zuess, Jonathan. *The Natural Prozac Program: How to Use St. John's Wort, the Antidepressant Herb*. New York: Three Rivers Press, 1997.

Ginkgo

DeFeudis, F. V. *Ginkgo Biloba Extract (EGb 761): Pharmacological Activities and Clinical Applications*. Paris: Elsevier Scientific Editions, 1991.

Foster, Steven. *Ginkgo: Ginkgo biloba*. Austin, Tx.: American Botanical Council, 1991.

Halpern, George. *Ginkgo: A Practical Guide.* Garden City Park, N.Y.: Avery, 1997.

Hobbs, Christopher. *Ginkgo: Elixir of Youth.* Santa Cruz, Calif.: Botanica Press, 1991.

Rothfeld, Glenn S., and Suzanne Levert. *Ginkgo Biloba: An Herbal Fountain of Youth for Your Brain.* New York: Dell, 1998.

Zuess, Jonathan G. *Ginkgo: The Smart Herb.* New York: Three Rivers Press, 1998.

Amino Acids

Braverman, Eric R., Ken Blum, Richard Smayda, and Carl Curt Pfeiffer. *The Healing Nutrients Within: Facts, Findings and New Research on Amino Acids.* New Canaan, Ct.: Keats, 1997.

Chaitow, Leon. *Thorson's Guide to Amino Acids.* London: Thorson's, 1991.

Erdmann, Robert, and Meirion Jones. *The Amino Revolution.* New York: Fireside, 1989.

Murray, Michael T. *5-HTP: The Natural Way to Overcome Depression, Obesity, and Insomnia.* New York: Bantam, 1998.

Nutrients

Balch, James F., and Phyllis A. Balch, *Prescription for Nutritional Healing.* Garden City Park, N.Y.: Avery, 1990.

Haas, Elson M. *Staying Healthy with Nutrition.* Berkeley, Calif.: Celestial Arts, 1992.

Hausman, Patricia. *The Right Dose: How to Take Vitamins & Minerals Safely.* Emmaus, Pa.: Rodale Press, 1987.

Hendler, Sheldon Saul. *The Doctors' Vitamin and Mineral Encyclopedia.* New York: Fireside, 1990.

Lieberman, Shari, and Nancy Bruning. *The Real Vitamin & Mineral Book.* Garden City Park, N.Y.: Avery, 1990.

Murray, Michael T. *Encyclopedia of Nutritional Supplements.* Rocklin, Calif.: Prima Health, 1996.

———. *The Healing Power of Foods.* Rocklin, Calif.: Prima Publishing, 1993.

Quillin, Patrick. *Healing Nutrients.* Chicago: Contemporary Books, 1987.

Essential Fatty Acids

Cunnane, Stephen C., and Lilian U. Thompson, eds. *Flaxseed in Human Nutrition.* Champaign, Ill.: American Oil Chemists Society Press, 1995.

Holman, R. T. *Essential Fatty Acids and Prostaglandins.* New York: Pergamon, 1982.

Siguel, Edward N. *Essential Fatty Acids in Health and Disease.* Brookline, Mass.: Nutrek, 1995.

Simopoulos, Artemis P., and Jo Robinson. *The Omega Diet*. New York: Harper-
    Collins, 1995.

Medical Texts

Clayman, Charles B., ed. *The American Medical Association Encyclopedia of Medi-
    cine*. New York: Random House, 1989.
Department of Drugs, American Medical Association. *Drug Evaluations*. 6th ed.
    Chicago: American Medical Association, 1986.
Gilman, Alfred Goodman, Louis S. Goodman, and Alfred Gilman, eds. *Goodman
    and Gilman's The Parmacological Basis of Therapeutics*. 6th ed. New York:
    Macmillan Publishing Co., 1980.
Julien, Robert M. *A Primer of Drug Action*. 3d ed. San Francisco: W. H. Freeman
    and Company, 1981.
Long, James W. *The Essential Guide to Prescription Drugs 1992*. New York: Harper
    Perennial, 1992.
PDR for Herbal Medicines. 1st ed. Montvale, N.J.: Medical Economics, 1998.
Physicans' Desk Reference. 49th ed. Montvale, N.J.: Medical Economics, 1995.
Robbers, James E., Marilyn K. Speedie, and Varro E. Tyler. *Pharmacognosy and
    Pharmacobiotechnology*. Baltimore, Md.: Williams & Wilkins, 1996.
Snyder, Soloman. *Drugs and the Brain*. New York: Scientific American Books,
    1986.

About the Tree of Life
Rejuvenation Center

The Tree of Life Rejuvenation Center, founded and directed by Gabriel Cousens, M.D., is an innovative rejuvenation, spiritual, eco-retreat center committed to the integration and renewal of body, mind, and spirit.

At the Tree of Life every aspect of lifestyle, including raw food, Kosher, organic, vegetarian, gourmet cuisine, organic gardening, building with solar energy, and interacting with heartfelt quality and spiritual energy, contributes to creating and sustaining a balanced life. Daily participants have the opportunity to connect with the rhythms of nature and their own unique healing rhythm through sunrise and sunset ceremonies, meditation, yoga, breathing exercises, and nature hikes.

In order to provide a supportive opportunity for growth, the Tree of Life Rejuvenation Center offers several self-healing courses and retreats, which empower participants to take responsibilty for their healing and awakened living. The Zero Point Process, a four-day psychospiritual healing course, and Arizona Live!, a two-and-a-half-day experiential workshop for learning the raw food vegetarian diet and lifestyle, are among these powerful vehicles for transformation. The center also offers medically supervised juice fasting and classes in raw food preparation and biodynamic organic gardening.

Personal optimal health evaluations are available with Dr. Cousens. This provides you with a holistic individualized plan of optimal nutrition, lifestyle change, and nutritional and medicinal supplements that will bring your body-mind-spirit into greater balance and harmony. In addition to the three-hour evaluation, a two-day Bio Brain Balance assessment is also. available to help you determine how to successfully individualize your diet, including a diagnosis of your fast or slow oxidizer constitution. Dr. Cousens combines the best elements of nutrition, Ayurveda, homeopathy, acupuncture, naturopathy, and other healing modalities for the healing of depression, the "addicitive brain," and other chronic degenerative diseases such as diabetes, hypoglycemia, chronic fatigue, arthritis, and candida. In addition, as a psychiatrist and family therapist, Dr. Cousens facilitates intensive individual, couple, and family therapy sessions.

The Tree of Life is located on 166 acres on a beautiful southern Arizona mesa, surrounded by the Patagonia Mountains. The campus includes an organic live-food café, casita-style housing units, a meditation sanctuary, gardens, and therapeutic hot tubs. The overall experience is a menu of awakened living inspiring people to become truly free so that they may experience the natural heartfelt joy of living and fully expressing their sacred design, celebrating an openheartedness to all of life.

Tree of Life Rejuvenation Center
P. O. Box 1080
Patagonia, AZ 85624
(520) 394–2520
E-mail: healing@treeofliferejuvenation.com
website: www.treeofliferejuvenation.com

Index

ADD (attention deficit disorder), xvii, 38, 145, 226, 229, 230, 231, 249–50
addiction, see alcohol, alcoholism; substance abuse
adenosine triphosphate (ATP), 64, 65, 100, 143–44
adrenal gland, 74–75, 136
adrenocorticotropic hormone (ACTH), 58–59, 74–75, 76
alcohol, alcoholism, xvii, 16, 26, 27, 28, 48, 86, 214, 220–34
   allergies and, 233–34
   conventional programs for, 221–24
   eating disorders and, 229–30
   epidemic of, 221–22
   foods and supplements for, 231–34
   GABA function and, 230–31
   genetic component of, 225–27
   holistic approach to, 224–27
   stress and, 227–29, 232
   tyrosine and, 95
allergies, 29–30, 80
   alcohol and, 233–34
   nutritional program for, 243–44
Alzheimer's disease, 9, 111, 112, 114, 116, 120, 132, 144
amino acids, xvi, 8, 11, 13, 19, 69, 80, 83–103, 163, 168, 231
   essential and nonessential, 84–85
   for serotonin imbalance, 239–40
   as supplements, 18
   therapeutic effectiveness of, 85–86
   see also specific amino acids
antidepressants, 3–4, 32–35, 39–40, 52
   see also specific antidepressants
anxiety, anxiety disorders, xiii, 12, 14, 25, 26, 36, 38, 64, 86
aspirin, 145–46, 157
ATP (adenosine triphosphate), 64, 65, 100, 143–44
attention deficit disorder (ADD), xvii, 38, 145, 226, 229, 230, 231, 249–50

Barnes, Broda, 73
bee pollen, 180
Birkmayer, Jorg G. D., 116–17
birth control pills, 56, 110
   vitamin B deficiency and, 104
blood sugar, see glucose
breathing techniques, 211–13
brewers yeast, 180
bulimia, xvii, 38, 229–30, 231
bupropion (Wellbutrin), 21, 27, 39

calcium, 122–23
carbohydrates, 17, 164–68, 214–15
carotenoids, 106–8, 155, 161
cellular respiration, 64–65
cholesterol, 149–50
choline, 114–15
chromium, 126–28
chronic mild depression (dysthymia), 23
citric acid cycle, 64, 65
clinical (major) depression, 22–23, 86
cobalamin (vitamin B$_{12}$), 111
cod liver oil, 157
coenzyme Q10 (coQ10), 121–22, 138
cooking oils, 173–75
cortisol, 58–59, 75, 83, 105
counseling and therapy, 236–37
cyanocobalamin (vitamin B$_{12}$), 111

depression:
   causes of, 25–32
   disease burden and, 43
   genetic basis for, 24, 26, 44–45
   as modern epidemic, 5–6
   personal biochemistry and, 79–80
   self-test for, 22
   sociocultural factors and, 45–46
   types of, 22–25
   underdiagnosis of, 48

DHA, *see* docosahexaenoic acid
diet, 19, 31, 65–66, 80, 162–99
    balancing of, 175–76
    carbohydrates in, 164–68, 175
    cooking oils and, 173–75
    EFA and, 139–40
    fat in, 170–73, 175
    glycerin index and, 164–68
    menus and recipes for, 178–79, 181–84, 186–99
    protein in, 168–70, 175
    serotonin effect and, 168
    transitions in, 199
    vegetarian protein sources for, 180
Dietary Supplement Health and Education Act
        (DSHEA), 159
docosahexaenoic acid (DHA), 142, 148, 152, 155,
        157, 171, 233
    effects of, 143–45
dopamine, 3, 7, 9–11, 33, 38, 80, 83, 84, 86, 92,
        93, 94, 95, 101, 116, 124, 130, 163, 168,
        227
    alcoholism and, 226, 230, 231
    deficiency in, 11, 238, 240–41
drugs, 20–42, 80
    addiction to, *see* alcohol, alcoholism
    magic bullet theory of, 21–22
    neurotransmitter revolution in, 33–35
    over-the-counter, 27
    prescription, 26–27, 239
    psychotropic, 38–39
    recreational, 27–28
    side effects of, 243–44
    for thyroid function, 71
    see also antidepressants
DSHEA (Dietary Supplement Health and Education
        Act), 159
dysthymia (chronic mild depression), 23

eating disorders, xvii, 38, 61, 229–30
EFA, *see* essential fatty acids
eleuthero, 136–37
endorphins, 7, 15–17, 18, 52, 80, 83, 86, 221
    alcohol and, 227–28
    deficiency and imbalance of, 17, 238, 243
essential fatty acids (EFA), 77, 139–61, 163, 173,
        233
    candidates for use of, 155, 156, 158
    cholesterol and, 149–50
    derivatives of, 141–42
    from fish oils, 156–58, 161
    from flaxseeds, 153–54, 155
    imbalance of, 78–79, 80, 140–41, 142, 149, 239,
        248–49
    minimal and optimal doses of, 151–52
    mood effects of, 148–49
    primary and derivative, 141–42
    prostaglandins and, 145–48, 163
    roles of, 142–43
    safety concerns with, 155, 156–57, 158
    from seed oils, 154–55, 159, 160, 161
    use of, 156, 157–58, 158–60
    see also omega-3; omega-6
estrogen, 55, 57–58
exercise, 60, 201–5, 214

fast oxidizers:
    dietary sources of, 176–77, 179, 181–82, 245
    glycemic index and, 164–68
    metabolism by, 63, 64–69, 80

    proteins and, 169–70
    self-assessment for, 67–68
fat, 76–79, 80, 163, 170–73, 175
    demonization of, 76–77
    imbalance of, 78–79
fatty acids, 19, 57
    in cooking oil, 174
    foods high in, 171–72
    see also essential fatty acids
FDA (Food and Drug Administration), 32, 37,
        87–88, 128, 159
Feingold, Benjamin, 29
5–hydroxytryptophan (5–HTP), 8, 9, 16, 85, 86, 88,
        90–92, 102, 110, 131, 230
flaxseeds, 153–54, 163
fluoxetine (Prozac), *see* Prozac
fluvoxamine (Luvox), 36, 39, 90
folic acid (folate), 8, 112
Food and Drug Administration (FDA), 32, 37,
        87–88, 128, 159
Freud, Sigmund, 32

gamma aminobutyric acid (GABA), 7, 52, 71, 83, 85,
        86, 97, 98–99, 102, 129
    alcohol and, 230–31
    deficiency of, 238, 242–43
GFT (Glucose Tolerance Factor) chromium,
        127–28
gingko, 105, 131–33
ginseng, 136–37
glucose (blood sugar), 10, 12, 13, 17, 63, 105, 163,
        221
    carbohydrates and, 164–68
    imbalance of, 239, 245–46
    oxidation of, 64–65
Glucose Tolerance Factor (GFT) chromium, 127–28
glucose tolerance test, 69
glutamine, 7, 83, 85, 86, 93, 96–98, 102
    deficiency of, 13, 238, 241–42
glycemic index, 164–68
goiter, 73, 170
Goodwin, Frederick, 59

Hamilton Depression Rating Scale, 17, 91
Hashimoto's thyroiditis, 71
hemp seed oil, 154–55
hormones, 18, 32, 63, 83, 163
    imbalance of, 76, 80
    stress-related, 74–76, 247–48
    thyroid, 70–71, 133–34, 170
    women and, 55–56
humor, 209–11
hydrogenation, 171
hyperthyroidism, 71
hypoglycemia, 63, 165, 199, 232
hypothyroidism, 69–70, 71, 73–74, 134, 170
Hypothyroidism: The Unsuspected Illness (Barnes), 73

I Don't Want to Talk About It (Real), 48
imipramine, 34, 101, 130
inositol, 113–14
insulin, 83, 90, 126, 168
iodine, 170
iproniazid, 33–34
iron, 124–25, 233

Kalmijn, Sandra, 149
Kaplan, Nathan, 115
Klerman, Gerald, 43–44

L-dopa, 124
lifestyle choices, 19, 31, 80, 200–219
    creative outlets, 207–9
    deep breathing techniques, 211–13
    exercise, 201–5, 214
    humor, 209–11
    personal and social relationships, 205–7
    relaxation and meditation techniques, 215–17
    sleep habits, 213–15
    spirituality, 219
    touching and massage, 217–19
lithium, 21, 32–33, 52, 71, 113
Luvox (fluvoxamine), 36, 39, 90

magnesium, 123–24, 140, 161
major (clinical) depression, 22–23, 86
manic depression, 24, 44, 52, 71, 114
MAO (monoamine oxidase) inhibitors, 12, 33–34,
    37, 39, 52
massage, 218–19
meditation, 215–17
melatonin, 8, 18, 24, 60, 75, 83, 86, 90, 105, 106,
    134–36, 214, 221
    SAD and, 51–53
    supplements of, 54
menopause, 57–58, 62
menstruation, 55–56
metabolism, 63–69, 86
    fast and slow oxidizers and, 63, 64–69, 80
    hypothyroidism and, 69–70
methylphenidate (Ritalin), 250
monoamine oxidase (MAO) inhibitors, 12, 33–34,
    37, 39, 52

NADH/Coenzyme 1, 115–18, 124, 129, 138
Nardil (phenelzine), 3–4, 34, 39
neurotransmitters, 3, 124, 163, 229
    alcoholism and, 230–31
    defined, 6
    fat imbalance and, 77
    natural biochemicals and, 17–19
    psychotropic drugs and, 38–39
    tricyclics and, 34–35
    see also specific neurotransmitters
niacin (vitamin B₃), 65, 110, 127, 140, 161
nonpsychotic major postpartum depressive disorder,
    57
noradrenaline (norepinephrine), 7, 14, 22, 71, 75,
    83, 86, 110, 130, 168
    addiction and, 227, 230
    amino acids and, 92–93, 94, 95, 163
    deficiency of, 12–13, 80, 238, 241
    prescription drugs and, 33, 34–35, 36, 38
nutrition, see diet; recipes

obsessive-compulsive disorders, 25, 64
omega-3:
    candidates for use of, 156
    classification of, 140–41
    dietary sources of, 170–71
    primary and derivative, 142
    prostaglandins and, 146–48
    safety concerns with, 156–57
    supplements and, 152–54
    use of, 157–58
omega-6:
    candidates for use of, 158
    classification of, 140–41
    dietary sources of, 171
    primary and derivative, 142
    prostaglandins and, 146–48
    safety concerns with, 158
    supplements and, 158–59
    use of, 158–59
opioids, 15, 16, 228, 229, 233

panic disorder, xiii, 25, 38
pantothenic acid (vitamin B₅), 110
Parkinson's disease, 10, 93, 101, 114, 116–17
Parnate (tranylcypromine), 34
Paxil (paroxetine), 36, 37, 39
phenelzine (Nardil), 3–4, 34, 39
phenylalanine, 10, 12, 16, 84, 85, 86, 92–94, 96,
    102, 168, 230, 231
postpartum depression, xiii, 24–25, 55, 56–57, 62,
    100, 143, 144
post-traumatic stress disorder (PTSD), 25, 226, 229,
    230
premenstrual syndrome (PMS), 38, 56, 95
prescription drugs, 239
    depression caused by, 26–27
    see also antidepressants; drugs
prostaglandins, 19, 77, 171, 233
    essential fatty acids and, 145–48, 163
    good and bad, 146–47
protein, 168–70, 214–15
    vegetarian sources of, 180
Prozac (fluoxetine), xiii, xv, xvi, xvii, 4, 8, 21, 34,
    39, 41, 42, 87, 100, 113, 129, 130, 214, 250
    discontinuing use of, 237–38
    popularity of, 36–37
    revolution of, 35–38
PTSD (post-traumatic stress disorder), 25, 226, 229,
    230
pyridoxine, 110–11, 140

Real, Terrence, 48
recipes:
    almond falafel, 189
    almond hummus, 192
    apple cinnamon nut sauce, 197
    buckwheat granola, 188
    carrot hijiki salad, 193
    creamy miso dressing, 198
    curry apple sunflax drink, 187
    daikon ginger salad, 193
    date oatmeal porridge, 188
    festive wild rice, 191
    heavenly garden soup, 196
    kimchee delight, 189
    lassi, 187
    minestrone soup, 194
    mixed greens and sprout salad, 192
    nori rolls, 191
    raita, 197
    red top salad dressing, 198
    spanakopita, 190
    Spanish salad dressing, 199
    spicy corn soup, 195
    spinach avocado salad, 194
    spinach salsa dressing, 199
    sun squash soup, 195
    tabouli, 190
    tahini apple dressing, 198
    three carrot soup, 195
    Tree of Life seven-fruit haroset, 186–87
    wheat treat cereal, 187
    yam burgers, 188

recipes (*continued*)
  zucchini sun dressing, 198
  see also diet
relaxation techniques, 215–17
riboflavin (vitamin B₂), 109
Richman, J., 209–10
Ritalin (methylphenidate), 250

S-adenosylmethionine (SAM), 85, 86, 99–102, 112, 234
St. John's wort, xvi, 4, 105, 129–31
Sears, Barry, 66
seasonal affective disorder (SAD), xiii, 18, 86, 119
  melatonin levels and, 51–53
  sleep disorders and, 50–51
  symptoms of, 54–55
  in women, 24, 50–51, 59, 60
selective serotonin reuptake inhibitors (SSRI), 8, 33, 35–37, 39, 42, 52
  adverse effects of, 37
  approved uses for, 37
selenium, 125–26, 140
Selye, Hans, xi
serotonin, xvi, 6–9, 11, 22, 33, 34–35, 38, 62, 71, 77, 80, 83, 86, 90, 101, 110, 146, 149, 163, 173, 221, 227, 230
  carbohydrates and, 168
  deficiency of, 9, 238, 239–40
  dietary sources of, 8
  effects of, 7, 168
  gender and, 49–50
sertraline (Zoloft), 36, 39
Siberian ginseng, 136–37
sleep, sleep disorders, xviii, 71, 86
  lifestyle and, 213–15
  SAD and, 50–51
slow oxidizers:
  dietary sources of, 177–79, 183–84, 245–46
  glycemic index and, 164–68
  metabolism by, 63, 64–69, 80
  proteins and, 168–69
  self-assessment for, 66–67
spirituality, 219
spirulina, 180
SSRI, *see* selective serotonin reuptake inhibitors
stress, 9, 11, 12, 16, 31, 63, 74–76, 111, 140, 203, 247–48
  addiction and, 227–29, 232
  hormones and, 74–76, 247–48
  women and, 47–48, 58–59
substance abuse, 48
  epidemic of, 221–22
  tyrosine and, 95
  see also alcohol, alcoholism
suicide, 5, 8, 18, 37, 41, 86, 148, 222
  dopamine activity and, 11
  MAOI drugs and, 34
  melatonin levels and, 52
supplements, 69, 80, 104–38
  addiction fought with, 231–34
  optimizing use of, 137–38

overview of, 128–29
  resources for, 252–54
  role of, 104–5
  see also specific supplements

T₃ (tri-iodothyronine), 70, 71, 73
T₄ (thyroxine), 70, 71, 73, 83, 133, 134
therapy and counseling, 236–37
thiamine (vitamin B₁), 109
thyroid gland, 59, 63, 69–74
  dysfunction of, 71–72, 80, 239, 247
  home test for, 73
  hormone production by, 70–71
  hormone supplements for, 133–34
thyroxine (T₄), 70, 71, 73, 83, 133, 134
touching, 217–19
tranylcypromine (Parnate), 34
Tree of Life Rejuvenation Center, 18, 181, 184, 216, 281–82
tricyclics, 33, 34–35, 39, 40
tri-iodothyronine (T₃), 70, 71, 73
tryptophan, 8, 9, 18, 84, 86, 87–90, 92, 110, 168, 214
  banning of, 87–88
  candidates for use of, 88, 169–70
  dietary sources of, 169
  safety concerns with, 89
  use of, 89–90
tyramine, 233–34
tyrosine, 70, 86, 92, 94–96, 102, 110, 124, 230
  alcohol and, 95

vegetarianism, 184
vitamin A, 106–8, 155, 161
vitamin B complex, 108–13
  see also specific B-complex vitamins
vitamin C, 105, 118–19, 124–25, 140, 161
vitamin D, 119–20
vitamin E, 120–22, 140, 161

Watson, George, 64
Weissman, Myrna, 43–44
Wellbutrin (bupropion), 21, 27, 39
women, 41, 43–61
  biochemical factors and, 49–50
  breathing techniques for, 212
  depression as learned behavior in, 47
  depression rates among, 43–45
  eating disorders in, 61
  gender-based depression in, 60
  hormonal changes and, 55–58
  negative life events and, 46–47
  SAD in, 50–51, 59, 60
  sociocultural factors and, 45–48
  stress and, 47–48, 58–59
  thyroid imbalance in, 71, 73–74
  treatment of, 60–61

Zoloft (sertraline), 36, 39
Zone, The (Sears), 36, 39